A guide to the restoration of nutrient-enriched shallow lakes

Brian Moss
School of Biological Sciences,
University of Liverpool

Jane Madgwick
Broads Authority, Norwich

Geoffrey Phillips
Environment Agency,
Eastern Area, Anglian Region

Contents

Preface   11

Acknowledgements   13

Introduction and Guide to Using this Book   15

Who needs this Guide?   15

The consequences of eutrophication   16

The role and scope of this Guide   17

Arrangement of the Guide   18

Chapter 1

How Lakes Work

Substances dissolved in water   21

Nitrogen and phosphorus   21

Catchments and trophic states   24

Morphometry   24

Light and the competition between phytoplankton and aquatic plants   26

Swampy fringes and the littoral zone   27

Nutrient cycling and the sediments   29

Nutrient cycling in plant beds   30

Control of the algal growth   31

Grazers of the periphyton algae   31

Grazers on phytoplankton   31

Fish feed on Daphnia   32

The refuge concept   33

On balance....   34

Grazers on the plants themselves   34

Birds, mammals and fish   35

Chaos and change   35

Chapter 2

A Spanner in the Works -
How Lakes are Altered by Human Activity

Sewage   39

Agriculture   40

Eutrophication   41

Eutrophication in shallow lakes -alternative states   42

The nutrient range for alternative states   45

Forward switches   46

Reverse switches   50

Loss of reedswamp and lilies   50

Filling in   52

Chapter 3

Restoration and Rehabilitation

Restoration   53

Why restore?   54

What should be restored?   55

Determining the histories of lakes from their sediments   56

Determining targets   57

Maximising diversity   58

Two principles   60

Targets for nutrient control   60

Determining the present nutrient sources and
the potential for their control   62

Chapter 4

An Overall Strategy for Restoration of Shallow Eutrophicated Lakes

63

Chapter 5

Steps in the Strategy (1) Detecting And Removing the Forward Switches

Reconstructing the past   65

Asking questions   65

Salinity   65

Herbicides   66

Introduced birds and other grazers   66

Destructive fish   67

Pesticides   67

Ensuring forward switch mechanisms are absent before
restoration begins   68

Carp problems   69

Bird removal   70

Next...   71

Chapter 6

Steps in the Strategy
(2) Nutrient Control

Phosphorus or nitrogen control - or both?	**73**
Three practical principles important in restoration	**73**
Point sources of phosphorus	**74**
Human sewage effluent	**74**
Stock wastes	**76**
Detergent phosphorus	**77**
Fish farms	**78**
Diffuse sources of phosphorus	**78**
Buffer zones	**79**
Point sources of nitrogen	**82**
Diffuse sources of nitrogen	**82**
Ploughing of grassland can also release a great deal of nitrate	**83**
Buffer zones again	**84**
Internal sources of phosphorus	**84**
Sediment sealing	**84**
The Riplox method	**86**
Sediment removal	**86**
Disposal of sediment	**88**
Should you remove sediment at all?	**90**

Chapter 7

Steps in the Strategy
(3) Biomanipulation

Piscivore addition	**93**
Water level manipulation	**94**
Fish-eating birds	**95**
Fish removal	**96**
How much needs to be taken out?	**99**
Where biomanipulation is difficult	**100**
Enclosure refuges	**102**
Complications: invertebrate predators	**103**
Wind induced turbidity	**104**
Finally, parasites!	**104**
A prognosis for the success of biomanipulation	**104**
A reminder	**104**

Chapter 8

Steps in the Strategy
(4) Re-establishment of Plants

The need for plant refuges	**107**
Problems in the re-establishment of plants	**107**
Problems of inimical sediment	**108**
Practicalities	**108**
What plants to introduce?	**110**
How much should be planted?	**112**
Sources of plants	**112**
Planting	**113**
Protection during establishment	**114**

Chapter 9

Steps in the Strategy
(5) Stabilising the System

Some guidelines for establishing permanency of a restoration   **117**

The new fish community   **118**

Uses and problems   **119**

Procurement of fish for replacement communities   **120**

Monitoring   **120**

Minimal monitoring   **121**

More detailed monitoring   **121**

Monitoring of external change   **122**

Chapter 10

The Collective Experience –
a Compendium of European Case Studies

Cockshoot Broad, UK   **124**

What was the problem?   **124**

What was the target for restoration?   **124**

What was done?   **124**

Why was it done?   **126**

Did it work?   **126**

What was then done?   **128**

Did it work?   **128**

What lessons were learned?   **129**

Lake Vaeng, Denmark — 130

What was the problem and what was the target for restoration? — 130

What was done and why? — 130

What happened? — 130

What lessons were learned? — 132

Little Mere, UK — 134

What was the problem and the target for restoration? — 134

What was done? — 134

What was the previous state of the lake? — 134

What happened? — 135

What was learned? — 136

Zwemlust, The Netherlands — 137

What was the problem and what was the target for restoration? — 137

What was done? — 138

What happened? — 138

What was learned? — 140

Lake Wolderwijd, The Netherlands — 141

What was the problem and target for restoration? — 141

What was done? — 141

What happened? — 141

What lessons were learned? — 142

Ormesby Broad, UK   **143**

What was done?   144

What happened?   145

What was learned?   145

Bosherston Lakes, Wales, UK   **146**

What was done?   147

What was learned?   148

Finjasjön, Sweden   **149**

What was the problem and what was done?   149

What was then done?   150

What was then done at Finjasjön?   151

What is being learned?   152

Barton Broad, UK   **152**

What is the problem?   152

What was done?   153

What happened?   153

What is being done now?   154

Detailed planning   155

Chapter 11

Expectations and the Future

References   **161**

Index and Glossary of Terms   **169**

Preface

Lakes are precious places. They are often beautiful and tranquil areas, offering a breathing space in busy lives. They can be rich in wildlife both above and below the water surface. Yet lakes are amongst our most vulnerable habitats and many of Europe's rare and threatened species are confined to just a handful of water bodies. As their potential to support nature has declined, so generally have other benefits to people - for example the quality of water for drinking, fishing and other forms of recreation.

Eutrophication is sadly the most extensive and pervasive threat to water bodies across Europe, affecting village ponds and vast lakes in the same way, with loss of diversity and value and sometimes an added threat of toxicity problems from blue-green algal blooms. Mostly, these changes have occurred over the past century and they have accelerated in the last fifty years as agricultural systems have intensified. But over the last twenty years or so, scientists and lake managers have been working hard to understand the eutrophication process and to develop techniques for reconstructing healthy, stable lake systems for the future.

This book stemmed from a long standing collaboration between scientists and managers in the Norfolk Broads in eastern England, a nationally protected wetland where there has been a growing commitment to restore the series of lowland lakes to good ecological condition, following a period of severe nutrient enrichment. The work in the broads attracted support from the European Commission through its LIFE programme over the period from 1993 to 1996. This enabled further research and experimental management work to proceed and encouraged European collaboration concerning shallow lake restoration.

The guide that follows presents the current status of knowledge and expertise on shallow lake restoration from eutrophication, drawing on the European experience. It offers advice on a step by step basis, highlighting the intrinsic complexity of lake ecosystems and promoting an ambitious but informed approach to any restoration project, large or small. Its authors share between them over 50 years of experience in lake restoration and this experience stretches from the fundamental science to the thoroughly practical. It is a guide that we hope will be added to continuously as this relatively new science develops and as more lakes are restored across the continent.

Aitken Clark
Chief Executive,
Broads Authority

Grainger Davies
Regional General Manager,
Anglian Region, Environment Agency

Acknowledgements

We are grateful to a number of people for reviewing the text and for provision of information. Robin Chatterjee of the EA read and commented on each of four successive drafts and made valuable contributions to Chapter 6. Marie Louise Meijer, Eddy Lammens, Marten Scheffer and Harry Hosper contributed details and an overall view, as did Paul Raven and Mark Everard. Ellen van Donk, Catherine Duigan, Deborah Dunsford, Helene Annadotter, Gertrud Cronberg, Julia Stansfield and Rob Andrews helped with details particularly of case studies. Jeremy Fox drew up the initial versions of the more complicated diagrams and flow charts, Karen Sayer was instrumental in bringing about the final production, and Fleur Bradnock made many improvements to the final text. Angharad Simlett Moss helped to prepare the index. This book is produced as part of a European Union Life Programme Project. Financial support to the overall project was provided by the European Union Life Programme, The Broads Authority, The Environment Agency, and the Soap and Detergent Industry Association Environment Trust.

Much of the book is based on research carried out by the authors over the last twenty-five years with the support of several organisations, including the former Nature Conservancy Council, and the Natural Environment Research Council (UK), in addition to those mentioned above, and the informal cooperation and much free interchange of ideas and results with our colleagues in mainland Europe. It is thus a personal view of lake restoration and the final responsibility for the views expressed rests with the authors and not necessarily with any of the sponsoring organisations.

Introduction and Guide to Using this Book

'Water attracts me as women attract men, as cherries attract blackbirds. I fall for it every time'.

H.E. Bates, Down the River, *1937.*

Who needs this Guide?

H.E. Bates understood and valued the relationships between men and women and the appeal of natural waters - the twin essentials of a civilised life! Though desert landscapes have their own special appeal, it is water that stitches together those elsewhere. We depend on freshwaters for our very existence but we enrich our lives also by them, whether it is through quiet contemplation, appreciation of nature, quiet or boisterous recreation. Bates was writing in 1937 and though many waters are still in an acceptable state, with reasonable clarity and diversity of their biological communities, there are many others that would now sadden him.

This book is for those whose role it is to restore ponds and shallow lakes which have been damaged by eutrophication. Eutrophication is the addition of more than natural quantities of the compounds of phosphorus and nitrogen that are algal and plant nutrients. It has consequences for the biological communities, which may be problems for some groups of people. One serious problem, in shallow lakes, is a change from clear water, dominated in summer by the larger aquatic plants, to turbid water, dominated for much of the year by a pea-soup of algae, and from which the plants have been lost.

Many people concerned with the management of lakes will not need to put in place the techniques described here. Their lakes will not be so seriously affected and may still have clear water, attractive lily fringes and a diverse community of aquatic plants, fish and water birds. Nonetheless, perceptive lake managers may learn from this guide about how the complex systems of shallow lakes work and thus become aware of possible threats to lake systems under their care. Some managers will be faced with quite serious problems and we hope that this book will help in their understanding and in finding solutions. A recent survey[36] of freshwater Sites of Special Scientific Interest in Britain showed about three quarters to have been damaged by excessive nutrient addition. Such sites are 'cherished' sites and receive more protection than others. The proportionate situation in the countryside as a whole may thus be worse. Similar problems are acknowledged throughout most of Europe by the new European Environmental Agency[109].

The productivity of a lake, and ultimately its conservation and amenity values, are largely determined by its nutrient supply. This is derived from the catchment and in an undisturbed area will depend on the natural fertility of the local rocks or glacial deposits, and the soils derived from them. Lakes thus vary in their natural fertility. Upland ones are generally less fertile than lowland ones, but pristine, infertile ones were common even in the lowlands amid glacial and other sands, and on crystalline rocks. The problems that we deal with in this book result from the increased fertility generated ultimately by people.

First, this may be a result of human waste, magnified in effect as a result of aggregation into cities. Here the essential removal of organic matter from sewage by conventional treatment results in an effluent concentrated in nitrate, ammonium and phosphate which reaches the freshwaters more rapidly than from an equivalent rural population served by septic tanks and ground seepage, where there is also the possibility of modification by soil processes.

This is a book for those wishing to restore severely damaged shallow lakes (those with pea-soup algal growth for much of the year and which have lost most or all of their water plants) for the purposes of conservation and amenity.

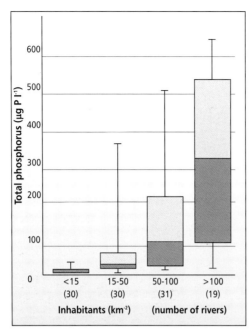

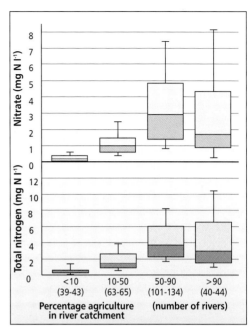

Fig 0.1 Total phosphorus concentrations in a large sample of European rivers, plotted against the number of people per square kilometre. Numbers in parentheses show the number of catchments in each sample. Box and whisker plots show the median and standard deviation (box) and range (whiskers). From Kristensen and Hansen 1995.

Fig 0.2 Total nitrogen and nitrate concentrations in a large sample of European rivers plotted against the percentage of their catchments devoted to agriculture. Numbers in parentheses show the number of catchments in each sample. Box and whisker plots show the median and standard deviation (box) and range (whiskers). From Kristensen and Hansen 1995.

Eutrophication is, in general, undesirable. It leads to reduced amenity and conservation value and may create economic problems.

In addition, intensification of agriculture has resulted in higher stock densities and increased fertiliser use, giving rise to problems with nitrate enrichment and potentially with phosphorus as the ability of the soil to bind it becomes exhausted [60a,60b,109a]. On average the concentrations of total phosphorus and total nitrogen have doubled in rural England and Wales since before World War II [99]. There are clear correlations **(Figs 0.1 and 0.2)** between the proportion of agricultural land in the catchment and the total nitrogen concentration in the receiving streams and between human population density and total phosphorus concentration [109].

The consequences of eutrophication

The consequences of eutrophication in lakes and other standing waters are many. The earliest symptoms include increases in growth of floating plants, or blanketing algae at the edges, and of suspended microscopic algae (phytoplankton) in the open water. The increased production may lead to deoxygenation of the deeper waters, undesirable changes in the fish community, and sometimes fish kills. Toxic algae may be produced and water for the domestic supply may become more expensive to treat. More algae will have to be filtered from it and greater quantities of undesirable taste and odour substances, which they secrete, will need to be removed. Clear water lakes will become cloudy, stones at the edges may become slimy and the general amenity will be impaired. The larger water plants may at first increase, clogging shorelines and

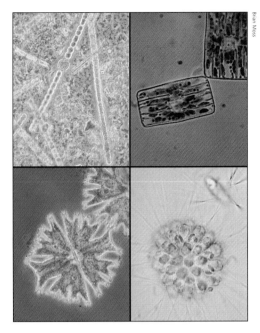

Under the microscope, algae are very intricate and beautiful. Shown here (clockwise) are a blue-green alga, *Anabaena*, which is also a nitrogen-fixer; a diatom, *Tabellaria*; a yellow-green flagellate, *Chrysosphaerella*; and a green alga, *Micrasterias*. The length of the filament of *Anabaena*, the diameter of the colony of *Chrysosphaerella* and the diameter of the cell of *Micrasterias* are all about 100 micrometres (one tenth of a millimetre). The cells of *Tabellaria* are each about 30 micrometres long.

Blue-green algal blooms are not uncommon on urban canals in The Netherlands. This was photographed in August 1994 in Delft.

casting up in piles at the edge after storms, but eventually are lost altogether. The biological diversity in general will be reduced and with it the amenity and conservation values of the habitat.

The role and scope of this Guide

In this is the crux of this guide. It is about the restoration of conservation and amenity value to freshwaters severely damaged by eutrophication. Specifically it is about the planning and execution of programmes for the restoration of relatively shallow lakes. They will have acquired dense phytoplankton growths (`pea-soup' water) where formerly much of their area was dominated by complex communities of aquatic plants, supporting diverse invertebrate, fish and bird communities in transparent ('gin-clear') water. The former state was clearly of much greater value for nature conservation than the turbid state.

Eutrophicated lakes occur everywhere in Europe. Many are in upland or piedmont regions, have been formed by the action of the former glaciers, and are deep. The solution to eutrophication problems in these has been to reduce the amounts of nutrients added to them. In particular, phosphorus control at sewage treatment works has been very successful. The shallow lakes, (water on average only about 1-3m deep) with which this book is concerned, are found mainly in the lowlands. For these, nutrient (usually phosphorus) control alone has proved disappointing in restoring much of their former amenity and conservation value. The processes of change in such lakes are more complex than in deep ones, and more than

Pristine shallow lakes are dominated by a diversity of aquatic plants, some of them emerging above the water, others with floating leaves and many totally submerged. Otis Lake, in Michigan, USA, is typical.

(Right) Shallow lakes which have become dominated by planktonic algae lose much of their diversity and attractiveness - a particularly damaged part of the system of lakes along the River Thurne in the Norfolk Broadland.

Theory is dealt with in Chapters 1 and 2. Practicalities begin in Chapter 3. No single prescriptive approach to lake restoration is likely to work and success will depend on an awareness of the fundamental approaches which shape lake communities.

nutrient change is involved both in their degradation and restoration.

These lakes are still not completely understood but enough knowledge has accumulated for attempts to have been made at restoration. Some have been very successful; others have failed miserably! The lessons that have been learnt, however, are enough to allow the production of this guide which should allow people faced with the need to restore a shallow lake to set about the task in an informed way. There are no magic formulae which will work in every instance, but there are general principles that can be applied and a wealth of practical experience on which to draw.

Arrangement of the Guide

This book does not provide simple prescriptive solutions to the restoration of any shallow lake. Such a 'recipe' book would fail to recognise the range of circumstances that any particular restoration attempt will need to address, and the uncertainties in our present knowledge. Rather it

tells how lakes work to allow those concerned to decide the most appropriate way forward.

The book may be used by a variety of people, some of whom may prefer to move straight to practicalities, which begin in Chapter 3. Others may first need to understand the theory in Chapters 1 and 2. This section thus maps the detailed contents.

To manage a lake successfully, it is essential to be aware of some of the important relationships that occur between the various organisms that live in the water. To provide this understanding, the book begins with a general account of how a pristine shallow lake works, introduces essential terminology and outlines the uncertainties of our present understanding (Chapter1).

One of the most important ecological discoveries in recent years has been the recognition that lakes (and perhaps other habitats) do not change smoothly from one condition to another in response to external pressures. Changes may be quite sudden and result in substantial disruption to the intricate networks that previously stabilised the lake's community. The changed community will then also develop stabilising mechanisms that create resistance to return to the former state. The importance of this to managers is twofold. First, simply removing the apparent cause of the problem e.g nutrient increase, is unlikely to give a complete solution and secondly, lakes which appear to be resilient at present could change rapidly with little warning.

This concept of alternative stable systems or states, some dominated by plants, others by microscopic algae, is developed in Chapter 2. Lakes dominated by water plants contain much more biological diversity (invertebrates, fish, birds) than those without them. The aim of restoration is often to increase biological diversity and hence conservation value by moving from dominance by algae to dominance by water plants. In relatively infertile and moderately fertile (eutrophic) conditions, only a clear-water plant-dominated state probably can persist. But once rates of nutrient addition (nutrient loadings) have increased sufficiently, either plant or algal dominance may exist over a wide range of such loadings. Within this range, stabilising mechanisms (buffers) tend to preserve the *status quo* and vigorous switches sometimes have to be applied to move the system from one state to another.

With moderate increases in nutrient addition, typical of intensively used lowland, switches from plant dominance (clear water) to algal dominance (accompanied sometimes by increased turbidity due to disturbance of bottom sediment) have coincided with destruction of the

Restoration involves an integrated, sequential strategy with both nutrient control and biological engineering (biomanipulation).

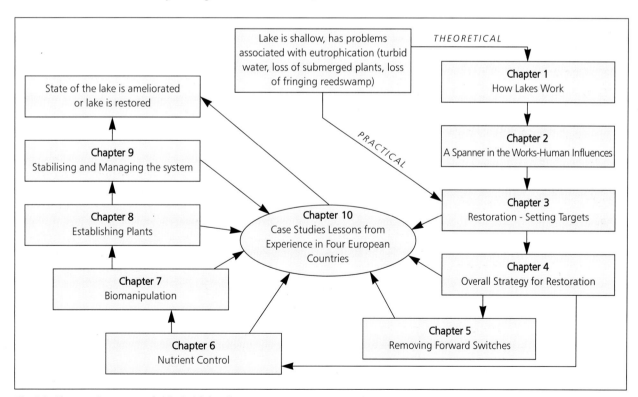

Fig 0.3 Chapter Structure of this Guidebook.

plants by severe cutting, boat damage, grazing by non-native vertebrates and use of herbicides. They have also involved destruction of invertebrate grazers (zooplankton), which remove phytoplankton algae as they develop, by pesticides, salt or changes in the fish community.

Switches required to restore the plants in these moderately enriched lakes include adjustment of the fish community to favour these invertebrate grazers, a process called biomanipulation, and introduction and initial protection of suitable plants. Biomanipulation is more effective, and the results more likely to be sustainable, if the nutrient levels are as low as possible within the appropriate nutrient range. At the concentrations caused by inadequately diluted sewage and other such effluents, it may be less effective. Methods of nutrient control appropriate to all lakes are thus relevant for maximal success and the general aim is to reduce total phosphorus concentrations to below 100 micrograms per litre. There may be an upper level of nutrient additions or other conditions in which only a phytoplankton community can persist and plants cannot survive in the face of uncontrollable plankton competition. This question has not been fully resolved but it is almost certain that stability of the plant-dominated state is greater, the lower the nutrient levels.

The restoration process is a sequential one (Fig 0.3) and the book develops in line with a strategy that moves from the initial step of deciding whether a problem exists and whether or not attempts should be made to solve it (Chapter 3), to the practical stages (Chapter 4). These are the removal of any extant forward switches (Chapter 5), nutrient control (Chapter 6), biomanipulation (Chapter 7), the reintroduction of plants (Chapter 8) and stabilising the restoration (Chapter 9). Experience from a large number of studies is incorporated throughout, but in Chapter 10, a selection of case studies is presented in a comparative way to illustrate particular lessons and issues. There is finally (Chapter 11) an overview of the realistic expectations for restoration schemes, references, and an index and glossary of technical terms.

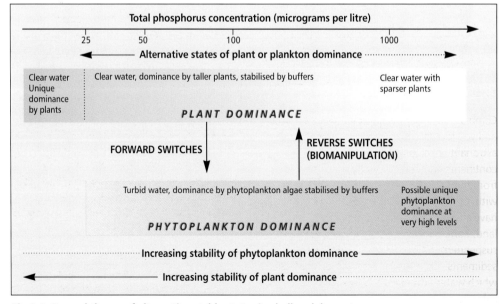

Fig 0.4 General theory of alternative stable states in shallow lake systems.

Chapter1

How Lakes Work

Climb a tree close to a shallow lake in summer and you look down on a microcosm of what an astronaut sees from the Challenger when the continents and ocean are in view. Water flows from the rivers to replenish the ocean, carrying with it the products of all the processes that have altered the rain that originally fell on the land. Some products are dissolved; others are suspended particles which become the ocean sediments. Likewise the catchment area from which water flows into the lake supplies substances in solution, fine particles of organic

matter from decomposition of vegetation, shards of soil and whole leaves.

The comparison is not exact, for the ocean is so large compared with the land surfaces that the variations in individual rivers have only local effects before they are obliterated by mixing into the huge mass of water. Local variations of the catchments, on the other hand, are supremely important influences on the nature of lakes.

Substances dissolved in water

Water dissolves almost everything to some extent. As a result, the notion of a natural 'pure' water is equally pure fiction. As rain forms in the air it picks up dust and gases, particularly carbon dioxide. When it penetrates soils, it dissolves a myriad of inorganic ions, derived ultimately from the rocks weathering underneath. As it comes into contact with the organic matter in the soil it dissolves a variety of organic substances that are intermediates of the decomposition of plant and animal material in the soil and the products of animal excretion.

There are thousands of different substances dissolved in any natural water and indeed no-one has yet fully analysed such a sample. Most of these substances will undergo further transformation when the water runs into a lake. Some may be nutrients to support growth of aquatic organisms; others may enter into reactions which maintain less soluble nutrients in solution. Yet others may be chemically inert but affect growth of plants and algae, by absorbing light as it passes through the water. Of all these substances, however, the compounds of nitrogen and phosphorus are of key importance.

Nitrogen and phosphorus

Living organisms require about twenty elements for growth. Nitrogen and phosphorus are of particular importance because their

Differences in the chemistry of the water determine much of the differing characters among lakes.

Nitrogen and phosphorus are of crucial importance to the condition of a lake.

natural supply in relation to that of the other required element is low compared with the amounts that organisms need. Nitrogen is required for production of proteins and nucleic acids (the components of genes), phosphorus for nucleic acids and substances which are used in the conversion of energy in cells.

Although there is a huge global reserve of atmospheric nitrogen gas, it is accessible in this form to only a few nitrogen-fixing bacteria. All other organisms must use combined nitrogen which has previously been fixed from the atmosphere into ammonium or nitrate ions. Phosphorus is relatively scarce in rocks and also relatively insoluble. It is easily bound to clays in soils and hence dissolves, as phosphates, only at low rates. Both nitrogen and phosphorus, in a variety of forms, enter the water that runs off from the land into lakes. These forms include dissolved inorganic compounds, such as nitrate, ammonium or phosphate ions, and dissolved organic compounds, such as the nitrogen containing amino acids or the sugar-phosphates.

There are also small particles, called colloids, such as clays and iron minerals, that contain absorbed phosphate, and fragments of organic matter usually referred to as detritus. All of these dissolved and particulate forms of nitrogen and phosphorus may become available for growth of algae and plants in the lake, either directly or following simple chemical reactions or transformation by bacteria. They are collectively referred to as *total phosphorus* and *total nitrogen* i.e. the total amounts of each element contained in all possible forms in a known volume of water (**Fig.1.1**). In the past, water companies and regulatory agencies have usually measured only one component of these stocks of nutrients - the soluble inorganic phosphate, or nitrate or its surrogate, total oxidised nitrogen. Measurements of these made in winter, when phosphorus and nitrogen are not being used for growth, are useful guides to subsequent fertility (though often severe underestimates), but may be very misleading if made from spring to autumn.

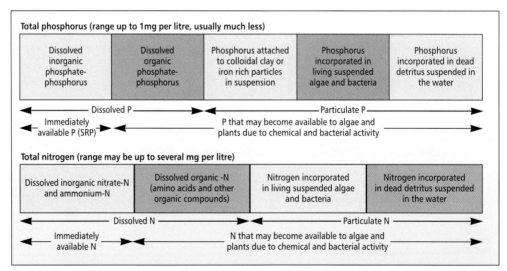

Fig 1.1 The meanings of the terms total phosphorus and total nitrogen. All that is included in the large boxes constitutes the total amounts of these elements in water samples. The sum of nitrate and the rarely occurring nitrite is often called total oxidised nitrogen by the Environment Agency and the sum of nitrate, nitrite and ammonium is similarly referred to as dissolved inorganic nitrogen.

Frequently, in a highly fertile lake, no soluble nutrients may then be detectable for all the nutrient is incorporated into plants or algae. This is a paradox that has puzzled many a schoolchild carrying out a project on a lake with high algal crops.

In pristine waters, total phosphorus concentrations will be of the order of a few micrograms to a few tens of micrograms, expressed as phosphorus, per litre. Total nitrogen concentrations will be about ten to twenty times as high, a few tens to a few hundreds of micrograms per litre. For comparison, a single grain of table salt weighs a few milligrams and a milligram contains a thousand micrograms. We are thus dealing with very low concentrations of nitrogen and phosphorus in pristine lake waters.

This is not surprising, for these same nutrients are required also by the ecosystems that develop on land **(Fig 1.2)**. They are just as scarce there and the ecosystems have evolved

mechanisms that conserve these scarce nutrients for continual cycling and re-use. There is thus very little that escapes to the run off waters from a fully developed intact land ecosystem. And since phosphorus compounds are less soluble than nitrogen compounds, phosphorus becomes more scarce and frequently limits the amount of algal growth that can be supported in a lake.

Nitrogen compounds, however, are more vulnerable to change once dissolved in the water. They can be converted by bacteria into nitrogen gas by a process called denitrification. These bacteria are particularly common in wetland and lake muds, where oxygen concentrations are very low or zero and where nitrate is used as an alternative oxidising agent for organic matter. As a result, much of the available combined nitrogen in lake water can escape back into the atmosphere.

In a pristine lake, therefore, phosphorus is usually scarcer than nitrogen in the open water,

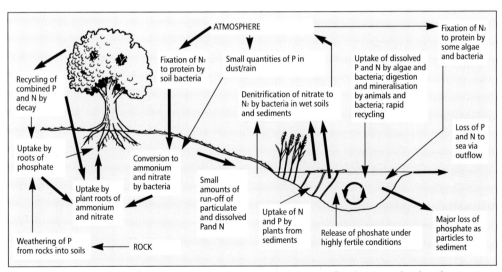

Fig 1.2 Major pathways of phosphorus and nitrogen during transfers between land and freshwater systems and the cycles within them. Thicker arrows indicate more important processes than thinner ones.

 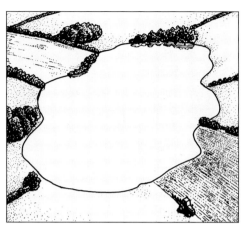

Fig 1.3   Infertile landscape (left) and fertile landscape

The geology of the catchment strongly influences the nature of the water, the shape and depth of the lake, and its consequent biology.

whilst in the sediments, because of denitrification, nitrogen may be scarcer than phosphorus. In both cases, both elements are fundamentally scarce. This scarcity will be greater in lakes in infertile catchments with poorly weatherable igneous or metamorphic rocks, or coarse sandstones or glacially deposited sands and gravels. It will be lesser in fertile catchments, underlain by sedimentary rocks with fine grain, such as shales, limestones, mudstones and glacially deposited clays and silts.

Catchments and trophic states

Catchments thus have considerable effects on the nature of the water that drains from them. A catchment with poorly weathered rocks and an intact natural ecosystem will produce a water with extremely low fertility, to which the term oligotrophic is commonly applied. A catchment with more reactive rocks and soils will produce relatively more fertile, but still absolutely infertile, water, providing it has an intact natural ecosystem. Such waters are often referred to as mesotrophic or eutrophic though these terms do not have precise definition and are used very differently by different people. They are referred to as trophic states, though in reality they form a continuum rather than

distinctive categories. These terms can be confusing and are best avoided. Disruption of the fertile catchment ecosystem, as will be seen in the next chapter, alters this picture. The nature of the catchment may also affect the lake in a different way, by determining its morphometry.

Morphometry

Morphometry is a useful word that sums up features of the shape, area, maximum and mean depths, volume and bed cross section (profile) of a lake. Poorly weathered catchments, if they are recently glaciated uplands, such as those in the Cumbrian Lake District, the Scottish Highlands or the Alps, may tend to have large, deep lakes with simple shoreline shapes and steep profiles. The basins have frequently been formed by the deepening of pre-existing valleys by ice as it gouged through the mountain passes.

Areas of softer, or more reactive, rock weather more rapidly to give subdued topographies that contain shallower depressions. Lakes may also form in basins left by the melting of icebergs buried in glacial drift deposits when the ice melted back. The North West Midland Meres of the UK and the many lakes of the plains around the Baltic Sea are good examples. Such areas also have rivers with wider floodplains, where

The resistant rocks of many upland regions produce infertile waters and lakes whose production is severely controlled by the availability of nutrients. The more western and northern lakes of the Cumbrian (English) Lake District are typical.

Lakes in the lowlands are generally naturally more fertile than those in the uplands because of the more easily weathered nature of lowland geology. Rostherne Mere is one of a group of lakes called the North West Midland Meres, situated in Cheshire, Staffordshire and Shropshire. They were mostly formed among the deposits washed out of the glaciers as they melted, by burial and subsequent melting, of huge, broken off icebergs.

cut-off meanders form shallow ox-bow lakes. They may be close to the sea where damming of streams by sand dunes or shingle bars (e.g Slapton Ley) can also form shallow lakes, often of complex outline. Lowland areas have also attracted greater human settlement, for their climates are more equable and their soils more cultivable. Lake basins formed by human activity are thus also common.

The eighteenth century saw the creation of many of these in the landscaping of the parks of the gentry (for example Bosherston Lake in

Pembrokeshire, see Chapter 10). There are more ancient examples in the mediaeval peat diggings of East Anglia, which formed the Norfolk and Suffolk Broads, and many of the lakes of the Netherlands.

An upland *versus* lowland correlation with deep, infertile and shallow, fertile lakes is imperfect. There are shallow lakes in uplands, poorly weatherable rocks in ancient lowlands

The widespread enclosure of the English landscape by fences, walls and hedges in the eighteenth and nineteenth centuries led to the landscaping of many estates. Central to many of these designed landscapes was an artificial lake, often shallow, but sometimes quite large. That at Blickling Hall in Norfolk, exemplifies the genre.

The Norfolk Broads are man-made lakes, whose basins were excavated as peat diggings between the ninth and thirteenth centuries. Martham North and South Broads lie to the north-east of the system of rivers and floodplains that contains them.

and young mountains of soluble limestones, but the generality is a useful one. Shallow lakes tend to be in the more fertile regions, and thus tend ultimately to be more vulnerable to human influence.

Shape and depth are features of particular importance in determining the potential for beds of aquatic plants to grow and the balance between plants and microscopic phytoplankton communities in pristine lakes. This is because of the effects that depth has on illumination of the bottom, and that shape has on the provision of bays sheltered from the effects of wind disturbance, especially in large lake basins.

Light availability is a particular problem for the larger aquatic plants.

Light and the competition between phytoplankton and aquatic plants

Natural waters absorb light quite quickly and after a few metres passage, only a few percent of the surface light will be left. An important measure of light penetration is the depth of the euphotic zone **(Fig.1.4)**, which is the depth at which growth of photosynthetic organisms is just possible. In north temperate regions this depth is that at which about 5% of the summer light at the surface remains, for aquatic plants, and 1% for the much less bulky microscopic algae. For a plant germinating or developing from small shoots on the bottom, the depth of water is critical. Development will not be possible in more than 3 or 4 metres of water in many lakes. The phytoplankton does not suffer from this problem because it is suspended in the water and circulated by wind-generated currents throughout the water column. Phytoplankton thus has a distinctive potential advantage in all lakes. A white disc, about 25cm in diameter, (called a Secchi disc after its inventor, an Italian admiral, who first used a dinner plate), when dropped on a line into the water, will eventually disappear from sight. This depth, the Secchi depth, is a measure of water transparency and approximates to the greatest

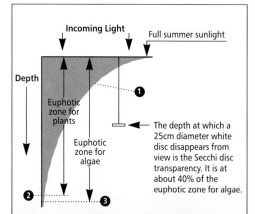

1 Light absorbed according to an exponential relationship - it decreases by the same percentage per metre with its penetration down the water column.

2 At about 5% of the surface light, bulky plants are only just meeting their requirements for maintenance and no new growth is possible. This is the lower limit of the euphotic zone for plants.

3 At about 1% of surface light, microalgae meet the same problem.

Fig 1.4 Major features of light penetration into freshwaters and definition of some important terms.

depth at which rooted aquatic plants will grow.

The aquatic plants may face further problems of light acquisition. Not only may they be shaded by the water itself, substances dissolved and phytoplankton suspended in it, but also by stirred up (resuspended) bottom sediment, especially in big lakes. Periphyton may cover them in all lakes. Periphyton is a complex microscopic community of algae, bacteria, mucilage and calcium carbonate particles (marl) **(Fig 1.5)**, which colonises plant surfaces and forms a shading layer several millimetres thick. Its light absorbing capacity may be as great as several metres of overlying water with phytoplankton.

Compared with the phytoplankton, therefore, the cards are somewhat stacked against the success of aquatic plants and indeed they are

Fig 1.5 The periphyton is a complex mixture of different algae with bacteria and small animals. The algae may be closely attached to the plant surface or they may be filaments or held on stalks projecting away from the plant's surface. Based on a drawing by Iwan Jones.

Reedswamp fringes provide habitat for fish and birds, organic detritus for other systems in the lake and an attractive edge. Ormesby Broad at dawn.

relatively unimportant in deep lakes. They do have one significant advantage, however, and that is access to nutrients in the interstitial waters of the sediments, which tend to be richer than the overlying water. In a pristine, shallow lake, only a few metres deep, therefore, submerged plants, with the help of the animal communities discussed below, may become predominant, but the balance is always precarious for them.

Swampy fringes and the littoral zone

From our viewpoint up a tree at the side of a pristine shallow lake then, we will see, in summer, a water dominated by the larger plants. There will be phytoplankton in the water but a microscope will be needed to see it. At the edge we will see the vegetation of the land grading imperceptibly into that of the water, with forests of oak, birch or ash acquiring alder and willow as the water table meets the surface of the soil. Beyond the trees, tall reedswamp plants take over in water that is perhaps a metre or more deep in winter, rather less in summer.

Dependent on place and accidents of coloni- sation, the community might be dominated by common reed (*Phragmites*), reedmace (*Typha*) or bulrush (*Scirpus* or *Schoenoplectus*), or even

sedges (*Carex*). Only space and mutual shading limit their growth for they live in a plant's ideal home. Water and light are not limiting, and as long as the shoreline is not being eroded by wind, sediments rich in soil particles, and their absorbed nutrients, will have accumulated. Thick stands of plants will have built up. The high production will be reflected in deposits of their remains as peat, and nutrients will be steadily released from these. Transfer from the dying shoots to the rhizomes in autumn will ensure much of the next year's nutrient needs for the plants.

Water lilies with their surface floating leaves, will become more abundant further offshore. They will be mixed with other floating and rooted plants - duckweeds, frogbit, bladderwort, stoneworts, hornwort and pondweeds, which will colonise the bottom as deeply as the light allows. Beyond that, a community of microscopic algae will occupy the surface sediments so that in a shallow lake virtually all the bottom will be photosynthetically productive. In deeper lakes, where parts of the bottom receive less than the nominal 1% of surface light necessary to support growth of microscopic algae, the bottom will be bare of photosynthetic organisms, but still colonised by

The fringing reedswamp occupies an almost ideal habitat for plants.

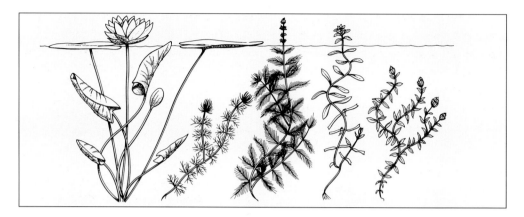

T Tilford, Press-Tige Pictures

For submerged plants in freshwaters, life is precarious.

The plant bed community is one of intricate biological and chemical relationships.

invertebrate animals and bacteria. These feed on the large supplies of organic particles which a beneficent gravity rolls down the slope from the upper regions of the lake.

That part of the lake where photosynthetic growth is possible on the bottom is called the littoral (shoreline) zone, and the term includes the overlying water as well as the bottom itself. The deeper areas and their overlying water are, correspondingly, the pelagial zone. They are not separate for, apart from the movement of organic matter, there is a circulation of water, with its suspended phytoplankton, between them. Movements of fish and water birds to feed and breed make further connections.

Life is precarious for the water plants that are partly or completely submerged, but evolution has produced a system which, in pristine lakes, promotes stability for the complex structure of the littoral. In the nooks and crannies, corridors and caverns that are created by the plant structures, niches for a myriad of animals abound. Most are small invertebrates, feeding on the plants themselves or on the periphyton attached to them or on the phytoplankton in the overlying and adjacent water. There will also be predators, both invertebrate and vertebrate. Together they help stabilise the plant community.

Our view from the tree, even with binoculars, will reveal only a little of this activity - the mating flight of damselflies, a swarm of midges recently emerged from their underwater larvae, the circlings of whirligig beetles feeding on the surface and the occasional leap of a small fish pursued by a bigger one. But there is much more going on than such casual observation can reveal[145]. In the intricacies of the littoral zone, even with special instruments, we sample like earth-moving machines demolishing a city. With the rush of water into bottles we destroy fine gradients, plumes of nutrients, only millimetres long, excreted by animals, or thousandfold changes in oxygen or carbon dioxide concentration close to plant and periphyton surfaces. With nets we obtain only

Whirligig beetles catch insects trapped in the surface film of water in quiet parts of the littoral zone.

the crudest idea of invertebrate and fish distribution and any sort of plant sampler crushes an important architectural structure and a finely distributed animal community into meaningless chaos. Such detail may explain why one organism is present here or another there, so it is not surprising that our understanding is meagre.

From what we do know, there are two important lessons. First, there is intense chemical activity in the littoral plant beds, with a regeneration of nutrients from animal excretions and from bacterial decomposition of organic matter falling to the sediment. And secondly, animals which might graze on phytoplankton in the adjacent water, perhaps at night, are abundant in the plant beds but are vulnerable to predators, particularly fish. Refuges, provided by the plants, are essential if such grazers and their predators are to co-exist. Each of these issues is crucial to the understanding of lake functioning and each will be examined in detail below.

Nutrient cycling and the sediments

Sediment varies greatly over small distances and is biologically and chemically very complex. Think of it accumulating on a lake bed without the complication of plants in the first instance. Foremost it is an accumulation of material - detritus, particles, carcases - for that is its essence. But then it may selectively return some of this material in processed form to the overlying water. There are billions of bacteria and single celled animals (Protozoa) in it that decompose organic matter. In doing so they consume oxygen which is not easily replaced by diffusion from the water. Sediment thus becomes anaerobic (oxygen-free) only a few millimetres below the surface and effectively forms a chemical processing factory with two storeys (Fig 1.6). In the anaerobic lower layer, bacteria continue to decompose organic matter, but, deprived of oxygen, they must use other oxidising agents such as nitrate and sulphate to complete the process. In doing so they convert any nitrate present to nitrogen gas (denitrification) and sulphate to sulphide. The former escapes eventually as gas, the latter usually combines with iron in the sediment to

Sediments contain large stores of some nutrients and are biologically very active. Depending on conditions the nutrients may be locked away as phosphate minerals, transformed to gas which escapes (denitrification of nitrate) or released to the overlying water (phosphate and ammonium ions).

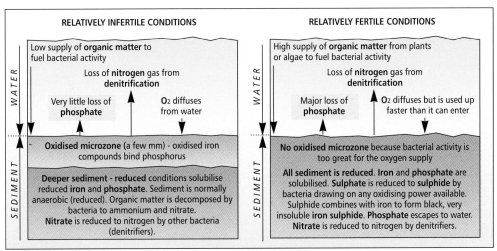

Fig 1.6 Some of the important chemical transformations that occur between sediment and freshwaters under relatively infertile (low production) and relatively fertile (high production) conditions.

form the very insoluble iron sulphide, the compound that gives anaerobic sediments their intense blackness. Phosphate is also produced from the decomposition, and under anaerobic conditions remains in solution at quite high concentrations (milligrams per litre, compared with values a thousand times lower in the lake water itself). Ammonium is also produced from the decomposition of proteins and similarly accumulates at high concentration, whilst some of the organic matter is converted to methane.

In the better-aerated, but thin, surface sediment layer, diffusion of oxygen from the overlying water allows aerobic decomposition to go on. The bacteria break down organic matter to carbon dioxide, water and inorganic constituents like ammonium and phosphate. The ammonium may then diffuse upwards into the overlying water, or may be converted by other bacteria to nitrate. Its fate is then usually to be denitrified back to nitrogen by bacteria before it can escape the sediments. Phosphate does not escape either, for in the presence of oxygen, it is tied up by iron as a brown complex which looks like rust and gives a brownish surface crust (the oxidised microzone) to such sediments.

Under these circumstances, all that escapes from sediments is a little ammonium, carbon dioxide and perhaps some methane from the anaerobic decomposition in the deeper layers. For phosphorus, the sediments are a sink not a source and for nitrogen they are a source, but mostly of nitrogen in unavailable gaseous form. The circumstances change, however, when the supply of decomposable organic matter is very high as it is in a dense plant bed in the littoral zone.

Nutrient cycling in plant beds

In dense plant beds, the processes are all potentially as described above, and towards the end of winter may be exactly as described. But once the plants and the associated invertebrate animals have established themselves, the drizzle of organic matter to the bottom intensifies to a heavy rain. As the plant roots permeate the sediments, they absorb some substances and move them into their shoots for growth. The additional organic matter so intensifies the activity at the sediment surface that oxygen diffusion from the water cannot cope and even the surface layer becomes anaerobic. All of the available iron may then become tied up as sulphide, and phosphate may diffuse upwards into the water. Sulphide formation depends on a supply of sulphate and this may be considerable especially when even small amounts of seawater (which is rich in sulphate) enter the lake from estuarine water or saline groundwater seepage. Under such low oxygen conditions, ammonium is also not so readily converted into nitrate and it too diffuses into the water above the sediments.

The sediment, receiving combined nitrogen and phosphorus in the organic detritus, has now become a source of available forms of these elements. The plant roots in the sediment, equipped with a number of adaptations to cope with the anaerobic medium, absorb both ammonium and phosphate from the plentiful supplies in the interstitial water. They also take most of the diffusing ammonium and some of the phosphate through their leaves. The periphyton also benefits from these supplies. Indeed there may be sufficient for quite a lot of phosphate to escape the plant bed entirely and become available to the phytoplankton in the overlying and adjacent waters **(Fig 1.7)**.

In open water, remember, nutrient scarcity is a major issue, limiting the growth of the phytoplankton, whose potential production can now increase. A shallow lake, with predominant waterplant beds, thus recycles nutrients that have entered from the catchment

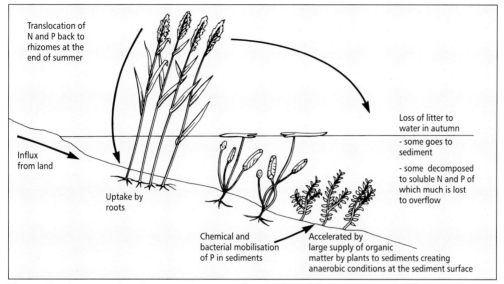

Translocation of
N and P back to
rhizomes at the
end of summer

Loss of litter to
water in autumn

- some goes to
sediment

- some decomposed
to soluble N and P of
which much is lost
to overflow

Influx
from land

Uptake by
roots

Chemical and
bacterial mobilisation
of P in sediments

Accelerated by
large supply of organic
matter by plants to sediments creating
anaerobic conditions at the sediment surface

Fig 1.7 Nutrient transfers that occur between plant beds and the open water in lakes.

and because of the stores it can build up in the sediments, can keep in circulation more than the current year's supply. To some extent, throughput of water may wash some of the phosphorus out, but throughput is generally low in summer when much of the release occurs.

Control of the algal growth

For the plants, these mechanisms could prove fatal if the growth of periphyton and phytoplankton, benefiting from the released nutrients, became so great that it shaded them and diminished their growth. This does not happen in a pristine lake because of mechanisms, dependent on the plants, which prevent the algae from reaching their potential maxima. Such mechanisms involve grazing by invertebrate animals. They may also involve the production of chemical inhibitors of the algae by the plants.

Grazers of the periphyton algae

The grazers of the periphyton are mostly snails, insect larvae and crustaceans. Some are quite large - a centimetre or two long, others, the

crustaceans in particular, are only millimetres or smaller in size. We may presume that, as in the intricate division of the available food between the antelopes, zebra, buffalo, mice and grasshoppers of an African savannah, there is much intricacy in how the periphyton, and some of the host plant, is divided among the grazer community, but we know surprisingly little. The animal community is very effective at keeping down the furry periphyton coating on the plants that would develop in its absence. This can easily be shown in experiments, when the snails, for example, are removed, but the intricacies of organisation among the community remain yet to be discovered [26,27].

Grazers on phytoplankton

In contrast we understand the phytoplankton grazers quite well. They are collectively called the zooplankton and come from two main animal groups, the crustaceans and the rotifers. The rotifers are tiny (mostly less than 200 micrometres), and since, in general, the effectiveness of a grazer is proportional to the square or cube of its body size, the rotifers

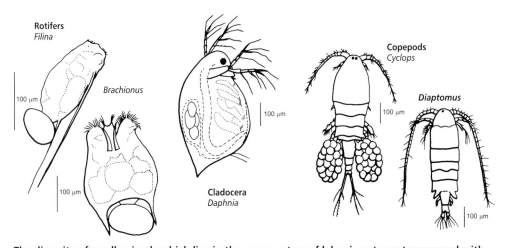

Rotifers
Filina

Brachionus

Cladocera
Daphnia

Copepods
Cyclops

Diaptomus

100 μm   100 μm   100 μm   100 μm   100 μm   100 μm

The diversity of small animals which live in the open waters of lakes is not great compared with those in the sea, but they are very important. There are three main groups of freshwater zooplankters. The rotifers (left two diagrams) are very small, form the food of the smallest fish just after they cease to be dependent on the yolk provided in the egg, but are not eaten by larger fish. They are also inefficient grazers on the phytoplankton. The cladocerans, or water fleas (centre), are prime fish food and also important grazers. Daphnia is the most important genus. Copepods are also important fish food, but more easily escape capture than the water fleas. They (right two diagrams) tend to graze on larger particles than the water fleas and filter the water less efficiently.

The water fleas, or Cladocera, are key players in the shallow lake system. Daphnia can prevent a phytoplankton algae community of any significance developing, but fish can remove the Daphnia faster than Daphnia can remove algae.

probably contribute rather little to the total grazing effort. The crustaceans, on the other hand are ten times bigger and thus, per animal, a hundred to a thousand times more effective at removing algae. They are of two main groups, the copepods, which are not particularly abundant in shallow lakes, though they predominate in big, deep ones, and the water fleas, or Cladocera, which are key players in the shallow lake system.

Some water flea species occur deep in the plant beds and may graze periphyton or phytoplankton brought in by currents of water and loosely caught up in the periphyton. Others, such as the well known *Daphnia,* prefer open water. They filter copious volumes through the beating of a series of limbs at their fronts, removing bacteria, algae and particles of detritus as small as one micrometre from the water, before conveying the amorphous mass to their mouths and guts for digestion. A moderate sized population of *Daphnia* (a few tens per litre) dispersed in a lake, can filter the

entire lake volume more than once a day at equable temperatures. These *Daphnia* can only survive if there is sufficient food. Their own activity quickly depletes the algal supply but they appear to be able to tide themselves over periods of low algal abundance by using other sources, such as bacteria and fine sediment particles, which are readily available in shallow lakes. Given the opportunity, therefore, *Daphnia* can effectively prevent a phytoplankton community of any significance from developing.

Fish feed on Daphnia

That opportunity is not easily given, however, for fish can remove the *Daphnia* as rapidly as *Daphnia* can remove the algae. Cladocerans move relatively slowly through the water, in contrast to copepods which can make sharp jumps out of the way when a fish attacks. Moreover, the larger cladocerans, such as *Daphnia* , are large enough to be easily seen by a fish, whose vision will be inadequate to make frequent successful attacks on smaller

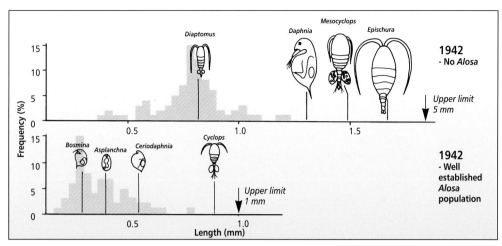

Fig 1.8 Fish and sometimes other predators are important influences in determining the nature of the zooplankton community. In a classic study made by John Brookes and Stanley Dodson (1965), the introduction of a zooplanktivorous fish, a shad, *Alosa aestivalis*, to Crystal Lake in Connecticut, resulted in a major reduction in numbers of all the larger species of zooplankton (mainly cladocerans and copepods) and a shift to predominance of much smaller cladocerans and rotifers. In general a community of smaller animals is less effective at grazing the phytoplankton algae than one of larger animals.

organisms such as rotifers. The energy used in attack is also barely compensated by the reward of such small prey.

Thus, placed in a large and bare tank, a few fish will rapidly change the composition of a zooplankton community from a mixture of large and small animals, in which *Daphnia* is predominant and with high grazing potential, to one of only smaller cladocerans, a few fast moving copepods, and a lot of tiny rotifers, collectively with little grazing potential[86] (**Fig 1.8**). Algae will then grow abundantly. Observe many bare aquarium tanks or garden ponds, with no filters but with abundant goldfish, and you will see an excellent demonstration of this.

Fish have other effects as well. They migrate a great deal within large lakes and when they move from the shallows, where they were spawned and grew, to the open waters, they may redistribute nutrients. Their excretion, as adults in the open water, may increase the availability of phosphorus to the phytoplankton and they may thus support a greater phytoplankton crop than would otherwise be present[100].

The refuge concept
Look at a pristine shallow lake, however, with abundant plant beds, and you will see clear water though there is no lack of fish capable of feeding on *Daphnia*. The edges of the weed beds, especially those of water lilies, will reveal swarms of this animal[204]. There will be small fish among them[191, 211] but insufficient *Daphnia* are taken to reduce the swarms to any marked extent. Extensive grazing can then still occur as the *Daphnia* disperse throughout the lake at night, when the fish cannot see them. By day, due to shading by the plants, the fish may not see the *Daphnia* well enough to risk an attack among the clutter of stems and leaf petioles in the plant beds, or they may be deterred from making too many obvious and risky movements in a place where their own predators, large perch and pike, may lurk. The

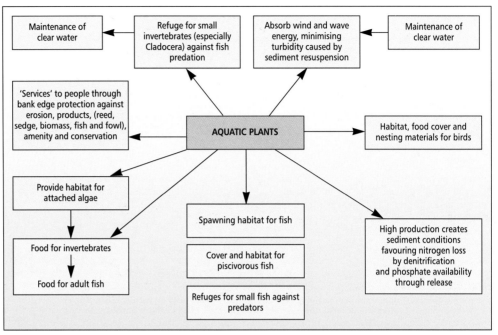

Fig 1.9 Links between aquatic plants and other organisms, including ourselves.

Aquatic plants may provide important refuges for Daphnia.

chemistry of the water may also deter them. Absorption of carbon dioxide by the plants raises the pH to values which may induce inactivity[9]. Aquatic plants, in these ways, provide refuges against predation for the zooplankton grazers[187].

On balance....

Thus the precarious position of the water plants is insured, and in a pristine shallow lake they persist and dominate. To their advantage is access to nutrients in the sediment and mechanisms of storing scarce nutrients by recycling them back to roots and rhizomes in the winter. To their detriment is the shading by the overlying water, and the periphyton and phytoplankton communities, and their very size and the problems it poses for the diffusion inwards of nutrients. But they have evolved insurance policies in their abilities to take up and store, in their large bulks, almost all the available supplies of ammonium and to create

conditions at the bases of their beds for most of the nitrate to be removed by denitrification, thus depriving the algal communities of nutrients.

In providing refuge for vulnerable invertebrate grazers to build up their numbers, plant beds can limit the growth of potentially damaging periphyton and phytoplankton. The separate strategies that allow each organism to persist have coalesced to form an intricate system with incidental but mutual benefit for all (**Fig 1.9**).

Grazers on the plants themselves

There are yet other components to this system, though we understand them far less well. Invertebrates also graze the plants, though each to a very small extent. The combined effects of large populations, however, can be devastating[108]. Water lily leaves, laced with the holes made by china mark moth caterpillars, are not uncommon. The plant compensates by continuous production of leaves throughout

Cormorant

Kingfisher

Grebe

Heron

Otter

Pikeperch

Perch

Pike

the season, completely replacing its structure more than once per summer. Larger fish than those that eat *Daphnia*, consume the plant grazers and the invertebrate predators of the periphyton grazers and reduce the populations to below fully destructive levels.

Birds, mammals and fish

Birds like coot, ducks, geese and swans also eat plants, but other mechanisms again prevent the populations reaching mutually destructive proportions. Pike take chicks; suitable nesting sites are limited. Fortunate accidents of migration minimise grazing pressures at critical times for plant growth. Some fish, like tench, eat plants but their populations are not great, perhaps because of their own predators, and their effects are minimised by a partiality for eating protein-rich invertebrates as well. Piscivorous fish, pike, large perch and zander may rapidly reduce the numbers of newly spawned coarse fish (roach, bream, rudd, small perch) that consume zooplankton.

Kingfishers, cormorants, grebes, herons and otters also have roles[217] in maintaining fish populations at levels which can co-exist with and not threaten the system. The bigger the organism, in general, the less we know about its precise influence and interactions, though much helpful natural history has been learned. But there will be intricate links no less important than those of the bacteria, algae and invertebrates yet to be discovered. Indeed there will be so many that we will never completely understand how the system, or any other natural system, works.

Chaos and change

Two factors - chaotic dynamics, and inevitable change combine to limit our ability to understand complex systems. Chaotic dynamics means that the composition of the system is not fully predictable. The existence or absence of a particular organism may be the result of the occurrence of environmental conditions appropriate, or otherwise, for it. But it may never have reached the site, especially in the

Chaotic dynamics and constant change preclude full understanding of any ecosystem.

short time that has elapsed since the devastating effects of the last glaciation. Or it may have been there but have been made locally extinct by some vagary of the past weather - prolonged ice causing a fish kill, or summer drought. There is some ordered expectation about what species one might find in a particular place but also a greater degree of uncertainty.

Because every species is at least slightly different from others with a broadly similar niche, the nature of its interactions will also vary. Take a choice of five aquatic plant species from a total potential of thirty, of a hundred algae from a thousand, fifty invertebrates from a hundred, ten fish from twenty and twenty birds from forty and work out all the possible

combinations. The number is unimaginably large and we have not yet allowed for the bacteria and Protozoa. There are over seventeen million such combinations of aquatic plants alone. We will thus have to content ourselves for the most part with considering functional groups - submerged plants, floating leaved plants, grazing zooplankters, fish-eating birds, for examples rather than the nuances of individual species. And our understanding may consequently be only coarse or biased by a particular concentration on a handful of particularly obvious or easily investigable species.

Then there is the problem of inevitable change. The system loses and acquires species faster than we can work out the details of its present state. This is especially true of shallow lakes for

Shallow lakes, left to themselves, fill in with the remains of their own vegetation and with sediment from the surrounding catchment. They become covered with wetland or even woodland vegetation. In the drier east of Britain, this vegetation would typically be alderwood (carr), perhaps with trees like oak. In the wetter west, as here at Abbott's Moss in Cheshire, the rainfall keeps the surface wet and acid. Bog vegetation, dominated by Sphagnum, heather and birch may be the result.

they do not represent climax communities, like deciduous forests. They are successional stages in the filling-in of temporary hollows in the landscape. Their natural fate is for a steady infilling with sediment and encroachment of organic remains (peat) at the edges. The littoral zone communities are so productive that decomposition cannot keep pace with accumulation.

Year by year, the reedswamp and fen communities encroach on the open water until the basin is filled by wetland and no open water remains. Dependent on the vagaries of changing climate, it may remain a wet alderwood or it may dry out if the water table falls, and develop into an oak, or ash or some other kind of woodland. If the weather becomes wetter, peat may continue to build up above the water table. In the acid conditions created at the surface by the leaching action of the rain, a bog with *Sphagnum* moss may develop but the former lake will have disappeared. Natural processes - landslides, or beavers blocking streams may create new shallow lakes, but in the natural course of events, pristine shallow lakes are doomed to disappearance.

However, we live in a period of history when many shallow basins still persist and we must consider a further organism that affects them - ourselves. The pristine shallow lake system can never have excluded us, though our role was small. We caught fish and birds for food, perhaps gathered reed for shelters, cut wood for fires and herbs for medicine, but our influence was probably almost indetectable, for our populations were low and our technology impotent. All that has changed. The pristine shallow lake no longer exists, though passable relics occur in remoter regions. The realities of shallow lakes in the now populous lowlands of Europe are the subject of Chapter 2.

Chapter 2

A Spanner in the Works - How Lakes are Altered by Human Activity

'O the hammer ponds of Sussex and the dew ponds of the west

are part of Britain's heritage, the part we love the best.

Every eel and fish and mill pond has a beauty all can share

But not unless it's got a big, brass broken bedstead there'.

Bedstead Men, Michael Flanders
& Donald Swann, *'At the Drop of Another Hat'*.

Climb again the hypothetical tree at the edge of a shallow lake and you may look down, not on a diverse waterscape reminiscent of a microcosmic Earth seen from space, but on a monotonous wasteland. For many shallow lakes are not pristine but greatly changed by the activities of more people than before and the demands they make on the environment for their comfort. Instead of a coherent fringe of reedswamp and swamp forest, you may see some remnant clumps backed by a ploughed field. The water will not be graced by lily flowers, nor will the damselflies sport over the surface. For the submerged plants, down whose stems they climbed to lay their eggs, will have gone.

So will the coot and ducks, unless they are domesticated ones fed on bread. The water will not be clear but laden with mud or algae and at the edges you may see the paint-like scum of a stranded algal bloom harbouring toxins[155] capable of killing farm or pet animals. And the local youth, facing an unrespectable devastation, may have contributed the odd shopping trolley, park bench, rubber tyre, or even a broken brass bedstead. This is the apparently unpromising subject that many would-be restorers of shallow lakes will have to face. Yet much is possible.

Sewage

Key to all the changes is that the flow of nitrogen and phosphorus from the land to the water has increased, though the story has greater complexities than this alone. Until the nineteenth century most of the population of Europe was dispersed in villages and hamlets. Their sewage was disposed of either direct to the nearest river or into pits.

With the industrial revolution and a movement of the population to the cities, pits were no longer an option, but disposal to the river remained so. The rivers suffered extreme deoxygenation, but it was the reality of cholera and typhoid epidemics that led first to the dumping of the sewage on land in sewage farms for it to rot. When this method was found to be incapable of coping with the amounts, the first sewage treatment works were constructed towards the end of the nineteenth century.

Sewage treatment works (**Fig.2.1**) remove the organic matter from sewage using a system of bacteria, Protozoa and other small inverte-brates, not unlike that which decomposes organic matter in sediments. Sewage is now an even more complex mixture than it was in the nineteenth century because it contains the products not only of domestic activities (now more chemically based and including detergents) but sometimes also industrial ones. As in the decomposition of organic matter in sediments, the products of sewage treatment

Many shallow lakes are not pristine but greatly changed by the increased activities of more people than before.

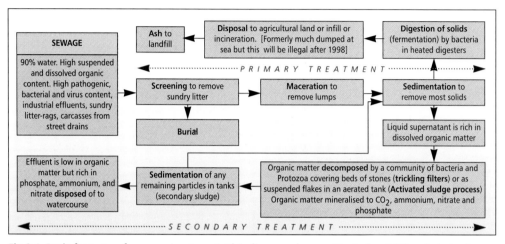

Fig 2.1 Basic features of sewage treatment. This diagram does not include additional stages for the removal of phosphate and nitrate (tertiary treatment) but includes features of conventional treatment in the UK.

are inorganic - carbon dioxide and methane, ammonium, nitrate and phosphate. An effluent, rich in the latter three (with concentrations at levels of tens of milligrams per litre), is discharged from the works to the nearest river or stream and thence to any lake basin that the river or stream may supply. The degree of dilution is often low but even if it is quite high, say 50 to 1, the concentrations of phosphorus in the water may be raised by ten or a hundred times that which would be found in a pristine stream.

The concentrations of ammonium and nitrate in the stream are also raised, but proportionately not by so much as those of phosphorus. This is because their background concentrations, in water draining from the land, are much higher than those of phosphorus on account of their high solubility. A properly functioning sewage treatment works (Fig.2.1) also includes a process in which ammonium is oxidised to nitrate, so that most of the nitrogen should emerge as nitrate rather than ammonium. This is desirable because high concentrations of ammonium, under certai n circumstances, especially at high pH, can be toxic to fish.

Agriculture

Far greater supplies of nitrate are delivered to the rivers from field agriculture and of ammonium from stock husbandry. Again this arises from understandable historic trends. The exigencies of war in the nineteen-forties led to an emphasis on home-grown food and thence on more efficient and intensive methods of production. Work on the land was hard and socially undervalued and this also promoted intensive machine-based methods. In turn, the capital needed to support such methods promoted specialisation on farms. There was a concentration on arable in some areas, on intensive stock-rearing in others. The time honoured principles of mixed farming, crop rotation and re-use of animal manures as fertilizer have thus been eroded.

New, high yielding varieties of cereals required fertilisation with nitrogen at levels fifteen or twenty times those used before the war, whilst annual cultivation of the fields has led to a reduction of the soil organic content which formerly bound up nitrogen. There has consequently been a major increase in the nitrogen content of the rivers gathering water from agricultural land [179].

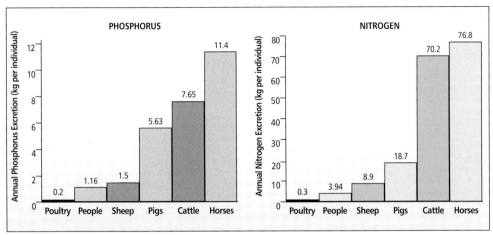

Fig 2.2 Annual excretion (including detergent use by people) of humans and domestic stock in western European countries.

With increasing numbers of animals, often intensively housed, livestock excreta are also a substantial nutrient source **(Fig. 2.2)**. Regulations and Codes of Practice should prevent direct leakage of excreta but eventually the manure must decompose. In doing so it produces ammonium and phosphate which ultimately enter the watercourses, unless partly bound in the soil by application to the land. There is evidence that the soil binding capacity has now become saturated in some areas[57,60a,60b,109a,196a]. In stock-rearing areas, the stock population provides equivalent loads of phosphorus to those provided by people in urban areas **(Fig 2.3)**.

Eutrophication

The very act of disturbing the natural vegetation cover from a catchment results in destruction of nutrient conservation mechanisms. The fertilizer and feed inputs of modern agriculture and husbandry inevitably leak to provide greater sources for runoff. This, in combination with treated sewage and other effluents, means that the amounts of nitrogen and phosphorus reaching our freshwaters have increased, particularly in the last few decades. Production of all the photosynthetic communities, algal

and plant, of pristine lake ecosystems was formerly severely limited by the supplies of these nutrients. This production has consequently increased.

Formerly phosphorus was in somewhat shorter supply than nitrogen (because of the greater solubility of nitrogen compounds) so that an injection of phosphorus alone could increase the production, particularly of algae, in the open water. Massive increases, however, eventually need both nutrients, as the limiting factor leapfrogs from phosphorus to nitrogen when phosphorus is increased. In large lakes, where larger plants are not important and phytoplankton dominates, eutrophication primarily by phosphorus has been a common phenomenon and losses of water clarity have been usual. There is a direct correlation [51,159,186,213] between the phosphorus concentration and the algal crop, measured by its content of the photosynthetic pigment, chlorophyll a in such waters **(Fig.2.4)**.

This has resulted in greater costs of filtration if the water is used for domestic supply. There may also be a loss of amenity, partly reflected in changing fish communities, which affects anglers, and partly in the production of surface

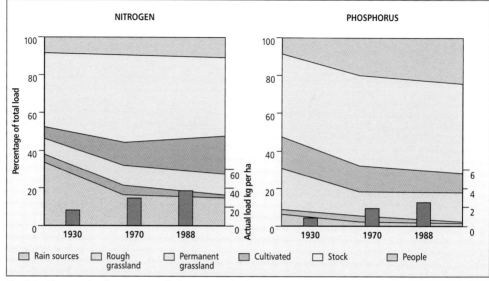

Fig 2.3 Changes in the sources of nitrogen and phosphorus supplied to streams draining ten rural British catchments between 1930 and 1988. The data are shown as percentages of the entire load for each year (main diagram) and the absolute load delivered is shown as a histogram at the bottom. On average loads have doubled since 1930. From Johnes *et al* 1996.

The relationship between nutrient levels and ecosystem structure is much more complex in shallow lakes than in deep ones. There are important questions of why it is important to reestablish plants, why such reestablishment is difficult, and why they disappeared in the first instance.

scums of algae, which may be toxic[155]. The solution has been relatively simple in a reduction of the phosphorus load by extra treatment at the sewage works, diversion of effluent away from the lake, or dosing of the inflows or the lake with chemicals such as iron sulphate which precipitate phosphate[72,180].

Eutrophication in shallow lakes - alternative states

The situation in the shallow, previously plant-dominated lakes, with which we are concerned here, has been more complicated and interesting. There is clearly a correlation between increased nutrient additions, increased phytoplankton growth in the water and, at first, increased plant growth. But then the plants disappear, leaving the stage to the algae and robbing the lake of most of the diversity with which Chapter 1 was concerned. Attempts to demonstrate a loss of plants with increased nutrient load in experimental ponds have generally failed[7,85,90]. Even with huge loads,

the plants thrive and the added nutrients do not build up in the water. They are sequestered into the sediments or plants, or are denitrified. Only if the plants are experimentally removed do the nutrients show an effect by stimulating further phytoplankton growth. Furthermore, sampling of a very large number of shallow European and American lakes has shown that over a very wide range of total phosphorus concentrations, hugely exceeding the pristine range, aquatic plant communities can persist, whilst other lakes within the same range can have lost all their plants and be dominated by phytoplankton[30,94,184].

The reverse is also the case. Just as adding nutrients does not inevitably displace the plants, because the mechanisms that insure their precarious position are powerful, reducing the nutrient loads invariably does not result in clear water and a return of the plants (**Fig. 2.5**). Partly this is because a lot of phosphorus leaks out from sediments laid down under nutrient-

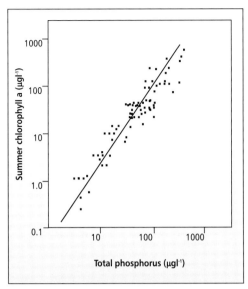

Fig 2.4 Typical relationship between the summer phytoplankton crop, measured as chlorophyll a and the total phosphorus concentration in a sample of lakes. The scales are logarithmic and this to some extent masks variation that would be more apparent with linear scales. Quite large ranges of chlorophyll a can occur for a given phosphorus concentration because of the influence of grazers in reducing the algal crop to below the potential set by the phosphorus availability. Based on Dillon & Rigler (1974).

Ditches (dykes), made in the wetlands of the Norfolk Broadland in former centuries, can be divided into separate ponds by wooden dams and used for experiments. These ponds at Woodbastwick, in the Bure Marshes National Nature Reserve, were used in the early 1980s to show that adding nutrients to a well established plant-dominated community did not, by itself, displace the plants and lead to plankton dominance. Only when the plants were severely damaged by raking them out did a plankton-dominated community develop, in ponds to which the greatest nutrient additions had been made.

polluted conditions, even after the external nutrient supply has been reduced[126,183]. But removing this sediment often results in no improvement. There are more subtle factors at work[7,87,150].

Just as mechanisms exist in the pristine lake to preserve the dominance of plants, even if nutrient loads are artificially increased, so also there are mechanisms which preserve phytoplankton dominance, even when the load is reduced (Fig.2.6). Prime among these is that in open water, unstructured by plant refuges, fish can easily remove all the large water fleas so that grazing pressure on the algae is minimal. This is also promoted by the greater ratio of zooplanktivorous to piscivorous fish that is

common in higher nutrient, phytoplankton-dominated lakes[94,171]. The reasons may include reduced average oxygen concentration, which disfavours active piscivores.

The absence of plants removes any competition for nitrogen or possibilities of the production of algal inhibitors. Once it is established, algal dominance is promoted by the earlier date in the year by which the algae are able to grow. In addition, algae do not need to support unproductive root and rhizome tissue but are wholly photosynthetic and can devote all their energy to production of more photosynthetic cells. Once established in spring, the shading by

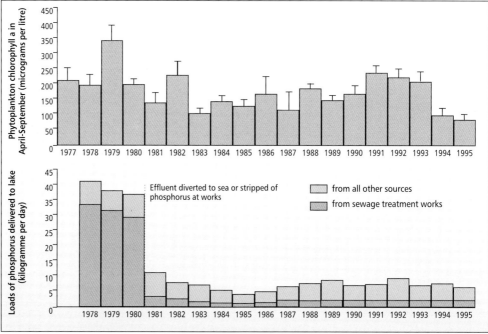

Fig 2.5 **The inputs of phosphorus to Barton Broad have been greatly reduced since 1981, but the water remains turbid with large phytoplankton growths.**

The nature of sediment is important. Muds laid down under plants are more structured and less easily disturbed than those laid down by algae.

the algae suppresses growth of any developing plant propagules at the sediment surface.

The sediment laid down by copious quantities of finely particulate algae differs from the more structured peaty sediments formed in plant beds. In large shallow lakes, the loss of plants may allow so much disturbance of sediment by wind that turbidity is created as much by this as by phytoplankton. The foraging activities of bottom feeding fish like bream may also stir up lots of sediment[25,112]. All of these will make plant growth difficult or impossible. Once decimated the plants are unable to recover easily for their propagules will be sparse and easily set back by wind and wave movement, bird grazing in spring and the shifting nature of anaerobic sediments no longer stabilised by plant roots.

We thus have two alternative systems, plant-dominated and phytoplankton-dominated,

each able to persist, once established, over a wide range of nutrient conditions, and each stabilised or buffered **(Fig.2.6)** by a variety of mechanisms. The key questions are then whether we can quantify this range of nutrient conditions and what happens outside it, and how the buffer mechanisms can be overcome

Bream forage in the bottom sediments and large fish may stir up considerable amounts. Small bream are zooplanktivorous. All ages of this species may then contribute to water turbidity.

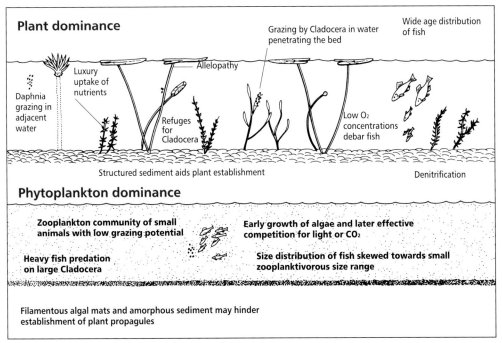

Plant dominance

Grazing by Cladocera in water penetrating the bed

Wide age distribution of fish

Daphnia grazing in adjacent water

Luxury uptake of nutrients

Allelopathy

Refuges for Cladocera

Low O_2 concentrations debar fish

Structured sediment aids plant establishment

Denitrification

Phytoplankton dominance

Zooplankton community of small animals with low grazing potential

Early growth of algae and later effective competition for light or CO_2

Heavy fish predation on large Cladocera

Size distribution of fish skewed towards small zooplanktivorous size range

Filamentous algal mats and amorphous sediment may hinder establishment of plant propagules

Fig 2.6 Some of the mechanisms which stabilise (buffer) aquatic plant - dominated and phytoplankton - dominated communities.

to switch the systems from one state to the other.

The nutrient range for alternative states

It is difficult to characterise the nature of a complex thing like water quality by a simple, single number, though frequently that is attempted. In recent years the practice has been to determine water quality, where eutrophication is concerned, by the total phosphorus concentration, though the total nitrogen concentration is equally relevant. Below about 25 to 50 micrograms of total phosphorus per litre, it seems that in shallow waters (less than 3m deep), aquatic plants will be able to dominate without threat of supersedence by phytoplankton. The pristine range for these conditions is more likely to have been lower than 25 micrograms per litre. The equivalent total nitrogen concentration would be about 250 to 500 micrograms per litre.

In this range, the smaller species of aquatic plant, which by their stature are least competitive, will thrive. They may include the charophytes, which are strictly large algae but have the equivalents of shoots and branches and an anchoring system in the sediments, the hollyweed, *Najas marina*, and some of the smaller pondweeds. Some of the charophytes are now very rare, for shallow lakes in this range are not common in the lowlands. Suitable infertile but bicarbonate-rich waters, that favour these plants, are fast disappearing.

Beyond about 50 micrograms per litre, either a plant-dominated or a phytoplankton-dominated system can exist as alternative states, though the higher the nutrient level, the greater the risk of the system being switched from plant dominance to algal dominance. The higher the level also, the greater the chance that some of the plant biomass will be draped

Below about 25 to 50 micrograms of total phosphorus per litre there will probably be dominance by aquatic plants. Above this range either plant or phytoplankton dominance may exist as alternative states.

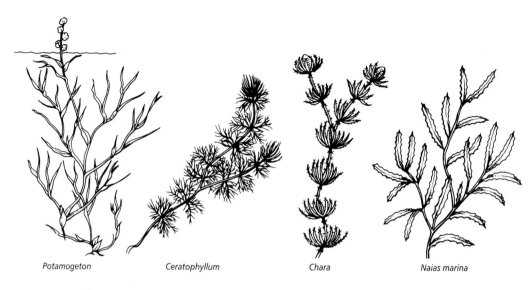

Potamogeton   Ceratophyllum   Chara   Naias marina

Forward switches promote the loss of aquatic plants provided the nutrient levels are sufficiently high. They include those that directly destroy the plants and those that interfere with the buffers that stabilise the plant community.

in competitive filamentous algae. The diversity of the plant community will also decrease at increasing nutrient levels, as highly competitive species like the hornwort (*Ceratophyllum demersum*) and sago pondweed (*Potamogeton pectinatus*) will come to dominate. The yellow and white water lilies are very tolerant and will also persist at increasing nutrient levels, but the bladderworts (*Utricularia vulgaris*), water soldier (*Stratiotes aloides*), frogbit (*Hydrocharis morsus-ranae*), and a great range of pondweeds (*Potamogeton* spp) seem to be less favoured with increasing concentrations.

The upper limit of the range of total phosphorus concentrations within which alternative states can exist is not known, but it is very high - several milligrams per litre. Water lilies and semi-floating plants like the amphibious bistort (*Polygonum amphibium*), the spiked water milfoil (*Myriophyllum spicatum*) and the duckweeds can grow in little diluted sewage effluent and may form substantial stands. Effectively then there is probably no upper limit, but the stability of the aquatic plant community may be low at such nutrient concentrations and much more prone to switch to algal dominance.

We can thus construct a diagram **(Fig.2.7)** which presents the state of unique plant dominance at

the lowest concentrations, and alternatives of plant-dominance or phytoplankton-dominance at all higher concentrations, set against a nutrient gradient, together with the mechanisms which stabilise these states. The question that must then be answered is what mechanisms cause switching between the alternative states.

Forward switches

Simple nutrient addition clearly can move the system from unique plant-dominance to the range where alternatives can exist. With increased nutrient loading, more vigorous species simply shade out the smaller charophytes and create dense weedbeds. Shading by increased periphyton may also be responsible[169]. Periphyton will also tend to increase on these more competitive plants but is continually removed by grazers. If this is not sufficiently effective, practices such as the sloughing off of periphyton-burdened leaves or the production of a leaf canopy towards the water surface, where light is most intense, may be used.

Some very vigorous plants, such as the water soldier (*Stratiotes aloides*), float in the surface layers in summer and lilies also deploy the effective device of having floating leaves.

Because nutrients, though they may change the composition of the community, cannot displace aquatic plants altogether, there has to be an additional switch mechanism for the plants to be displaced and for phytoplankton to take over. Such switches will be called forward switches as opposed to reverse switches which catalyse the conversion of phytoplankton-dominance back to plant-dominance.

Two groups of forward switches are known or suspected[142]. One group removes the plants themselves to a damaging extent; the second interferes with the stabilising buffer mechanisms, particularly the grazing Cladocera. Direct loss of the plants may be by simple mechanical removal - an over-zealous raking out for amenity purposes or to create open swims for fishing. The propellors from repeated boat passages may cut so much biomass that the plant fails to recover. Deliberate use of herbicides to control the plants[209], or run-off of herbicides used on the land may be responsible. In some cases, the raising of water levels has displaced plants, presumably by reducing the light available to them for growth from their propagules on the bottom[3,19,20,21].

Finally, grazing by vertebrates may throw the switch. Most instances involve exotic species, introduced from elsewhere, whose burgeoning populations are uncontrolled by natural predators. The common carp (*Cyprinus carpio*) is associated with loss of plants and turbid water[29,42,46,60,110,122,128].

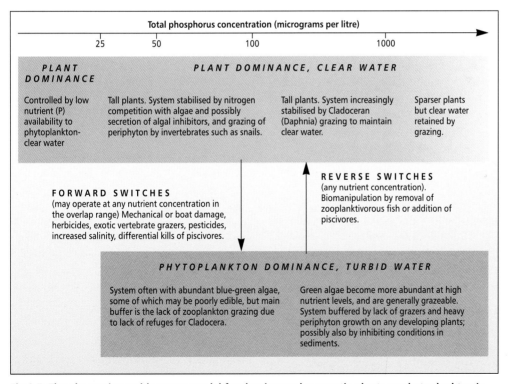

Fig 2.7 The alternative stable states model for dominance by aquatic plants or phytoplankton in shallow lakes, over the gradient of total phosphorus concentrations that includes both pristine values and those encountered in polluted conditions.

Many mechanisms can contribute, singly or in combination to switch a shallow lake from plant dominance to algal dominance. They may include: introduction of carp; large numbers of Canada or greylag geese, or coypu; herbicide or pesticide run-off; boat damage; or selective fish kills, under winter ice or in summer stagnation, that alter the balance of piscivores to zooplanktivores among the fish.

Carp were introduced into the British fish fauna during the mediaeval period, or possibly earlier by the Romans. They are not a problem so long as their numbers and sizes are small. Hitherto they have bred only infrequently and been a problem only when they have been heavily stocked for angling. That situation may be changing as climatic changes favouring carp reproduction take hold, giving warmer summers. It is possible also that stocking of bream together with carp is a particularly damaging activity for the plants, for carp eats plants and mobilises phosphorus from the sediment, both disturb sediment, and the young of bream are voracious feeders on *Daphnia*.

Chinese grass carp (*Ctenopharyngodon idella*) would be equally damaging if introduced into a ·lake. Indeed they are used specifically to control plants in canals under carefully prescribed conditions[54]. Among birds, Canada geese, and large numbers of mute swan may displace plant communities and feral flocks of greylag geese must be regarded with suspicion. Of mammals, only the coypu[23,66,198] seems a likely candidate.

The second group of forward switches generally removes the zooplankton grazers[201]. There are yet no known examples, but crustacicides and molluscicides, used on a lake or washed in from its catchment, could seriously reduce the numbers of periphyton grazers; organochlorine pesticides, now banned but widely used in the 1950s and 1960s have been shown to decimate *Daphnia* populations. Cladocerans are much more sensitive to these substances than other aquatic animals[181]. Cladocerans can also be removed by salinities increased to above about 1000 milligrams of chloride per litre, or about 5% of sea water[6,95,144].

This might not seem a significant risk for inland freshwaters, but there are many shallow lakes close to the coast in the Netherlands and around the Baltic sea and in East Anglia. Salt may enter through floods arising from increased

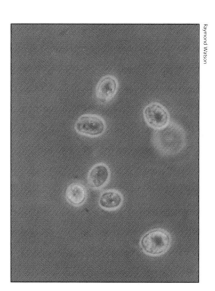

A tranquil scene that hides a severe problem. Drainage in the centuries previous to this one was modest in scope and powered by wind. The old wind pumps, often ruined, sometimes restored, are now admired features of the landscape. Their steam and diesel powered successors were also relatively ineffective. Modern electrically powered pumps, such as that housed in the small brick building here at Horsey, in Norfolk, are able to move vastly greater quantities of water from the wetlands. If the area is close to the sea, salt water may then be sucked into the freshwater system and cause major shifts in the river and lake communities.

Above, centre: Fish kills, caused by a very small alga, *Prymnesium parvum*, were common in the Broads around the River Thurne in Norfolk in the late 1960s and early 1970s. They were probably associated with increased salinity in the area, coupled with enrichment in nutrients from black-headed gulls. The latter have declined in numbers and the kills are now less frequent.

Above, right: *Prymnesium parvum* is only about ten micrometres long but can occur at densities of up to a million per centimetre cubed. It has two flagella by which it swims and a short additional projection, the haptonema, between them. The function of this is unknown, but it characterises a group several of whose members can produce a toxin that kills fish, either in brackish waters or the sea.

sea levels or pumped drainage of the surrounding land. Paradoxically, in one well documented example at Hickling Broad, in the UK, the rising salinity seems to have favoured a particular alga, *Prymnesium parvum*[79], which produces toxins that kill fish. The death of the fish might be expected to have favoured the growth of cladoceran populations, but did not because of the counteractive effect of the increased salinity[6,89,149].

A major alteration in the fish community, particularly in the balance of piscivorous and zooplanktivorous fish[28], may also result in increased predation on the *Daphnia*. Deoxygenation occurs under prolonged ice in winter, or during the night in summer, when the respiration of a large biomass of aquatic plants may be sufficient to remove most of the oxygen in the water. This generally affects the piscivores more than the zooplanktivores because the piscivores are very active, fast-moving fish with high oxygen demands. The zooplanktivores, dependent on less active prey can afford to be less active themselves. This list is undoubtedly incomplete and there may be other ways in

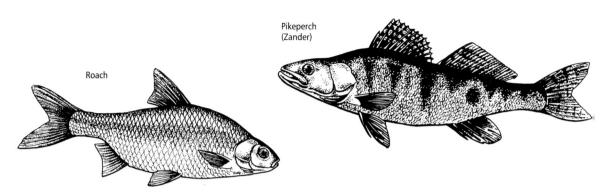

Pikeperch
(Zander)

Roach

Piscivores, like the pikeperch or zander, are generally more streamlined than their prey, such as the roach. They are also demanding of higher oxygen concentrations in the water to support their bursts of hunting activity and thus more susceptible to deoxygenation in the water.

Reverse switches amount to reinstatement of the zooplankton community through manipulation of its predators in the fish community. This is called biomanipulation.

Reedswamp as well as submerged plants may be lost with eutrophication.

which the buffers that stabilise the plant community can be overcome.

Reverse Switches

In attempting to restore a plant community, the buffers stabilising the phytoplankton must be overcome and those stabilising the plant community must be reinstated. It is these processes, and the management options for furthering them, that are the main subjects of this book and which will be dealt with in some detail in subsequent chapters. Basically they amount to reinstating the grazer pressure, through manipulation of the fish community, and reinstatement of plants under conditions in which they can flourish.

The first technique is called **biomanipulation** [192,194] and involves removal of all fish, selective removal of zooplanktivores, or addition of piscivorous fish to reduce the numbers of zooplanktivores. The establishment of plants may involve protection against physical disturbance and bird grazing. In the final restoration of the plant-dominated system, however, it is essential that coexisting communities with both fish and birds should be reinstated. Otherwise all that is being achieved is management, not restoration.

Loss of reedswamp and lilies

The discussion so far has centered on the disappearance of submerged plants. In lakes that have been switched from aquatic plant-dominance to phytoplankton-dominance, there has frequently also been a loss of fringing reedswamp, of such resilient species as the white water lily (*Nymphaea alba*) and of the floating duckweeds such as *Lemna minor*. These plants are not so vulnerable to increases in the phytoplankton as those that are totally submerged or have both floating and submerged leaves.

Reasons for the loss of the duckweeds are perhaps explained by nutrient competition with the phytoplankton because the duckweeds depend entirely on nutrients that they absorb from the water. Dense algal growths make considerable demands even on the increased supplies that come in from sewage effluent or agriculture and in summer, in such conditions, nitrogen compounds are usually completely depleted. Duckweeds, small as they are, are nonetheless much bulkier than microscopic algae and thus suffer from problems of slow diffusion of nutrients into their roots or joints (the technical name for the green part of floating duckweeds).

The loss of white water lilies, and even more the normally vigorous reedswamp plants, is less easily resolved. Both have substantial reserves of energy in their overwintering rhizomes and ready access to nutrients in the sediments. These energy reserves are adequate to allow early growth in spring to bring the shoots above the water surface whence they are immune to the effects of phytoplankton or any other turbidity in the water. Loss of these plants therefore can only be ascribed to mechanical damage by wind and water erosion or grazing by birds or mammals.

The loss of the submerged plants, with their capacity to absorb wave energy, may make the more brittle lilies and reed vulnerable. If they do not break directly they may be undermined by erosion of the peats and sediments in which they are rooted. The loss of more nutritious submerged plants with their low lignin content, their associated invertebrates and seed production may force geese and swans to turn to the reeds and other emergent plants. The coypu, a mammal introduced to several countries for fur farming, easily destroys reedbeds on which it preferentially feeds (if it cannot find sugar beet or some other very palatable crop!). Loss of reed by this means, however, is a separate issue to that of eutrophication.

Different explanations for its loss are needed where reed forms floating mats, as it does when it is growing vigorously in sheltered conditions. If the nitrate loading is high, reed produces plants that are top heavy in green shoot material but which invest less energy in roots and rhizomes. Such mats may be prone to topple if disturbed and may then break up and be washed away in riverine lakes or capsized in deeper water. Much of the reedswamp area lost in the Norfolk Broads was floating 'hover' of this kind (**Fig 2.8**)[22]. Other explanations advanced for the loss of reed

The Common reed, *Phragmites australis*, is a prominent plant in the lowlands of eastern England. When loss of fringing occurs (reed die-back) it may affect several species, but is most obviously manifested by *Phragmites* because of its usual prominence in undisturbed sites.

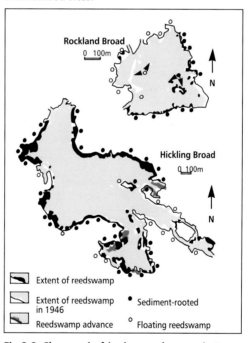

Fig 2.8 Changes in fringing reedswamp in two of the Norfolk Broads between 1946 and the 1980s. Black areas indicate reedswamp present in 1946 and still extant. Green areas are reedswamp that has developed since 1946. Clear areas denoted by a line are reedswamps that have disappeared or have strongly regressed since 1946. Solid dots indicate firmly rooted swamp; open symbols indicate floating mats. It is in these areas that most of the regression has occurred. (From Boar *et al* 1989).

1839

1881

1946

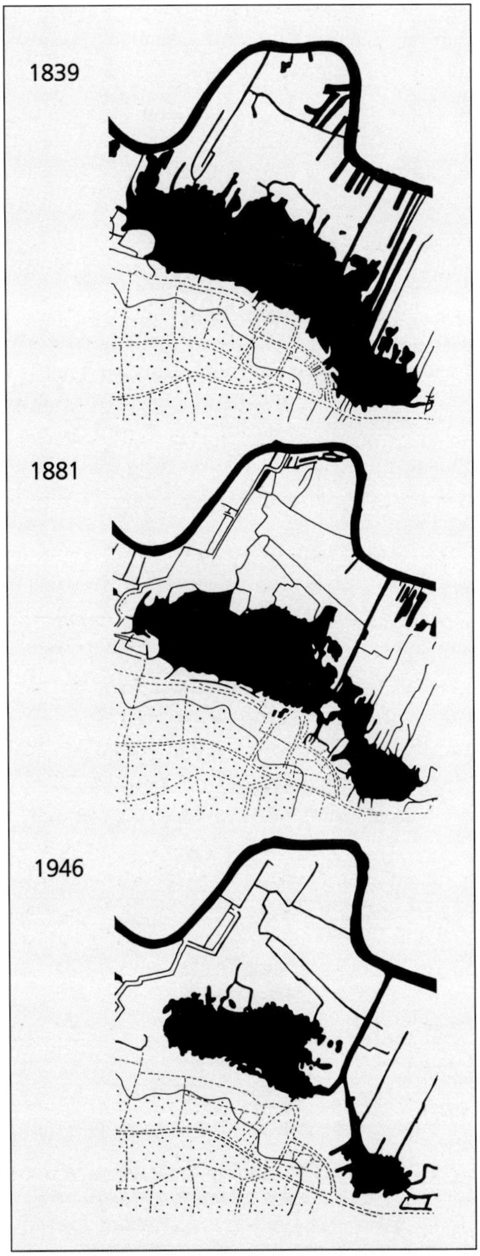

Fig 2.9 Decrease in open water in Ranworth Broad, Norfolk, due to infilling by reedswamp between 1839 and 1946. Since then reedswamp regression has reversed the process to a state intermediate between those of 1881 and 1946. From Ellis 1965.

The irony is that had aquatic plants and reedswamp not been lost to eutrophication, we would be facing the problem of loss of water space due to plant succession.

during eutrophication include mechanical smothering of the shoots by filamentous algae developing in response to increased nutrients[106,107,125,188,205]

Filling in

This brings us to a final irony. Had not the shallow lake systems been damaged by eutrophication, acting in concert with the forward switches discussed above, they would be in the process of infilling with reedswamp and succeeding to woodland. Indeed the Norfolk Broads, by the 1940s, were filling in so rapidly that there was serious concern for the extent of open water that would soon be available for recreational boating and sailing. The conversion to algal dominance has deflected this problem for the loss of lily and reed beds has increased the area of open water and arrested the succession **(Fig 2.9)**.

Restoration of the plant-dominated state, a goal widely held to be desirable, is thus not to solve all problems of management and nature conservation, but to deflect the problem to that of getting natural succession back on track and coping with its consequences. This raises issues of goals as well as techniques and the determination of appropriate goals will be the topic of Chapter 3.

Chapter 3
Restoration and Rehabilitation

'One of the penalties of an ecological education is that one lives in a world of wounds. Much of the damage inflicted on land is quite invisible to laymen. An ecologist must either harden his shell and make believe that the consequences of science are none of his business, or he must be the doctor who sees the marks of death in a community that believes itself well and does not want to be told otherwise.'

Aldo Leopold, *'Round River'*.

Restoration

Restoration is a fine-sounding word. It carries connotations of bringing back the past in all its glory. It has a ring of idealism about it. But what exactly does it mean and what precisely is possible? Visit any demonstration site that purports to be a restored ecosystem and your high expectations will generally not be met. We are better at restoring buildings and art works than we are at natural systems, for we have much less control over and understanding of the latter.

The problem is also that we all have pictures in our mind's eye that are coloured by a wealth of images acquired from books, from childhood idealism, from ideals and hopes, especially now in the obviously damaged land- and waterscapes of much of Europe. Aldo Leopold was writing in the nineteen-forties, which might be regarded as still in a golden age for nature conservation. Goodness knows how he would view the present.

We cannot 'restore' an ecosystem for two reasons. First we cannot know exactly what it was like in the past, though various sources of information may give us a general idea. Secondly, ecosystems do not exist as boundaried units, separate from other bits of land. They have a context and are part of a continuous landscape that has changed under natural and human influences and will keep changing. They themselves change and so there is no single ideal state that can be defined as the target for restoration. There is also an important lesson that we should protect those lakes that are close to a pristine state, because to restore them, once they have been damaged, may not be possible.

Usually we cannot restore, although we use the term; strictly speaking we rehabilitate the habitat to something more acceptable than its present state (Fig. 3.1). Therein lies a further problem - acceptable to whom? The pea-soup pond may be greatly valued by a myriad of mothers and old people. It is kept that way by the feeding of large populations of ducks and swans, which excrete the nutrients brought in with the food, thus stimulating algal growth, and prevent any plant colonisation by stirring up the bottom. The daily visit to the pond may

Strictly speaking, we rehabilitate a habitat to acceptability rather than restore to some former state.

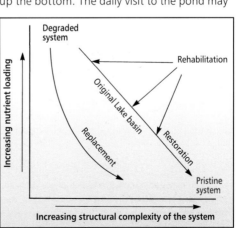

Fig 3.1 Relationships between restoration, rehabilitation and replacement in lake basins.

be part of a comforting daily routine and ducks are much more fascinating to children than a diverse plant population.

A lake stocked with carp may look dreadful to a conservationist, but acceptable to a fishery manager and attractive beyond the riches of Croesus to an avid specimen angler. One of us was once shown two lakes in China. The first was algal-dominated, grass carp having been introduced, and fast motor boats roared all over it, giving trips to tourists, against a background of noise from shooting galleries at the lake edge. The other was a clear water, plant-filled lake which perfectly filled the image of what a natural, diverse shallow lake should look like. It had rich bird populations and a picturesque setting with traditional bamboo fish traps gracing the scene. It was this latter, though, that the Chinese talked of restoring - so as to get the maximum fish crop out, with the least trouble, and make some money from the motorboats. They had tried introducing grass carp, but 'unfortunately', they had yet had no effect.

Why restore?

Restoration, then, carries social as well as scientific issues and it is essential to know from the outset why a restoration is desirable as well as what it is intended to restore. To conser-

vation organisations, it will usually seem self-evident that plant communities as diverse as attainable should be re-established, for much diversity of invertebrates, fish and birds is associated with such communities.

Nature conservation is fundamentally about diversity, although a number of other criteria, such as rarity, representativeness and typicality influence the choice of sites for conservation by statutory bodies such as English Nature. Particular reference is made to the need to restore communities that are being lost from once moderately fertile (mesotrophic) lakes in the European Union's Habitats Directive, and this is reflected also in the UK Biodiversity Action Plan.

Amenity bodies, on the other hand, may place more emphasis on an attractive lily fringe and clear water. Local health authorities will wish to be rid of toxic algal blooms, especially where these accumulate at the edge. Many recreational anglers will value a variety of fish to catch. For all of these interests, restoration of the clear-water, plant-dominated state will be self evident. For specialist anglers, yachtsmen, and other boat operators, this may not be so. And most of the general public will be indifferent.

Perceptions of what constitutes a desirable state vary among different people. In this pair of lakes in Inner Mongolia, the Wulansuhai has a rich aquatic plant community, clear water and a prolific bird life. It is fished by traditional methods. The Havahai has been converted to an alga dominated lake by addition of the Chinese grass carp and supports a more mechanised fishery and a tourist trade based on power boats of various sizes. Local opinion was that the desirable state was represented by the Havahai. This book is about restoring lakes to the state of the Wulansuhai!

An important point is that it is usually impossible to meet all aspirations in a single lake. Without aquatic plants, algae will dominate a shallow lake and a dinghy sailor is unlikely to be able to sail in weed-free water without the risk of encountering blue-green algae. Yet he or she may volubly curse the plants when they impede progress, especially in races.

Similarly, the village or municipal park pond, teaming with carp and populated by ducks fed on bread and cake, will never contain the desired crystal clear water. At the start of any restoration project, the reasons for doing it should be carefully set down. These will be the basis for justifying the funds to be spent and the removal of what might have been a cherished resource for some people.

There is a third 'r' in the habitat improvement directory. This is replacement, the creation of an entirely new habitat perhaps with the abandonment of the former one, now so damaged as to be very expensive to restore. There is every reason to create new lakes,

provided they do not displace valuable and diverse wetland vegetation, but as additions, not replacements. A lake is more than a bag of biodiversity. It has a historic and geomorphic context that may be culturally important. The Norfolk Broads, for example, are ancient mediaeval peat pits. To restore them is not only to recreate amenity and conservation assets, it is to respect also a cultural significance and to recognise that the lake basins are only part of a greater landscape.

What should be restored?

The next stage is in deciding what should be restored. What, in general, should the new system look like? What features should it contain? Experience in many habitats has shown that it is sensible to attempt to restore the plant structure of the system and that the associated animal communities follow by natural colonisation if the habitat is suitable. In some cases, conditions have been altered to favour a particular group or a rare or endangered species and this seems inherently laudable. However, such attempts may mean

Old photographs, diaries, oral accounts and scientific techniques can help determine the range of former states of a lake.

Old photographs, especially labelled postcards can give insight into the former states of shallow lakes. This photograph, of a shallow lake, Salhouse Broad in Norfolk, taken about sixty years ago shows extensive beds of lilies and a fringing reedswamp that are no longer present.

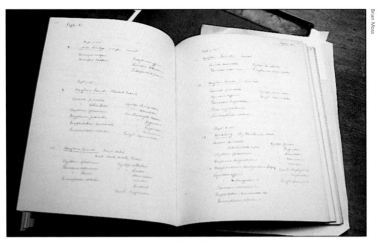

Brian Moss

Formal scientific records of the states of lakes do not usually extend back very far. The notebooks of local naturalists, however, date back to the early part of this century or earlier and can give valuable insights. In the Castle Museum in Norwich, UK, are the records of Robert Gurney, a landowner, gentleman-naturalist, and then contemporary authority on several groups of crustaceans. His records from Hickling Broad in the first two decades of this century were very important in piecing together the reasons for major changes in the Broad fifty years later.

distorting the features of the habitat and creating something that is overall less diverse and less attractive than it otherwise might be. An over-enthusiastic devotion to wader scrapes in bird reserves is a good example.

In restoring the plant structure, it will not be possible to predict exactly what will grow and what will not, but as much information should be gathered as possible on previous states of the site. Was the reedswamp of common reed or of reedmace, sedges or a mixture? What was the extent of lily beds? Old photographs, documentary accounts (the proceedings of local natural history societies; diaries of local naturalists) and talking to older people familiar with the site over a long period can all be helpful. Less direct techniques can also be useful, but more expensive.

Determining the histories of lakes from their sediments

These indirect techniques are those of palaeolimnology[139], which is the study of the history of lakes as revealed in the chemical and fossil contents of their sediments. Sediments are laid down in a chronological sequence. Though there may be a few years of disturbance at the sediment surface, once the sediment is covered by several more millimetres of newer sediments, it becomes relatively stable. Dependent on the conditions in the lake under which it was laid down, each sediment layer will carry a great deal of information from which changes in water chemistry and community structure can be deduced.

Particularly useful are the remains of a group of algae called the diatoms, which are very abundant in most lakes. They are very well preserved in sediments because their cell walls are of silica, which, although it may dissolve

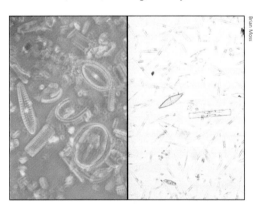

Brian Moss

Diatoms, graced by the scientific name, Bacilliariophyceae, are brown coloured algae whose cell walls are made of silica. The walls are readily preserved in sediments as a record of the diatom flora at the time the sediments were laid down. Here are shown some living diatoms, which move over the surfaces of sediments, and the remains of an assemblage, from the sediments of Strumpshaw Broad in Norfolk, that lived about two hundred years ago, attached to the surfaces of aquatic plants.

under very alkaline conditions, does not rot as organic walls would. Particular species of diatoms are characteristic of different habitats within a lake - the phytoplankton, the periphyton or the surface of the bottom mud, for example, so that an index of the balance of these different habitats can be obtained **(Figs 3.2, 3.3)**. A shallowing of the lake might be reflected in an increase in periphyton and mud diatoms and a decline in phytoplanktonic species for example .

Use of sophisticated statistics, and a knowledge of the present day correlation between occurrence of particular species and measures of water chemistry, can convert a species list identified from a sediment layer to an estimate of the value of that particular determinand at the time the sediment layer was formed. In this way changes in pH, total phosphorus, total nitrogen, and salinity can be back-calculated[8,15,203]. The precision of the calculations is high for pH, yet less so for other determinands, but is continually increasing in its sophistication.

Analysis of pollen, which is also preserved in sediments, gives very useful information on the plant communities previously present in the lake as well as those of the surrounding area. Palaeolimnological investigations require specialist laboratories and expertise. They are fairly time-consuming but inexpensive, however, compared with the engineering costs of many restoration projects.

Determining targets

Palaeolimnological, documentary, photographic and oral evidence will all help to build up a picture of the lake at various stages in the past and can only be a help in planning a restoration project. They cannot, however, substitute for the making of decisions about the targets for restoration. It is impossible to recreate the past exactly, for the context will

Brian Moss

Fig 3.2 A sediment core taken with a drainpipe from Hoveton Great Broad in Norfolk. The core is a little over a metre long and is distinctively stratified. The lowermost layer (bottom of photograph) is of the peat from which this man-made lake basin was formed in the thirteenth or fourteenth centuries. Above this is a light coloured sediment with many snail and charophyte remains. This phase ended in the mid nineteenth century when increasing enrichment with sewage and sewage effluent upstream changed the plant community to one dominated by taller, more vigorously productive species. This community laid down a darker sediment, coloured by the black iron sulphide which forms in anaerobic conditions brought about by intense bacterial activity when large amounts of organic matter are incorporated into the sediments. In the 1960s this plant community was displaced by a planktonic algal community and the upper, brown, amorphous sediments are partly alga-derived and are partly of sediment moved from elsewhere in the system, now that there are few plants to stabilise it.

have changed. What has to be decided is an appropriate target for the future. This may rest on the future use to be made of the lake - as a place for swimming and recreation or water supply, in which clear water unhampered by aquatic vegetation may be desired, or as an amenity with visually attractive lily fringes but little overall diversity, for example.

Decisions on future use should always bear in mind the existing nature conservation value of the lake. There is a range of conservation contexts, from purely local importance to international significance, to be considered. Previous presence of a rare species or community may suggest restoration of it as a priority target. However, if the lake is one of a group, complementary targets might be set among individual sites, so that conservation and amenity uses are balanced with those for sports or angling. Table 3.1 gives a check list of general sources of information useful in the setting of targets in relation to the uses to be made of the lake.

Maximising diversity

One of the most demanding targets will be that which restores the maximum biological diversity and thus the maximum variety and complexity of biological structure within the lake. There may be conflicts in deciding whether to strive for increased diversity overall or to promote conditions favourable for a particular rare species.

Environmental factors and cost will influence this for one or other may need much more stringent (and costly) nutrient control and different sorts (and costs) of subsequent management. Generally, unless there is a remnant population of a rarity, or reintroduction has been successfully tried in similar lakes, recovery of rare species should be subordinate to the pursuit of increased overall diversity.

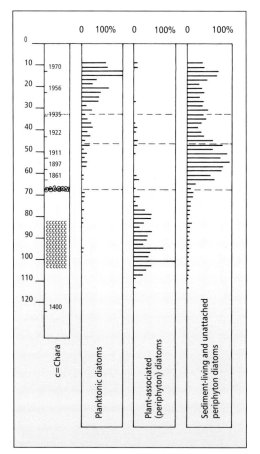

Targets must be feasible, reasons must be clear, and ambition is better than timidity.

Fig 3.3 Some details from the core illustrated in Fig 3.2 from Hoveton Great Broad, Norfolk. The depth of the core is shown in centimetres at the left, together with dates obtained by lead 210 dating. The symbols at around 72cm show the upper limit of layers with rich snail remains. These are associated with plant dominance, though absence of them does not necessarily preclude it. Under very fertile conditions their shells are not so easily preserved. Plants were present in the broad until the 1960s. Charophytes disappeared early as nutrient loadings increased and a number of specifically associated epiphytic diatoms became scarce from then on. Diatoms which live on sediments or freely move over plant surfaces were most abundant after the charophytes declined and other plants took over. Latterly planktonic diatoms have taken over and plants have disappeared. From Moss 1988a.

FUNCTION	INFORMATION SOURCE	KEY INFORMATION	LINKS TO TARGETS
Nature Conservation	(i) Statutory and voluntary bodies	(i) Designations and survey data	Ideal objectives for communities and species based on the ecology of the lake and its former state
	(ii) Published literature and unpublished data from research institutes and universities (especially current monitoring and paleolimnology)	(ii) Priority communities and species	
	(iii) Informal sources such as historical and anecdotal records and photographic evidence	(iii) Former state of the lake	
Recreation and amenity	(i) Landowners	(i) Public and private rights to navigation, mooring, shooting etc	Establish constraints on conservation objectives and future management, e.g. area required to be 'weed-free', depth needed for established uses, opportunities for wildfowl refuges, priority species for angling
	(ii) Parish Councils	(ii) Traditional uses, e.g. swimming, skating	
	(iii) Local clubs, eg. angling, sailing	(iii) Seasonality of use and any legal conditions such as zoning or close season for angling	
		(iv) Previous management such as stocking with fish, dredging, weedcutting	
Public water supply and land drainage	(i) Water companies and regulatory bodies	(i) Water resource and quality needs, effects on lake	Establish existing constraints on water level fluctuation and quality targets such as algal concentrations for potable water use
	(ii) Drainage and flood defence bodies	(ii) Licence conditions	
	(iii) Local authorities	(iii) Any agreed objectives, e.g. in water level management plans	
		(iv) Location of control structures and operating rules	
		(v) Responsibility for monitoring and regulating water levels	

Table 3.1 Checklist of information useful in setting targets related to the intended functions for a lake.

Great structural diversity leads to increased species diversity. Thus, a lake with fringing reedswamp, floating and submerged plants is highly desirable from a nature conservation viewpoint as it benefits all other groups of organisms. Variation in physical features - depth, profile and sediment type - is also desirable. Shallow, muddy margins are favoured by dabbling ducks while sandy or gravelly areas may support charophytes.

The existing situation, however, will determine the lake's potential and no matter how desirable, certain physical features may be simply incompatible with the local environment, whilst dredging and recreational use may diminish the possible range of structure and hence of diversity.

Paradoxically, however, in some situations, diversity is a poor criterion for nature conservation value. For example, extensive beds of one or two *Chara* species may be more desirable than more diverse higher plant communities at higher nutrient concentrations. Charophyte beds are increasingly scarce so it is again important to establish the context of the lake in the region or wetland in setting targets.

Two principles

Nonetheless, the principle of maximising diversity should usually guide the project and the most stringent goals, though not easily achieved will give better results than modest aspirations.

A second principle is thus that ambition is better than timidity. Bold, often large projects are more daunting than small but have a proportionately greater effect, if succcessful, in promoting even more such projects to the ultimate general good. What are the ground rules for doing this? They fall into the categories of environmental feasibility, intended function, and cost.

Feasibility first of all means that the project is possible. It will not be so if the lake is a heavily stocked carp fishery, privately owned and profitable to its owner, unless the site is first purchased. It will not be feasible if the first stage in restoration, the removal of any forward switches (see Chapters 4 and 5) is simply impossible and it will not be feasible without considerable enthusiasm to achieve a restoration on the parts of those paying for it, directly through committees and agencies or indirectly through public taxation.

Beyond all that, the practicable target must be determined. This will be a function of the nutrient loading currently entering the lake and the extent to which it can be reduced by the various means available. The latter is not always easy but there is no point in attempting a restoration target that is unattainable even with the greatest nutrient reduction possible.

An important consideration, also, is that the greater the benefit of the restoration project in

A simple technique (Table 3.2) allows you to determine the flows of nutrients to a lake as a desk study.

terms of environmental and recreational improvement, the more the investment that can be justified. Cost-benefit analysis of water quality improvements will be increasingly used in the UK prior to spending of funds. Where there is still uncertainty of results, this has the effect of constraining the goals of restoration. In such a case, plans should still be bold but phased progressively so that further works may be justified by the results achieved in earlier steps.

Targets for nutrient control

It will generally not be possible, though not impossible [197] in intensely farmed areas of lowland Europe, to achieve the diverse charophyte waters that require less than about 25-50 micrograms of total phosphorus per litre. Only catchments with less than about 10% of agricultural land and no ingress of sewage effluent will be able to sustain such low concentrations. Values of 100 micrograms of total phosphorus per litre, on the other hand, are attainable. They will permit reasonably diverse plant communities, though often at a high biomass that may cause problems for users other than those concerned with conservation and casual angling, and sometimes even these. At progressively higher total phosphorus concentrations, plant communities can still be restored, but they will be of increasingly lower diversity and will be more and more prone to switch back to phytoplankton dominance.

It is comparatively easy to determine the total phosphorus concentration in a laboratory set up to do such analyses. The value is not constant throughout a year and at least six samples spaced throughout the year will be necessary to obtain a reliable estimate. It is less straightforward to decide what has to be done to reduce the nutrient inputs sufficiently to give the desired concentrations in a restoration programme.

To calculate the current total phosphorus and total nitrogen concentrations for the inflows to a lake, you need to know:

(i) the amount of water that enters it, on average, each year (the mean annual discharge of the streams plus any ground water inflow);
(ii) the number of hectares of land in cultivation (cereals, beet, oil seed rape, vegetables etc), the number of hectares in temporary grass, and the number of hectares in permanent or rough grass, woodland or other natural or semi natural habitat;
(iii) the number of cattle, sheep, pigs and poultry in the catchment;
(iv) the number of people in the catchment and whether they are mainly served by mains sewerage or mostly by septic tanks.

The discharge can be estimated from the annual rainfall minus the annual evaporation (equal to the net run-off), each expressed in metres. These values are obtainable for the general area from the Meteorological Office and will be given in millimetres so conversion is necessary. If the net run-off is expressed in metres and multiplied by the area of the catchment in square metres, the run-off in cubic metres per year is obtained.

The different areas of land use and the numbers of stock may be determined by a field survey, which need not be exhaustive and detailed. Alternatively, the results of the Annual Agricultural Surveys are recorded on a Parish basis. These data are available from the Agricultural Development and Advisory Service. Some adjustments will be needed if the catchment occupies several parishes and the results must be apportioned to the area of the catchment in question.

The numbers of people can be determined from the most recent ten-year population census, which is widely available in local government offices and libraries, again on a parish or other basis which will need adjustment to the area of the catchment in question. Whether the population is served by main sewage treatment works or not will usually be obvious, but in cases of difficulty, the appropriate water company will know.

Given this information, the total load of phosphorus can be calculated by multiplying the total hectarages of land use, the total numbers of each sort of stock and the number of people by the values given in the table below and adding them to give the total load in kilograms per year. The amount originating from the atmosphere (in dust and rain) must be included also. By dividing the annual total load in kg by the annual stream discharge in cubic metres and multiplying by a million, you will obtain the concentration in the stream in micrograms per litre. This value can then be compared with the values in the text to determine the extent to which nutrient control may be desirable. The data will also tell you what the main sources of phosphorus at present are likely to be.

By altering the land uses, stock headage or population numbers, the effects of changes in any of these can be readily calculated and the effects of diverting sewage effluent, or removing 80% of the phosphorus from it (see Chapter 6) determined. The same sorts of calculations can also be made for nitrogen.

Annual amounts of total phosphorus (kg per ha or per individual) delivered from various land uses and animals				Annual amounts of total nitrogen delivered from various land uses and animals (kg per ha or per head)			
	Upland areas (Extensive farming)	Lowland areas (Intensive farming)	Very flat lowland		Upland areas (Extensive farming)	Lowland areas (Intensive farming)	Very flat lowland
Atmospheric (rain, dust)	0.2	0.2	0.2	Atmospheric (rain, dust)	25	35	25
Cultivated	0.2	0.9	0.4	Cultivated	10	50	30
Temporary and permanent grassland	0.3	0.8	0.4	Temporary and permanent grassland	2	30	10
Woodland, rough grazing natural/semi natural	0.02	0.07	0.03	Woodland, rough grazing natural/semi natural	1	13	3
Cattle	9	18	12	Cattle	40	80	60
Pigs	6	6	6	Pigs	19	19	19
Sheep	1.5	1.5	1.5	Sheep	10	10	10
Poultry	0.2	0.7	0.4	Poultry	0.6	0.6	0.6
People (largely mains sewerage)	1	1	1	People (largely mains sewerage)	4	4	4
People (largely served by septic tanks)	0.4	0.4	0.4	People (largely served by septic tanks)	2	2	2

Table 3.2

Determining the present nutrient sources and the potential for their control

Each source of nutrients is called a load, the list of different loads constitutes the income part of the nutrient budget, and the total load divided by the amount of water carrying it (discharge) gives the concentration. A technique called export coefficient modelling[98,99] allows you to estimate the total phosphorus and total nitrogen concentrations in inflow stream water. It needs knowledge of the general geography of the catchment, and the average stream discharge and calculates the loads from land use, livestock and the human populations in the catchment. Table 3.2 gives all the steps necessary to make calculations for a particular lake.

Such desk calculations will be inexpensive and will give an indication of the feasibility of restoration. They will indicate the primary targets (the biggest sources) for nutrient control and allow decisions on strategies for achieving such control by the methods discussed in Chapter 6. An assessment of the political and economic realities of such deployment will then indicate the limits of what might be possible. Currently, in England and Wales, the Environment Agency is developing a national strategy to guide such assessments.

The model (Table 3.2) gives the concentrations that might be expected from loads in the catchment. These are called external loads. The concentrations in the lake will also be affected by internal release of phosphorus from the sediments. One of the uncertainties is that we do not fully understand whether or not this load may be part of the cause of changes in the lake or a consequence of them. The chances are that it is a consequence generated by increased external loading. But for a lengthy period, even after reduction of external loads,

there may be considerable internal loading. In summer this can be as great as the external loading, if the lake has received high external loads for many years. A sensible assumption will be that the summer concentration will be doubled by internal loading and that the annual mean concentration will be increased by a half. In making feasibility calculations as to the effects of nutrient reductions in the catchment, the calculated concentration should thus be increased by 50%.

The calculated concentration might, in some instances, suggest the possibility of restoration of the lowest nutrient state, with diverse charophyte communities and a guarantee of clear water. In other cases only modest reductions may be possible, or none at all. The general principle to be applied, however, is that of trying to achieve the greatest possible reduction in nutrients if the restoration is to be diverse and lasting. The higher the nutrient concentrations, the more prone the system will be to switch back to phytoplankton dominance, and the greater the risk of a disappointing failure. The lower the nutrient concentrations, the more stable the system will be and the less the future recurrent costs of maintaining it. The greater also will be the chance of a successful restoration. On the other hand, the greater the degree of nutrient control attempted, the greater will be the cost and the political difficulties of attaining it. In each instance a specific choice will have to be made in the light of the local circumstances.

The setting of appropriate targets for a lake is thus complex, needing an interplay between what is desirable and what, in practical, political and economic terms, is feasible. All of these aspects must be considered together because, without clearly agreed objectives for the desired condition and use of the lake, it could be vulnerable to damaging changes in the future.

The higher the nutrient concentrations, the more prone the system will be to switch back to phytoplankton dominance and the greater the risk of a disappointing failure. The lower the nutrient concentrations, the more stable the system will be and the less the future recurrent costs of maintaining it.

Chapter 4

An Overall Strategy for Restoration of Shallow Eutrophicated Lakes

'προαιτεισθι τε δει αδυνατα εικοτα μαλλον ηδυνατα απιθανα'

'Probable impossibilities are to be preferred to improbable possibilities'.

Aristotle, Poetics.

We discussed the feasibility of restoration in the previous chapter. Some view will then have been formed as to the extent to which a given lake might be restored and a general target will have been decided. This will take the form of a decision to restore plant communities to a high degree of diversity or to accept a less ambitious target. Whatever the target, the general overall strategy is similar and takes the form of a series of graded steps (**Fig.4.1**). These are:

(i) Forward switch detection and removal

(ii) External and internal nutrient control

(iii) Restructuring the ecosystem by a reverse switch (generally biomanipulation)

(iv) Plant establishment (including reedswamp fringes)

(v) Stabilising and managing the restored system

The reasons for these steps emerge from the general model of change in shallow lakes and

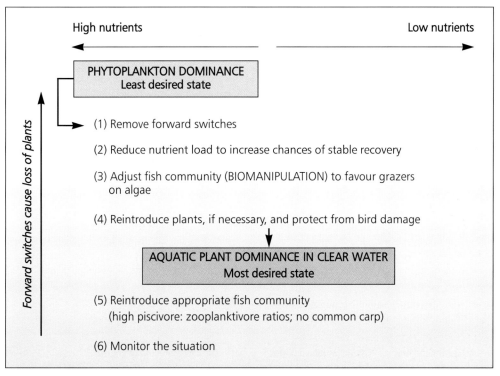

Fig 4.1 The strategy for moving from phytoplankton-dominated, turbid water to plant-dominance in clear water, adopted in this handbook.

the existence of alternative stable states. We explained the concept of alternative stable ecological states within a gradient of nutrient enrichment in Chapters 1 and 2. Two important conclusions were drawn. First, control of nutrient input is essential for satisfactory restoration of a eutrophic lake. But secondly, unless inputs can be made extremely low (unlikely in most cases), the desired results will not be obtained unless other factors (forward switches) acting against the plants have been eliminated.

Steps (i) and (ii) must be considered during the initial planning. There is no point in considering how to reduce nutrients until the nature of the forward switch (or switches), that have catalysed the loss of plants, has been determined. This may not be easy. It is possible to omit the nutrient control step and move immediately to biomanipulation, though this is inadvisable.

Omission of nutrient control assumes that there is no upper limit to the nutrient concentrations at which alternative states may exist. There is some controversy about this and there may be circumstances where biomanipulation will not be effective unless nutrient concentrations are reduced or other environmental changes are made. These issues are discussed in Chapter 6. Except in extremis, nutrient control should be attempted because restorations are unlikely to be stable when nutrient loadings remain high.

Step (iii), biomanipulation, or application of other reverse switches, will clarify the water, and until this is done there is no point in attempting reestablishment of plants (step iv). They will not survive. It is possible that residual seeds or other propagules of plants will be available and deliberate introductions will not be necessary. Step (iv) may thus be unnecessary but will often have to be taken.

The final step (v) of stabilising and managing the system will have a greater or lesser importance dependent on the degree of nutrient control that has been achieved and the extent to which local circumstances in the catchment may be continuing to change.

The more stable the restoration, the less will be the need for continued management. Management is usually costly and the need for it an expression of failure. The ultimate aim should be to eliminate any need for it.

However, it can never be assumed that the system can be left completely to look after itself, though this would be the ideal. Agricultural techniques are still changing and new nutrient inputs or new pesticide and herbicide risks may come from these; new housing estates may be built and new flows of nutrients may come from these. As in all conservation issues in a society not primarily dedicated to conservation, eternal vigilance is necessary!

In the following Chapters, each of these steps is examined with practical details emphasised. Decision trees are given at the ends of each chapter. These summarise the major issues covered.

Chapter 5

Steps in the Strategy

(1) Detecting and Removing the Forward Switches

'History is a distillation of rumour'.
Thomas Carlyle History of the French Revolution Bk 7 Ch 5.

'History is a nightmare from which I am trying to awake'.
 James Joyce, Ulysses.

'History is more or less bunk' .
Henry Ford, Chicago Tribune , 25 May 1916.

'En effet, l'histoire n'est que le tableau des crimes et des malheurs'.
Voltaire, L'Ingenu.

'Great abilities are not requisite for an Historian... Imagination is not required in any high degree'.
Samual Johnson, Boswell's Life of Johnson.

Reconstructing the past

Determination of what forward switch might, in the past, have operated can be difficult. Indeed the accurate reconstruction of history is always a problem, which is why there are always so many interpretations of it and why rival historians have such jaundiced views of one another. But it is essential to identify what switch or switches have operated, or at least to be sure that none of the known switches is engaged before proceeding further with a restoration.

Documentation will usually be poor or absent; different individuals with knowledge of the site will have different recollections - and often mutually opposed views. Palaeolimnology may give clues but only if analyses are directed at particular suspects such as pesticide or herbicide residues. Common sense can however be applied. Remember also that there may be more than one forward switch. Bird grazing alone may not damage an otherwise strong reedbed, but if the reed is being eroded by boat wash, the birds may deliver a *coup de grace*.

Asking questions

First look for obvious changes. Have there been increases in water level as in the Swedish lake Krankesjon[1] (**Fig. 5.1**), where an alternation of plant-dominated and phytoplankton-dominated states has coincided with a relatively small alternation between low and high water levels? Has there been any deliberate management of the plant communities? The local angling club, fishing the lake, and the land owner or tenant should know this if it was recent, but it may have occurred in the unremembered past. Are there motor boats operating? In the canals of some Dutch towns there is a very clear distinction between the turbid waters of the routes along which boats move and the clear waters, with lilies, in canals from which boats are excluded. Has there been an increase in boat activity? Local enquiry should sort out this possibility.

Salinity

If the lake is close to the sea, and if the surrounding land is pump-drained for agriculture, salt may be entering the lake as sea water is sucked into the drains. A part of the Broadland in Norfolk is so affected. Chloride concentrations were around 600 milligrams per litre at the turn of the twentieth century (**Fig. 5.2)** when pumping was by wind and steam. Powerful electrical pumps have now increased

It may be very difficult to establish what forward switches have operated. It is more important what switch mechanisms might currently be in operation.

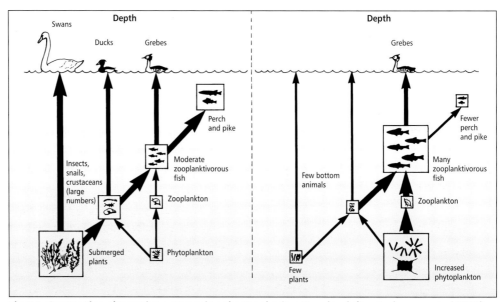

Fig 5.1 Contrasting alternative systems in Lake Krankesjön, Sweden (after Andersson et al 1990).

Forward switches may include mechanical damage, boat damage, exotic grazers, herbicides, water level increase, salinity increase, pesticides and selective fish kills.

this to well above the 1000 mg per litre which tends to exclude *Daphnia* species[6] . Enquiry of the local drainage board or the Ministry of Agriculture, or their equivalents in other European countries, will reveal when pumps were replaced and whether their rating was increased. Salinity can be readily determined if a laboratory is available but if not, a few drops of silver nitrate solution (2%) will give a dense, cloudy white precipitate (as opposed to only a hazy gray one) to indicate dangerously high salinities. If a portable conductivity meter is available, conductivities of 4000 microsiemens per centimetre correspond to about 1000 mg per litre of chloride in freshwater contaminated with seawater.

Herbicides

Past herbicide effects are more difficult to discover. Especially if there has been misuse, or clandestine attempts to use herbicide to remove weed, honest answers to questions cannot be expected. Sometimes, however, there has been deliberate and authorised use

by drainage boards to remove weed from ditches and if the ditches connect with the lake, there will certainly have been a possibility of contamination.

Introduced birds and other grazers

If large numbers of exotic vertebrates have been present, there will usually be local knowledge of it. Indeed such animals will still be present unless they were such a pest elsewhere that they have been controlled. The coypu falls into this latter category, Canada geese and ornamental waterfowl into the former. Coypu escaped from fur farms into the wetlands of East Anglia in the 1930s. They feed predominantly on reed rather than submerged aquatic plants, but could have been partly responsible, in concert with other switching agents, for the loss of plants in the Norfolk Broads. Coypu, because they were an agricultural pest have now been eliminated from the wild in the UK by exhaustive trapping (at very high cost).

Semi-domesticated mute swans, Canada geese,

greylag geese, tame mallard, domestic ducks, and conceivably Egyptian geese, may also develop artificially high populations that can damage vegetation (reed in the case of geese, submerged plants also in other cases) beyond

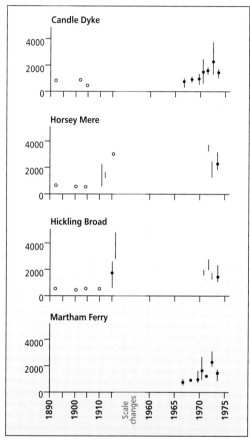

Salinity has increased in some of the Norfolk Broads close to the sea as a result of ingress of sea water through the porous sand deposits which separate the lakes from the sea. This results from increased drainage using more powerful pumps in recent decades, which suck sea water into the freshwater system and pump it into the river and broads. In the 1950s there was a temporary increase due to breach of the sea defences during heavy storms. Martham Ferry is a place on the River Thurne, Candle Dyke is the outlet to Hickling Broad and Horsey Mere which are connected. From Holdway *et al* 1978.

recovery if they are present in sufficient numbers. The same is true of aggregations of a huge variety of waterfowl that may be kept in or attracted to reserves and sanctuaries. Where geese and swans are artificially fed to attract spectacular numbers it is impossible to maintain plant dominance because of physical disturbance, let alone grazing. Such aggregations will be more than obvious.

Destructive fish

Fish are less obvious. Local anglers, however, will know what species are present if a netting survey is not possible. The presence of common carp should always ring alarm bells, for even a few large carp can disturb the sediments as they forage, uproot and eat plants and mobilise phosphorus from the sediment through their feeding and excretion (see Chapter 2). Exotics like grass carp should not be present, unless illegally. A severe shortage of piscivores, such as perch and pike should also be regarded as a sign that there have been undesirable alterations to the fish community that may have caused the system to switch.

Enquiries of the Environment Agency (the Scottish Environmental Protection Agency in Scotland) as to permissions given for movement of fish and restocking may reveal recent introductions. Under Section 30 of the UK Salmon and Freshwater Fisheries Act (1975) the Agency must give permission for stockings as part of its role in the limitation of the spread of fish diseases. Local anglers and fishery managers of the Environment Agency should also know about recent fish kills, though not necessarily of those in the more distant past. Information on fish kills is not held in the public registers of the Agency and hence can be difficult and expensive to obtain.

Pesticides

The subtle effects that organochlorine pesticide residues may have had on *Daphnia* and other crustacean grazers are perhaps the most difficult to discover. The effects may have been felt thirty or so years ago when the dangers of these substances had not been fully realised and they were used with some liberality. The evidence for their importance is based on the effects of recorded spills and on detection of residues in sediment cores, coincident with changes in the composition of the zooplankton community. Such substances are no longer used in most of Europe but there is always the chance that new pesticides or other industrial substances may prove to have similar effects. Several thousands of new chemicals are introduced into the environment every year as a result of industrial developments. Some are by-products unrealised by the industry producing them. Unequivocal linking of these to effects in lakes is an impossible task without very intensive research but the possibilities of problems must be acknowledged, especially as spray drift from farmland ploughed very close to the edge of waterways must inevitably occur.

When all eventualities have been examined, almost certainly a list of several suspects for past switches will have been compiled, but it will not be possible to draw absolutely certain conclusions. For the purposes of restoration, this does not matter. The possibilities will be a useful guide for the next stage, which is more important: that of making sure that none of the known switch mechanisms, at least, are still operating. In this respect perhaps Henry Ford was right.

Ensuring forward switch mechanisms are absent before restoration begins

In gaining such assurances lies a knot of potential problems. The first step must be to convince, as appropriate, the land owner, tenant, any management authorities, fishing clubs and, in some cases, the general public that the restoration should be attempted.

The removal of forward switches can be very difficult.

Some may want to keep the carp, the ducks or the salt-seeping drainage. Compromise to reduce the risk of switches continuing to operate may be more likely than outright removal of certain activities.

Thus, you are more likely to obtain agreement to rigorous abidance with accepted codes of practice for the use of herbicides and pesticides than agreement to discontinue their use. And zoning of boat activity, through voluntary agreement, to protect particular lake areas, may be sufficient to minimise mechanical damage until such time as the plant beds will create their own protection through inaccessibility.

Agreements to discontinue weed management or to change water levels should not be difficult once the principle of restoration is agreed, but the issue of salinity may pose more difficulties. Increases in salinity, as have occurred at Hickling Broad in Norfolk, arise from vigorous drainage of arable marshes in the catchment.

Broads Authority

Environmentally Sensitive Area arrangements can promote farming practices with potentially significant improvements in natural waters in those areas.

Fishponds were created at many mediaeval monasteries and priories to house the introduced common carp as a source of food. Little now remains of St Benet's Abbey in Norfolk, but the rectangular layout of the old fishponds is still prominent.

The concept of drainage as a desirable procedure is deeply engrained in the national agricultural community. Agreements under the Environmentally Sensitive Areas (ESA) scheme (EC Regulation 797/85, implemented under the Agriculture Act 1986 in the UK) may allow compensation to farmers to convert arable to grassland and so drain less vigorously. This will maintain higher water tables and hence less marine seepage in the catchment. A potential opportunity exists to use ESA legislation for lake restoration in the Hickling Broad area but this has not yet been taken up by landowners. Approaches such as flushing with fresh water to reduce salinity, as alternatives to tackling the cause, are also problematic, usually owing to lack of sufficiently large supplies of water of appropriate quality.

Carp problems

The exotic vertebrates pose equal problems. In practical terms there is no difficulty with their removal from a lake, but such removal, particularly of carp, may be opposed. Carp have not been a severe problem, so far as is known, until recently. Indeed they are normal members of fish communities on mainland Europe. The change has resulted from a much more competitive approach to angling, in which the catching of large fish that do not passively accede to being caught is increasingly prized. Carp do not breed regularly in British waters, which hitherto have been too cold in summer, but the present tendency to introduce them to more and more waters, in sufficient numbers to provide widespread sport, is extending their effects. The presently rising global temperatures may also mean that carp reproduction

Karen Sayer

Ducks, swans and geese, attracted by bread and cake, may build up large populations, which can severely damage the vegetation by feeding, trampling or other disturbance.

becomes more successful. The fish are long lived and old and large carp have been described as the fish equivalent of bulldozers, for the damage they do in uprooting plants and in disturbing the bottom sediments.

There are some misunderstandings in the UK dependent on the different aspirations of anglers and fishery managers on the one hand and conservationists on the other. The former often take the view that as long as there are many fish to catch, the state of the ecosystem must be good. The fish are seen as recipients of the resources that the habitat provides and not as potential controllers of its quality. Provided the fish to be put in are healthy, there has been little resistance to proposals for stocking. Increasingly this view is being challenged by research which shows a very considerable 'top down' influence of fish on lower levels of the food webs [12,33,63,76,81,170].

However, despite growing evidence for the effects of fish on the ecosystem, fisheries management strategies, including stocking,

generally do not take it into account. The duty of the Environment Agency to further conservation in the UK Environment Act (1995) may help to ensure that the effects of fish stocking policies on conservation are more fully appreciated.

It will, nonetheless, take a little time to convince anglers and their advisors that their ideals of plenty of large, hungry carp in a diverse community of pleasant aesthetics are mutually incompatible. The conflicts of some forms of fisheries management with the restoration of a lake must be acknowledged and resolved. Offers of compensation to anglers for loss of carp fishing might help. Preferably this should be in the form of other desirable fish species, such as tench perhaps, and in the possibilities of more diverse fishing in a pleasanter environment.

Bird removal

The removal of birds is equally contentious in the UK, perhaps less so on mainland Europe. Mute swans are much prized, as are the flocks of ducks which come to be fed with bread and cake. Mute swans have now returned to their former numbers[41] following their decline through lead poisoning from angling weights[190], and may cause damage in the future; ducks are very abundant. As a rule of thumb such birds are unlikely to be a problem if they must depend on natural resources for their food and breeding sites. But artificial feeding or nesting provision will increase the chances of damage. It will be almost impossible to obtain agreement to remove these birds, or to stop people feeding them. The restoration of shallow lakes in public parks may thus be infeasible.

Where remoter lakes, perhaps amid farmland or on nature reserves are concerned, the problem is likely to be one of Canada or greylag geese, which have established non-migratory populations in many parts of the country. The effectiveness of Canada and greylag geese in destroying aquatic plants in shallow lakes is not fully known, for their main food supply is short terrestrial grasses, but they will eat young or fringing reeds and may cause physical disturbance.

It is now illegal to introduce Canada geese further into the wild under the Wildlife & Countryside act (1981) but the stable door is already open. The goose is of North American origin and was first introduced around 1665 by agents of King Charles 1. It bred to populations of around 3000 by the 1950s and was then redistributed to other areas in the hope that small manageable populations would be formed and controlled by wildfowling. However, it is a rather tame species, not prized by wildfowlers or saleable as meat, and is found in about a thousand sites in the UK. The birds can be rounded up during the annual wing moult and shot, but their tameness and occupancy of lakes in country estates and parks open to the public has provoked vigorous public outcry in some places, despite public education campaigns. Their numbers are also increasing in mainland Europe, where there is less compunction about shooting them.

It is usually necessary to seek permission or licence from authorised bodies (in the UK, this is required from English Nature, the British Trust for Ornithology, or the Ministry of Agriculture, Fisheries & Food) before attempting any removal or control of wildlife outside any agreed shooting season. This is especially true when Sites of Special Scientific Interest, Special Areas of Conservation, or Special Protection Areas are concerned.

Control of geese is, in any case, difficult. The first approach is by habitat manipulation. Predation of eggs and nestlings is much greater on mainland sites than in islands in a lake, so

removal of islands may help. Removal of nesting cover, provision of low fences around the lake, and increasing local disturbance (gas bangers, scarecrows, kites to keep the geese airborne, lights at night, rockets, humming wires and tethered balloons) may also be effective. Geese avoid feeding in enclosed areas which might harbour predators and in amenity lakes shrubs may be planted to create such areas.

All of these techniques will need to be applied year on year and may also disturb desirable species. Populations may be more effectively controlled by shooting in the established winter season (at least 20% per annum over a number of years is necessary to begin a reduction in most populations). Egg control by removing eggs from nests and replacing them with dummies, pricking them, or coating them with light mineral oil can be effective locally if thoroughly carried out. Birds are unlikely to re-lay if a clutch is lost after three weeks of incubation.

The most effective method is to round up the birds on land during their annual summer moult and quickly and humanely kill them then. Clearly a large proportion must be removed for there to be a significant effect, as other geese will quickly move in from elsewhere. Similar considerations apply to the less numerous feral flocks of greylag geese, of which there are about 10000 at present in the UK, compared with 60000 Canada geese. In some areas, for example the Norfolk Broads, greylag (2500) are however, the predominant ones, with only 800 Canada geese.

Next....

At this stage, the restoration project may have to be abandoned, because an obvious potential forward switch agent is present and cannot be removed. If there seems to be no such impediment, the strategy proceeds to the stage of considering what degree of nutrient control may be practicable.

Decision tree for forward switches

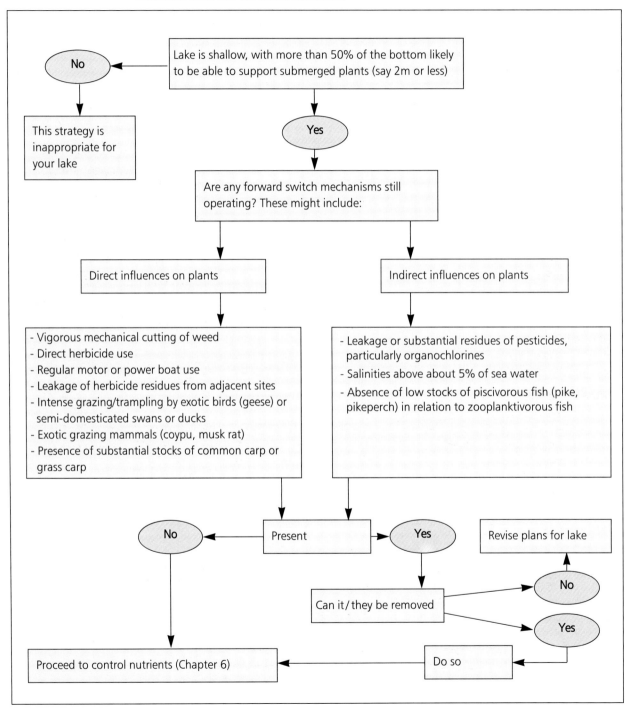

Chapter 6

Steps in the Strategy

(2) Nutrient Control

Except in the remoter northern and mountain regions, where acidification is the problem, European land and waterscapes have become suffused with nutrients. Over-fertilisation is the most pervadent problem for conservation of both natural and semi-natural systems on land and all of the aquatic systems to which the waters drain.

Phosphorus or nitrogen control - or both?

From the 1940s, when the problem was first recognised as such[73], it became widespread, with the intensification of agriculture, the provision of mains sewerage for a population that was increasingly aggregating in cities and towns, and the invention of laundry detergents that used sodium tripolyphosphate as a major, and very effective, component.

The development of increasing crops of algae needs phosphorus and nitrogen to be supplied in a ratio of about 1 to 10, if one of the nutrients is not to become scarce and unilaterally limit the growth. However, the relative scarcity of phosphorus, in comparison to nitrogen, in many pristine lakes, has focussed eutrophication control on phosphorus because nitrogen supplies are deemed to be in surplus.

David Schindler[185] argues that eutrophication can be driven, in any case, by increase in phosphorus alone because the condition of combined nitrogen scarcity, that an addition of phosphorus generates, will cause an increase in the growth of nitrogen-fixing algae. These are all members of the blue-green algae which can take dissolved nitrogen gas and convert it ultimately into the nitrogen component of proteins.

The activity of these algae will then rebalance the nutrient supplies without benefit of an increase from external sources of ammonium or nitrate. This is theoretically true, but in practice the development of blue-green algal nitrogen fixers in lakes is slow and the phytoplankton as a whole may be strongly nitrogen-limited during mid-summer [146,150,168,174,175,176].

It would therefore be a mistake to think of eutrophication only in terms of phosphorus. Beyond the first stages, in many lakes, nitrogen is equally important and in some lakes it may be increases in the availability of nitrogen compounds that initiate the process. Because of the phosphorus that might be naturally regenerated from the sediments in dense plant beds[164,202], even pristine ones, it is possible that the eutrophication of shallow lakes has been primarily driven by nitrogen.

Three practical principles important in restoration

Whatever the balance of nitrogen and phosphorus entering a lake and the interaction with nitrogen-fixers, three practical principles are important in restoration. The first is that whatever nutrient may be limiting growth at a particular time, or whatever nutrient has driven the process, growth can be greatly reduced by severely restricting the supply of only one of them. This is analogous to the fact that since cars need both oil and petrol to move, absence of either will immobilise them.

The second is that it is far easier to control phosphorus in external sources than nitrogen. Phosphates are comparatively insoluble, can be easily precipitated and mostly come from a few concentrated sources (point sources - sewage treatment works and intensive stock units). Nitrates and ammonium are very soluble, cannot easily be precipitated and emerge in a diffuse way from hundreds of thousands of field drains and seepages.

Increase in phosphorus usually drives eutrophication in freshwaters, though ultimately increased supplies of both phosphorus and nitrogen are needed.

For several reasons it is sensible first to attempt to control phosphorus supplies.

The third is that, within a lake that has been receiving nutrients for many years, there will have been a much greater build up of phosphorus, which may be released from the sediment, than nitrogen. Nitrogen will, in general, have been denitrified or more easily washed-out because of the greater solubility of its compounds. The practical conclusion to be drawn from these principles is that it is sensible to attempt nutrient control first through phosphorus control.

Because nothing is ever quite so simple, however, it is wise also to remember that nitrogen cannot be ignored. Certain problems, for example the loss of fringing floating reedswamp, may be a direct consequence of increases in nitrate[22]. And, given the availability to plants of phosphorus from the sediments, through their roots, increases in nitrogen are likely to reduce the diversity of aquatic plant communities. This has been the general pattern when land plant communities have been fertilised. The more vigorous and competitive species will take advantage of the increased supply and suppress other species. Ultimately, control of both phosphorus and nitrogen is thus desirable, although initially the most practical way forward will have to be phosphorus control.

There is a large range of options for reduction of nutrient loading [72,180]. It will usually be pointless to do much about internal loads from the sediment until external loads, which are responsible ultimately for increased internal loads, have been dealt with. Among the external loads, a practical approach will be to identify the most important using the nutrient budget technique described in Chapter 3 and then to proceed with others in the order of their importance. This might not always be possible. Sometimes the greatest loads are the most intractable. In restoring shallow lakes, however, any significant reduction is probably

Phosphorus may come from external point sources, external diffuse sources and internal sources - the lake sediments.

worthwhile, in that the stability of the restoration is likely to be greater, the lower the nutrient level.

We will deal with available techniques in the order: external point sources of P; external diffuse sources of P; external point sources of N; external diffuse sources of N; internal sources of P. In each case we will indicate relative effectiveness, relative cost and potentially helpful legislation[58,216].

Point sources of phosphorus

Occasionally there may be industrial sources (for example food factories) but the main point sources of phosphorus are excretal - human sewage effluent, and, because cattle produce ten times as much phosphorus per head as people, large stock units. Guanotrophy, fertilisation by flocks of birds, is not unknown[117,149] but probably not a widely serious problem.

Human sewage effluent

Sewage effluent will normally contain 10 to 30 milligrams of total phosphorus per litre and there are two options for dealing with this. One is to divert the effluent to below the lake or to a river not supplying lake basins or direct to the sea. This is only possible where the works is close to such a sink, for pipelines are expensive. It is not a proper solution in that the problem is displaced not removed. Large rivers and coastal waters can also suffer from eutrophication problems. In summer the loss of the carrying water may also be significant for the hydrology of the lake. Reduction of flushing can promote growth of species of algae [193], such as blue-green algae, that are less easily grazed [48,64,65,152].

The second option is to remove the phosphorus from the effluent before discharge, a process called precipitation or stripping. It is a routine part of sewage treatment in many parts of mainland Europe (Switzerland, Sweden, Norway, Denmark, the Netherlands, for example) but more sporadic elsewhere, including the UK. The most common technique is for the phosphate to be precipitated either from the raw sewage, or more usually the final effluent, with iron salts, calcium hydroxide or aluminium sulphate. The precipitate is removed as sludge, which is bulked with other sludges produced by the works, and either spread on the land or buried in a waste tip. The efficiency of the process can be high (>95%) with careful control and efficient plant, but is more usually 80 to 90%. The concentration of total phosphorus in the final effluent can be reduced to 1 milligram per litre or lower.

There has been much pressure for installation of phosphorus stripping in mainland Europe, especially in Scandinavia and countries blessed with large lakes that form the focus of tourism. The phosphorus contents of many mainland lakes and rivers have fallen as a result. An EC Directive, the Urban Waste Water Treatment Directive (91/271/EEC) sets phosphorus standards for sewage treatment works serving more than the equivalent of 10,000 people, which discharge to waters subject to, or at risk from, eutrophication. There is a problem in that the Directive does not define 'sensitive to eutrophication' and allows individual governments flexibility in doing so.

In the UK, the Directive has hitherto only been applied to some thirty-three *Sensitive Areas (Eutrophic)*, the majority of which are large lakes, frequently drinking water reservoirs. Although city populations are served by large sewage treatment works that may be regulated under the Directive, many areas have smaller works that are not. A recent survey of sites of conservation significance[36] showed that very few could potentially benefit from this legislation and that small shallow lakes are likely not to benefit at all in the UK. More comprehensive approaches prevail elsewhere,

Phosphate can be easily be precipitated from sewage effluent by adding a concentrated solution of ferrous ammonium sulphate, shown being dripped in here at a Dutch sewage treatment works. The iron phosphate precipitate so formed is allowed to settle then disposed of to the land or to a waste tip. It might also be profitably recycled back to the chemical industry.

but not everywhere, in mainland Europe, where some countries have (in scientific terms quite correctly) designated all of their area as subject to eutrophication.

Although the Urban Waste Water Treatment Directive is a useful mechanism to start the process of phosphorus control, its uniform standard for effluent (1 or 2 mg per l) may be insufficient to reduce the phosphorus load on a lake sufficiently because of other smaller discharges to the same lake, that cannot be controlled under the Directive. In these cases, phosphorus control can only be achieved in the UK by a consent under the Water Resources Act 1991. These consents are usually based on an Environmental Quality Standard (EQS) set for the receiving water, but none have yet been agreed for phosphorus, although proposals relating to sites of conservation interest (Special Ecosystems) are being considered. In any event, our understanding of eutrophication suggests that phosphorus addition should be minimised and that the concept of an EQS may be inappropriate for systems with alternative stable states. In many lowland catchments, diffuse phosphorus sources will already provide higher concentrations than a currently discussed proposal for a suitable EQS of 100 micrograms per litre.

A better approach may therefore be to minimise the input of phosphorus using the BATNEEC (best available technology not entailing excessive cost) approach to minimise phosphorus inputs from controllable sources. Whilst this can lead to long debates about what is 'best' and 'excessive', the BATNEEC concept has been used in the Anglian region of the National Rivers Authority to introduce additional treatment at a range of sewage treatment works discharging to the Norfolk Broads. These will be regulated by a Water Resources Act consent, with a discharge limit of 1 mg per litre, measured as an annual average. Although apparently not a very demanding standard, it represents a substantial improvement on the 2 mg per litre UWWTD standard for smaller works.

The Wildlife and Countryside Act 1981, again in the UK, gives English Nature and the statutory conservation bodies in Wales and Scotland, powers to control *Potentially damaging operations* (PDO) in Sites of Special Scientific Interest (SSSI). Where eutrophication threatens the integrity of an aquatic SSSI, these powers may potentially be used to drive nutrient control. The EC Habitats Directive (92/43/EC), enabling the designation of Special Areas of Conservation (SAC) in which rare and endangered habitats and species must be protected, will extend these powers on a European scale. In addition, while the Ecological Quality of Waters Directive (94/C222/06/EC) is not yet in force, it is likely to include a specific requirement for excessive

plant growth (taken to include algae) to be absent from surface waters.

In any instance, justification for incorporating phosphorus into consents will be increased if there is an associated lake restoration plan. The new requirement for the Environmental Agency in the UK to consider the relative benefits and costs of any proposal will also affect decisions on consents.

An alternative to the statutory controls above, is to pursue site-specific, voluntary agreements for phosphorus removal with Water Companies. Because phosphorus stripping inevitably increases the costs of sewage treatment, this approach is most likely to be successful where the company can include these costs as 'discretionary expenditure' within its five year Asset Management Plan. This has been done in parts of the Norfolk Broads.

Stock wastes

The problem of stock wastes is more intractable. Animal manure is best disposed of by ploughing it into the land, or spreading it on the surface in periods of light rainfall to promote its incorporation. A 'Code of Good Agricultural Practice for the Protection of Water' has been drawn up by the Ministry of Agriculture, Fisheries and Food and the Welsh Office for use in England and Wales. It emphasises to farmers their legal responsibilities not to pollute under the Water Act 1989, Water Resources Act 1991 and regulations deriving from them.

However, the definition of pollution revolves around 'noxious matter or solid waste' and tends to be interpreted as gross organic waste. Much of the Code thus deals with the storage of slurries so that they do not leak into streams and cause deoxygenation, and with the storage and use of pesticides. Phosphorus is not mentioned as such and the term does not appear in the index. The conventional wisdom of the agricultural industry has long been that nutrients are a good thing and, though attitudes are changing, the concept of them as pollutants is not easily accepted. There is yet no legal precedent that has established that nutrient run-off from agriculture is an offence under the Water Act.Nonetheless, adherence to the Code must go some way to minimising delivery of phosphorus to waters. The phosphorus production of large stock units is, however, so considerable that disposal methods that are the equivalent of the nineteenth century sewage farms for the human population cannot be regarded as a solution. In many rural catchments, especially in the wetter, more hilly areas, stock are the major sources of phosphorus. In these areas, unless recycling back to the land, effectively a resumption of traditional mixed farming, can be shown to reduce nutrient losses from the

The Ministry of Agriculture, Fisheries and Food has produced a code of Good Agricultural Practice which advises farmers of their obligations under the law and also suggests ways of minimising fertilizer run-off.

land, we may need to accept that nutrient control is not possible or consider the phosphorus stripping of stock effluent in the same way as that of human effluent.

Detergent phosphorus

There has been considerable controversy about the phosphate content of domestic laundry detergents. From the 1950s to the 1980s nearly half of the phosphorus content of human sewage was due to detergents, the remainder being from excretal waste. There were pressures in many countries to replace the phosphate during the 1970s and 1980s and bans have been enforced in some. Others negotiated voluntary agreements to reduce the phosphate content. The detergent and chemical industries resisted attempts to create a Europe-wide legal ban, because in most ways phosphate is an ideal component of detergents, and have hitherto been successful in this.

Phosphate, as sodium tripolyphosphate, is used as a builder to combine with calcium and magnesium hardness in the water. This would otherwise bind with the surfactant to form a scum and prevent the surfactant removing fatty matter from the laundry. Phosphate is non toxic, non corrosive and non hygroscopic - a desirable attribute of a free running powder that must not cake in the packet, or clog pipes in a washing machine, or poison the infants who, for unfathomable reasons, occasionally eat it.

Much of the cost in phosphate stripping is in the chemicals used, and in theory, if detergents contribute a proportion of the phosphate (formerly about 40%, now probably closer to 20%), they contribute the same percentage to the costs of treatment. In practice this is not entirely true for more chemical is needed to remove a given amount of phosphate, the lower the concentration of phosphate. Most of

It is more difficult to reduce diffuse sources of phosphorus than point sources.

the cost is in removing the last few milligrams, not the initial bulk. Removing phosphate from detergents would thus reduce the costs somewhat, but not proportionately.

Alternatives to phosphate have been much discussed and include nitrilotriacetic acid and zeolites. The latter have found much favour, have few problems but are not as effective, bulk for bulk, as phosphates. It is possible, though unlikely at the expected environmental concentrations, that some alternatives may poison invertebrates in freshwaters. In the absence of a solid understanding of the environmental risks of alternative builders, however, calls for statutory removal of phosphate detergents from the UK market are being resisted. The detergent industry in the UK has, nonetheless, for some time been (quietly) marketing dual lines of detergents, some with zeolite, others with phosphate. The detergent contribution to the phosphate content of sewage is probably now only half what it formerly was.

The ability to remove phosphorus in sewage treatment is an advantage in favour of continued use of phosphates but the limitations of the Urban Waste Water Treatment Directive dictate that most works in the UK will not have phosphorus removal stages. On balance, therefore, there could be advantages in a complete replacement of phosphorus in detergents. Or alternatively, a comprehensive installation of phosphorus removal at sewage treatment works, together with sale of the precipitated phosphorus back to the detergent industry, could have advantages to industry, consumers and the environment.

Fish farms

One point source of phosphorus may become more important in the future, that of the effluent from fish farms. There has been an increasing establishment of rainbow trout farms on rivers in southern England and there are some problems in northern England and Scotland. It is unlikely that such a farm would be situated in a shallow lake for there would be too much danger of overnight deoxygenation on a still summer night. Fish are given nitrogen and phosphorus rich feed. The effluent from the holding ponds is also rich. Where it proves a significant part of a nutrient budget to a shallow lake, there will be need to control it, but unless the discharge is from a fixed pipe there is no requirement for a discharge consent. It may be possible to reduce problems by gaining agreement to limit food additions. There is yet no specific technology for treating fish farm effluents, except for some removal of solids in ponds prior to discharge, though in principle they are no different from the wastes of other animals.

Diffuse sources of phosphorus

External diffuse sources of phosphorus have hitherto been believed to be relatively small compared with the point sources. They have been mostly of phosphate absorbed on particles, that erodes from agricultural land and that which may be washed off when animal slurry or inorganic fertilizer is applied too heavily to fields, or in very wet weather. However, it is now becoming apparent that soils in intensively cultivated areas have a surplus of phosphorus and that their retention mechanisms are becoming saturated. Much more is running off as soluble phosphorus than previously [57,77,196]. Increasing awareness of the problem is likely to result in pressure to develop more sophisticated approaches to matching crop demand and fertiliser use. Meanwhile, adherence to the Code of Good Agricultural Practice, especially with respect to the need for soil analyses to determine the real, as opposed to presumed requirements of particular soils, should minimise these losses. Nonetheless,

G. A. Maclean, Oxford Scientific

The effluent from fish farms, where the animals are intensively housed and fed, may contain very high quantities of nutrients, which are later released to a nearby stream.

much will run off for some time yet. Detailed studies of catchments reveal that there is a heterogeneity in the sources of nutrients. Sometimes the bulk of the load comes from only a small area, which can be targeted for improvement. In attempts to reduce the effects of diffuse sources, an immediate safeguard may be the establishment of buffer zones alongside inflow streams and around the lake.

Buffer zones

Buffer zones are areas of uncultivated, ungrazed (by stock) land which consequently develop semi-natural or natural vegetation. In principle they retain particulate phosphorus and one method of treating effluents is to run them through a bed of buffer wetland. The case for their use as nitrogen filters (see below) is well established for they promote denitrification, provided that they are wide enough and continuous. They do not retain soluble phosphorus compounds permanently, and may become sources of these in summer. Nonetheless, there are many arguments for using buffer zones, in terms of retaining sediment, reducing nitrogen loading,

recreating wildlife corridors, providing nesting habitat for birds, providing some protection against pesticide spray drift and general amenity.

There is controversy about how wide such zones need to be and the best sort of vegetation for them to contain. 'Vegetated filter strips' up to 262 m wide in the USA were effective in removing 80% of total N and total P from concentrated effluents from intensive cattle raising and ratios of buffer area to source area of 1:1 have been found necessary for land to which chicken manure was applied. Such ratios will generally be impossible to provide but smaller areas will suffice if used in conjunction with other means of nutrient control. Strips up to 9m wide have been tested for control of nutrients from cereal crops. They were: more effective at removing sediment than nutrients; less effective after heavy rain; ineffective for large source areas; most effective when new; good at removing N but not P; and useful only for relatively short spans [50,121].

A minimum of 5m to each side of the stream

Buffer zones must inevitably be helpful in reducing diffuse nutrient loading, especially of nitrogen but the land take involved is more than a token.

channel is suggested by Harper & Pacini[72] on the basis of a literature review, but this figure is likely to be notional. Widths of only 2m appear to be effective in retaining eroded particles in some places. Common sense would suggest however, that there is little point in having a few 50-metre stretches, each a couple of metres wide along kilometres of stream in an intensely agricultural catchment[103], though that is the way more extensive schemes may need to start. Any buffer zone will be compromised if there is under-surface tile drainage delivering water to the stream.

Complete coverage, with vegetation, of the soil in a buffer zone is desirable and vegetation that is actively building up biomass, such as young woodland seems to be most effective at removing sediment. Reductions of up to 500 kilograms of N and 40 kilograms of P per hectare have been recorded under ideal conditions. With export rates of around 40 kg of N from agricultural land, this would imply ratios of buffer zone to source area of at least 8%[214,215].

More effective is a buffer of natural riparian wetland vegetation, either of reedswamp or woodland. Again nitrogen and sediment are removed more effectively than phosphorus and ratios of wetland to source area of about 1% appear to be effective, at least in the short term. The wetlands may be those of the stream floodplain, which may need reinstatement if they have been drained, or they may be specially constructed and the stream led through them. Water levels in such cases need control as all the nutrient retention processes need contact between water and the vegetation and bottom.

Such constructed wetlands will fill in rapidly with peat and sediment and may become

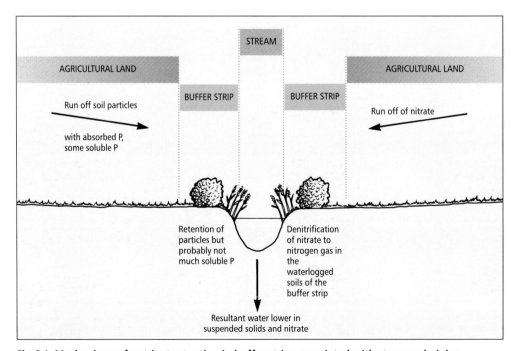

Fig 6.1 Mechanisms of nutrient retention in buffer strips associated with streams draining agricultural land.

sources of phosphorus mobilised from particulate sources in time [61]. They will generally remain effective as nitrogen filters so long as they remain wet and water tables are allowed to fluctuate. Guidance on the design of constructed wetlands is given in [37,70,74,] and [133].

In the USA, the ideal system for cereal and other field crops is thought[121] to be one with about 25m of natural wetland spanning the stream channel, a further 45m of wetland used for forest management to either side of the natural wetland, and a further 5m of vegetated filter strip of ungrazed grassland, taking coarse sediment debris, to the outside. The width of the entire system would thus be 125m for streams only a few metres wide.

There is no legislation in Europe directly requiring land owners to establish buffer zones, though from a conservation and amenity point of view such legislation would be a major advance. The set aside schemes (EC Regulation1765/92, 2293/92 and 2296/92, UK Set Aside Regulations) of recent years were designed simply to take agricultural land out of production, not specifically to use it positively. There was an option in the regulations for creation of 'water-fringe habitat' and some schemes were set up though in very few areas. Currently, Environmentally Sensitive Area Schemes (EC Regulation 797/85, Agriculture Act 1986) could include more provision for buffer strips. Some encourage the leaving of thin strips of grassy vegetation near watercourses in arable areas. A further possibility lies in the Countryside Stewardship scheme set up in the UK by the Countryside Commission and now transferred to the Ministry of Agriculture. This scheme is intended directly for environmental benefit, whilst the ESA scheme is intended more to maintain traditional farming systems and the landscape

Brian Moss

Natural streams in temperate areas have a riparian (bank edge) vegetation that is dominated by trees or wetland vegetation. Such vegetation acts as a filter for sediment, promotes denitrification of nitrate to nitrogen gas in the wet soils, especially where there is frequent fluctuation in water levels, and provides a variety of habitats for wildlife. Re-establishment of such buffer zones where they have been lost is desirable for many reasons. This example is from New Zealand.

qualities they engender. A voluntary scheme, the 'waterside habitat scheme', promoted by English Nature to encourage farmers to establish such zones alongside rivers that are Sites of Special Scientific Interest has not been widely taken up. It is probable that future success of buffer strip schemes will depend largely on specific legislation or compensation payments.

Point sources of nitrogen

Most sources of nitrogen are diffuse. However, nitrogen compounds are by no means absent from sewage effluents, and there may be several tens of milligrams per litre. Mostly this should be in the form of nitrate but in works not running at high efficiency, the effluent may be equally rich in ammonium. The Urban Waste Water Treatment Directive provides for the removal of nitrogen as well as phosphorus from works which fall under its regulations. But for the reasons given above, the Directive is unlikely to contribute as much help as it might in some parts of Europe, including the UK.

Removal of nitrate from effluent is more expensive than phosphorus removal, requiring the use of ion exchange resins, though where land is available, much can be removed by denitrification in artificial wetland systems, through which the effluent is trickled. For large works, however, the land required for this would have to be very extensive (tens of hectares). The proportionate contribution to lake loadings of nitrogen from effluents is generally much smaller than that from agricultural sources and so where priorities must be drawn, investment in phosphorus control must come first.

Diffuse sources of nitrogen

Agriculture and, increasingly, the atmosphere are the major sources of nitrogen to lakes. Both are diffuse sources and therefore difficult to control. The atmospheric source is the nitrate produced by oxidation in the atmosphere of nitrogen oxides produced particularly by vehicle engines but also some industrial processes. In extreme cases rainfall may contain several milligrams per litre. The reduction of this source is a national matter, requiring new transport policies and clearly is not within the immediate remit of those planning a restoration project. There are local atmospheric sources that come from the volatilisation of ammonia from intensive stock units. To some extent this can be reduced by storing manure in covered dumps and by adding water to it in storage.

Beds of reed can be used to improve water quality, if the bed is large relative to the water flow. Nitrate is denitrified to nitrogen and soil particles eroded from the land can be filtered out. The reed, however, progressively lays down peat and the effectiveness of the bed will diminish as it dries out. Reedbeds will thus need surface stripping and re-establishment from time to time, especially if they are receiving heavy loads of silt. Their long-term effectiveness in retaining phosphorus is open to question.

In the lowlands, and in agricultural catchments of the uplands, field sources are, for the moment, much greater sources of nitrogen than the atmosphere. The main problem is simply that nitrate, added as fertilizer, or produced by decomposition and mineralisation of organic matter stored in the soil, is very soluble and is easily washed out to the streams. The greater the source, the intensity of cultivation, the slope and the amount of rain that runs off the fields, the more will be the losses. About 58000 tonnes of nitrate-nitrogen are lost to streams each year, in England and Wales, following applications in autumn and winter [67].

Ploughing of grassland can also release a great deal of nitrate

Strategies for minimising nitrate losses therefore should minimise fertilizer additions and use nitrogen sources that release nitrate progressively as the crops require it. Farmers should apply the fertilizer in damp, as opposed to very wet weather, and plough it in, and they should maintain a crop or stubble cover on the field for as long as possible. This minimises the period of fallow, when bare soil is exposed. Ploughing should be across slopes or along contours and not down slopes, so as to minimise water run off. Strip cropping of alternate bands of hay and cereal also minimises such run off. Overall, controlling the amount and timing of manure spreading, converting arable back to permanent grassland and using green cover crops to avoid bare land in autumn are the most effective measures in reducing nitrate leaching[67]. The Code of Good Agricultural Practice in the UK makes suggestions along these lines.

The problem for the lake restorer is in making sure that good practice is always followed. Measures to minimise nitrate run off are beneficial to the farmer in that fertilizer costs should be reduced, and labour costs saved by minimal cultivation. There is, nonetheless, plenty of scope for weather, marketing techniques and human error to foil the best laid plans.

Legislation has not helped greatly in minimising nitrate losses. There is a European Union Directive on Nitrate (991/676/EEC), which is intended to protect drinking water supplies, for nitrate is suspected of causing some human disorders. It may also be used to control nitrate applications where waters are eutrophic or may become so if action is not taken. In both cases there is provision for creation of Nitrate Vulnerable Zones (NVZ). NVZ have been created mainly in drier areas of freely draining soils over porous rocks supplying groundwater aquifers or on heavier land draining to rivers used for abstraction. They are mandatory where drinking water abstractions have concentrations of greater than 50 milligrams per litre of nitrate (11.3 milligrams per litre as nitrogen). Within them the timing and rate of application of fertilizer and manure is limited. The rate is still high from a conservation point of view (210 kilograms per hectare for the first four years, thence 170 kg/ha) and no compensation is payable because these levels are intended to supply a productive crop, but no more.

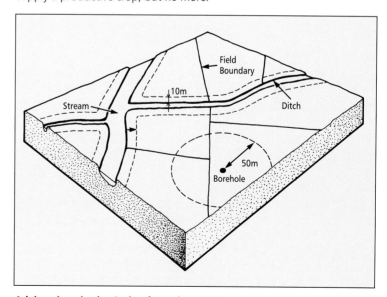

Advice given in the Code of Good Agricultural Practice concerning spreading of manures and sludge on land associated with streams, or boreholes used for drinking water abstraction. Manure should not be spread in areas between the hatched lines and the water.

So far no such zones have been created in the UK to solve eutrophication problems, only to protect drinking water. The concentrations of nitrate that contribute to serious eutrophication are far below those likely to be responsible for health problems.

There is provision in the Water Resources Act of 1991 to create nitrate sensitive areas (NSA) where fertilizer use is severely curtailed. Compensation is payable to farmers because the levels of application may be lower than those considered to be good practice, from a purely agricultural point of view. Mostly these concern the recharge zones of groundwater supplies where nitrate concentrations may be very high indeed. Few have yet been designated in the UK and none to protect surface supplies. The Nitrate Directive has thus not yet been used at all in the prevention of eutrophication in the UK although it offers scope for this to happen.The best opportunity for reducing diffuse nitrate run-off for lake restoration is in designated Article 19 areas (Environmentally Sensitive Areas (ESA) in the UK), where fertilizer restrictions may be easily included in return for compensation payments. In the grazing marshes of the Broads ESA, applications have been reduced by about half compared with levels in the 1980s. Since fertilizer application has increased by twenty-fold in the last fifty years in the more intensively farmed areas of western Europe, however, even the reduced application rates are still likely to be uncomfortably high from the point of view of loading on a lake.

The regulations for environmentally sensitive areas offer a legislative opportunity for control of diffuse nitrogen loads.

Buffer zones again
In view of all this, it will always be desirable to separate any lake and all its inflow streams from cultivated land by buffer zones. Extensive areas of wetland are of particular value because rates of denitrification are high in waterlogged soils. It is not yet possible to state exactly how wide or extensive such buffers should be in specific instances. Common sense and experimental data would suggest that the wider and bigger the better, and that token bands are unlikely to be very helpful.

Internal sources of phosphorus
There is little point in doing anything about internal sources of nutrients until external sources have been reduced, for ultimately the external sources provide the stocks of those released internally. There may also be an argument, which is presented later, for delaying internal control or not attempting it at all. That having been said, there are four basic approaches to minimising the effects of internal loading of phosphorus: washout, sediment sealing, sediment removal and biomass removal [55,180].

The first and last can be dispensed with immediately. Flushing the lake with low phosphorus water is likely to be impossible for lack of a suitable supply, although theoretically it should speed up the ultimate loss of phosphorus stored in the lake. This may still be very slow. Removal of nutrients by biomass removal is only practicable for aquatic plants. Although it may be useful once plants have been restored and perhaps are growing so vigorously as to clog the lake, it is clearly a technique for eventual management and not for immediate restoration. Even then it is a dangerous practice for it could constitute a forward switch for loss of the vegetation again.

Sediment sealing
This leaves sediment sealing and sediment removal. Sediment sealing means the physical or chemical isolation of the sediment from the water. The former has been achieved by use of plastic sheeting and by the dumping of a relatively thick layer of pulverised fly ash (the solid waste product from coal burning power stations). Such techniques have been used to minimise algal bloom problems in lakes used

primarily for unquiet recreation such as power boating or for industrial water supplies, but are clearly inappropriate for conservation purposes, where a bottom supportive of aquatic plant growth is needed.

Chemical sealing has been successful when alum has been added to the water to form a phosphorus-binding blanket at the sediment surface [40]. The costs are reasonable (about 1200 to 2400 ecu per ha) but alum is likely to be toxic to aquatic plant roots and therefore inappropriate in sites of conservation and amenity importance. It has so far been unacceptable in the UK. A more subtle approach is possible, however, when an attempt is made to mimic the natural processes that promote retention of phosphorus in the sediment.

Thus iron sulphate may be added as a dense solution to the water near the sediment surface, or dosed at the inflows [47]. There is no absolute shortage of iron in the environment, but in heavily eutrophicated lakes most or all of the incoming supply may be tied up as insoluble ferrous sulphide in the sediments, leaving none to bind phosphorus. The principle of adding iron salts is thus acceptable (though under certain circumstances, iron salts are regarded as List 2 substances under the EU Dangerous Substances Directive). In practice the technique has not been entirely satisfactory. To be really effective, the amount of iron used must be considerable and unsightly orange deposits tend to be formed around fringing plants. Invertebrate diversity may also be reduced and a blanket of iron floc must also have a detrimental effect on plant diversity, though suppporting data are few.

The technique has been used mostly on drinking water reservoirs, without the essential prerequisite of reducing the external phosphorus loading. The amount of iron used,

therefore, has had to be considerable for it is intended to precipitate phosphate from the incoming water as much as suppress its release from the sediment.

The industrial iron salts used may be contaminated with other metals and addition to water bodies requires the consent of the regulatory authority (the Environment Agency in the UK). It would be far more desirable to use the same iron salts to remove the phosphorus at the sewage treatment works!

There have also been problems with making sure that the iron persists in the sediment surface. The sediments under lakes which have lost their aquatic plants may be more fluid at the surface than those stabilised by plant debris and roots. Iron salts may then mix downwards easily and be bound up as sulphide, or the iron may be exchanged much more readily with the overlying water. In shallow riverine lakes with considerable water movement, it may be difficult simply to prevent undue dilution with the overlying water. In lakes close to the sea, with substantial sulphate concentrations due to tidal flow or even the ingress of sea spray through rain, there may be enough potential sulphide formation to tie up very large added quantities of iron.

Internal sources of phosphorus may be large and may need to be controlled. This is usually expensive and the need should be carefully considered.

Sediment in Ranworth Broad being treated with iron salts.

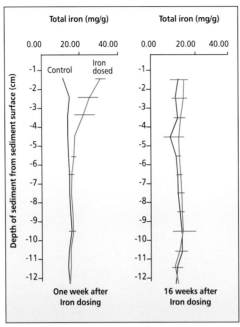

Fig 6.2 Changes in the iron content of sediment in cores taken from Ranworth Broad after it had been injected with iron sulphate. Results are the means from three cores and standard deviations are shown. Although increased iron levels could be shown in the dosed area after a week, this was no longer the case after 16 weeks, when dosed areas were not significantly different from control areas. (From Madgwick and Phillips 1996).

The technique gave disappointing results **(Fig 6.2)** in the Norfolk Broads , even though the iron sulphate was carefully injected into the sediments through nozzles. Almost all factors there, however, would mitigate against success. The sediments are fluid, the sites are affected by sea water and the extent of the eutrophication is considerable.

The Riplox method
Chemical sealing elsewhere, under more favourable circumstances and using a different technique, has been more promising. There is a patented process called Riplox from the name of

its inventor, Wilhelm Ripl[178], and the fact that it attempts to oxidise the sediment surface, thus favouring the formation of ferric phosphate (see Chapter1). The oxidising agent used is nitrate, and specially designed equipment injects a concentrated nitrate solution into the sediment. This minimises the risk of increasing the nitrogen concentration in the water **(Fig.6.3)**. Calcium and iron salts may also be used, respectively to improve the conditions for denitrification and to increase the phosphorus binding capacity of the sediment.

In theory this is an ideal technique because nitrate is an oxidising agent that naturally functions in sediments. It is not persistent, being denitrified in supporting the bacterial decomposition of organic matter at the sediment surface. This reduces future bacterial activity and allows the oxidised microzone at the sediment surface to re-form. Riplox has been successfully used on a number of small Swedish lakes, all of them relatively sheltered with stable sediments and modest degrees of eutrophication **(Fig.6.4)**. Good results were obtained for Lake Lillesjøn (4.2ha), in Sweden, but not at Lake Trekanten (13ha), despite a cost of 50000 ecu per ha, though iron was not used in this case.

The disadvantages of the Riplox method are its need for specialist operators and equipment, and the cost of the chemicals. As in all attempts to reduce internal loading, it is only a temporary expedient if external loading is not reduced first and the rate at which organic matter is delivered to the bottom thus curbed.

Sediment removal
Any chemical technique is likely to be expensive in materials and its potential success or failure will not be known until the money has been spent and the job completed. There is thus merit in the idea of insuring against the risk of failure, or only temporary success, by removing

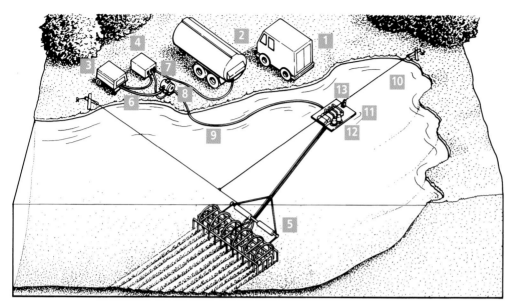

Fig 6.3 Equipment used in the Riplox method for dosing sediments with iron chloride to reduce the rate of phosphate release. 1 is a field laboratory; 2, a chemical supply tank; 3, a portable compressor for bubbling air into the chemical mixing tank; 4, mixing tank for the chemicals (calcium nitrate, ferric chloride); 5, harrow-like device to loosen sediment with compressed air and inject chemicals; 6 and 7, air feed lines to mixing tank and to drive pumps; 8, air-driven pump; 9, supply line for chemicals; 10, guide line for pulling chemical injector across bottom of lake; 11, air driven dilution pump for mixing chemicals with water and injecting mixture into sediment; 12, dilution water intake; 13, pneumatic winch.

the sediment entirely, or at least taking off the more phosphorus-enriched surface layers.

This should not be undertaken lightly. It is expensive in that the wet sediment is bulky and though it can be readily sucked from the bottom and conveyed by pipeline out of the lake, this is slow and the sediment has to be disposed of somewhere. To remove each successive centimetre of sediment, from a fifty-hectare lake, means disposal of at least fifty thousand tonnes of sediment slurry, which will settle to five thousand tonnes of wet sediment and then dry out to about five hundred cubic metres of material.

It is thus first desirable to work out the absolute minimum of sediment that must be removed, but this may be difficult. All sediment is relatively rich in phosphorus compared with overlying water, simply because phosphorus,

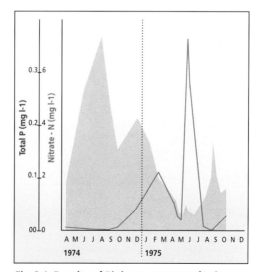

Fig 6.4 Results of Riplox treatment of Lake Lillesjon, Sweden. Injection of nitrate in 1974, some of which appeared in the water, led to falls in phosphate concentration in the subsequent year. (After Ripl 1976).

Suction dredging is expensive and requires careful planning. Disposal of the sediment over large areas of land is more useful than dumping in a lagoon.

being insoluble, tends to be bound into sediments. Below the surface, all sediments are anaerobic and so phosphorus is easily mobilised.

There is always some loss of phosphate from the sediment surface by diffusion, despite the chemical binding mechanisms, even with oxidised surfaces. There may also be an upward diffusion within the sediment so that even after removal of phosphorus-rich surface sediments, the residual, formerly less rich, deeper sediments may acquire enriched surface layers through diffusion. There is also increasing evidence that

M Timms

Analysis of sediment cores is desirable in planning a restoration. Short surface cores can be removed by a variety of samplers. Sediment up to a metre or so deep in lake basins with peaty bases can be removed intact using a drainpipe that has been cut longitudinally in half then taped together with waterproof tape. The pipe is thrust into the sediment, then stoppered at the base with a rubber bung as it emerges from the water. In a small boat, on a windy day, insertion and removal can be an interesting business!

under some circumstances, e.g of high temperature, certain forms of disturbance by burrowing animals, or increased pH stimulated by photosynthesis, there may be substantial aerobic release of phosphorus. In general then it is sensible, despite the cost, to be generous in the amount of sediment removed rather than parsimonious.

Removal and disposal will cost a lot anyway, and this cost, per unit of sediment removed, will decrease with increasing amounts. Costs of up to 72000 ecu per ha have been reported. Sediment cores should be taken during the planning of such operations and fairly detailed analyses carried out for phosphorus and other indicators. For example, in the Norfolk Broads, the successive ecological changes in the lakes are reflected often in prominent layering of the sediment. The sediment laid down by pristine, charophyte-dominated communities can easily be seen and more recent layers identified for removal.

In more amorphous, visually uniform sediments, it will be necessary to investigate the diatoms contained in them. Predominance of genera that are periphytic will identify layers that were deposited in plant dominated conditions. Any attempts at sediment removal should at least go as deep as these layers and preferably well into them.

Disposal of sediment

Disposal of the sediment is a major problem. Even for lakes near the sea, marine dumping may become illegal under the Directive on Urban Waste Water Treatment, which prohibits sewage sludge dumping at sea, after 1998. Lake sludge might be construed as being ultimately of the same nature, though there have yet been no test cases. Dumping on land is likely to be the rule.

The usual technique has been to create a lagoon within a raised bund in nearby flat land and to run in the sediment slurry through a pipe which

Suction dredger at work in Hoveton Little Broad, Norfolk. The dredger works along a line moved systematically across the lake. The mud slurry is pumped away through pipes in the background.

Sediment lagoons prepared for drying of sediment from Barton Broad, before eventual restoration of the land for agricultural uses.

is moved from time to time to prevent burial and to distribute the sediment evenly. The water drains away and the sediment settles. When the lagoon is full to the top with drained sediment, it is allowed to dry, whilst a second lagoon is filled, if necessary. After drying, more sediment may be layered onto the first lagoon. The lagoons are unsightly and should be screened by woodland, if possible. They should not occupy land of great conservation value for, although the dried sediment will colonise relatively rapidly with plants, these will be of a vigorous nature, like nettles and willows, and diversity will be low.

Siting should be done with care, for the water draining from the lagoon may be extremely rich in phosphate and sometimes ammonium or nitrate. It should not be allowed to run straight back into the lake, though its effects are likely to be insignificant in the disturbance caused by sediment removal. The nutrients released during this will ultimately be washed out (though some might re-enter the sediment). Design of the drainage pattern within the lagoon system to maximise the length of path taken for the water

to pass through will ensure maximal retention of suspended solids. Use of a reedbed system in the final stages will also 'polish' the effluent of some remaining solids and combined nitrogen compounds. In some schemes, such as at Lake Trummen in Sweden [2,10,17,18,43,45], the water has been treated with iron sulphate in additional lagoons before return to the lake, but this increases the costs. Sediment lagoons are also potentially dangerous until they are dried out because deer, other wild mammals and intrepid youth, venturing onto them, may become mired down, panic and drown. There may be legal requirements for suitable fencing and provision of life saving equipment.

The disposal of waste must usually be licensed by the Environment Agency but material dredged from lakes or rivers may be exempt. The conditions that apply are complex and any dredging proposal should be discussed with the Environment Agency. In lakes in urban areas that have been receiving industrial effluent, there may be significant concentrations of heavy metals, hydrocarbons or other toxic materials in the sediment. Sediments should be analysed at an early stage when planning a dredging programme. If toxic material is found in significant concentrations, disposal to land may be difficult and the material may have to be removed to a licensed site.

Where sediment can eventually be spread over agricultural land, as currently it is at Barton Broad in Norfolk, many of the long term problems of lagoons can be avoided. Through spreading over a wide area, the sediment will dry out more rapidly and can then be ploughed in. It should not be spread heavily on slopes where a sudden rainstorm may wash it back into the lake nor preferably on fields directly abutting the lake unless a substantial wetland buffer zone intervenes. The area of land needed

will depend on the nature of both receiving soil and incoming sediment, and specialist advice should be taken from the Agricultural Development and Advisory Service, or equivalent bodies, about this. There may also be legal difficulties to be overcome as the land may need to be licensed for landfill and subject to landfill tax. The Environment Agency should be contacted for advice.

Should you remove sediment at all?

Any technique for reduction of internal loading will be very expensive. Moreover, some major schemes, such as that at Lake Brabrant (see Chapter 10) in Denmark have yet to show much reduction in total phosphorus concentration in the water. On the other hand it seems

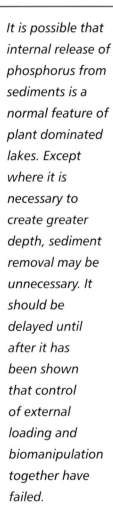

It is possible that internal release of phosphorus from sediments is a normal feature of plant dominated lakes. Except where it is necessary to create greater depth, sediment removal may be unnecessary. It should be delayed until after it has been shown that control of external loading and biomanipulation together have failed.

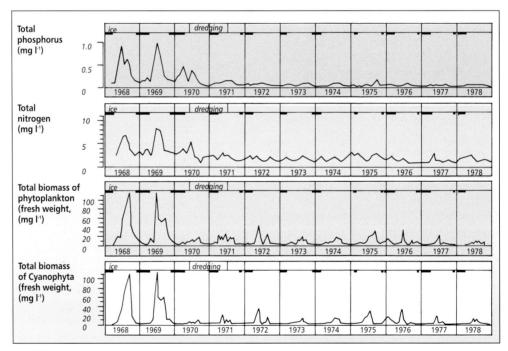

Fig 6.5 Changes in Lake Trummen, Sweden, following sediment removal in 1970/71. In previous years, phosphate removal was carried out on incoming sewage effluent but there had been little change in the lake. Sediment removal led to falls in total phosphorus, total nitrogen, phytoplankton biomass and the biomass of blue-green algae (Cyanophyta). This apparent success of sediment removal is comparatively unusual and may depend on the very infertile earlier sediments, derived from an infertile catchment, left in the lake. There is some evidence that it may have resulted from a fish kill and inadvertent biomanipulation of the lake. (From Bengtsson et al 1975).

that Lake Trummen in Sweden was not restored by external nutrient control alone and that sediment removal on a fairly large scale did contribute to initial recovery [17,18] (**Fig. 6.5**).

One possible explanation for such restoration of Lake Trummen may be that nutrient levels were sufficiently reduced to limit phytoplankton growth strongly, though available data suggest that they are as high as 100 micrograms per litre in summer. They are less than half of this in winter and spring, however, and these may be the more important values. The complete explanation may be more complex. There was a severe winter in 1969-70, with a major fish-kill under the ice [43,44]. The major changes that occurred in the lake following suction dredging in 1970/71 may thus have been a result of this natural biomanipulation rather than removal of mud. The fish stocks recovered, following recolonisation from another lake, downstream, and experiments showed a major importance of top down effects [1]. Despite the sediment removal and continued stripping of phosphorus at the sewage treatment works, the lake has since moved back towards its former state, though algal growths are not as great as before nutrient diversion [44].

Insufficient data are yet available for certainty but it is possible that internal loading with phosphorus is a normal feature of many shallow lakes even when they are dominated by aquatic plants. This is especially so when external nutrient loading brings concentrations into the range in which alternative stable states of plant or phytoplankton dominance can exist. Plants slough off a great deal of organic matter during the growth season and a huge amount when they die back in autumn. Water movements are also stilled within the bed, so that diffusion of oxygen is slowed, and the sediment surface is dark, through shading by the plants and cannot benefit from oxygenation by algae living on it. At night the respiration of the plants themselves creates a substantial oxygen deficit within the bed.

Sediment surfaces under plant beds therefore experience all the conditions that are needed for release of phosphorus at an anaerobic surface. Rates of phosphorus release in a plant-dominated lake may be at least as high as in a eutrophicated and algal dominated one[202]. Release of nitrogen as ammonium, however, may be greater in an algal-dominated lake for there is not the substantial plant biomass available to take it up. If this is so, algal growth may be given an extra boost by internal loading and it may be worth removing the sediment.

Our advice would be that sediment removal should be delayed until after it has been established that control of external loading coupled with the steps to be described in the next two Chapters (biomanipulation and plant establishment) has failed. If they succeed without sediment removal, all well and good and a great deal of money will have been saved. If they fail for reasons that can be attributed to the nature or activity of the sediment, then only a year or two of time and the costs of fish removal, will have been lost. On the other hand, sediment removal will not be detrimental, even if unnecessary for nutrient control. If the lake has filled in so much with sediment that only decimetres of water are left, sediment disturbance by wind may inhibit plant establishment and may preclude additional uses of the lake such as sailing. It may thus be desirable to remove sediment for these reasons alone, but in all cases it is a procedure that causes much disturbance and expense and should be considered with great care.

Decision tree for nutrient control

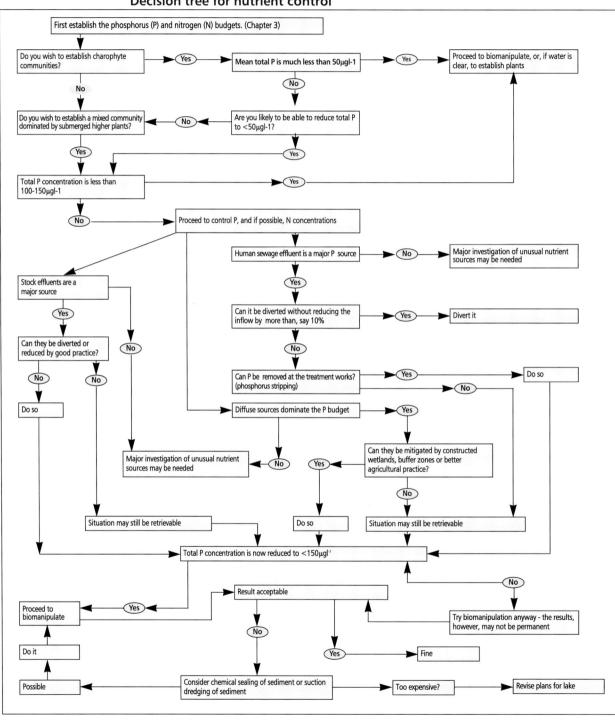

Chapter 7

Steps in the Strategy
(3) Biomanipulation

'Biomanipulation' strictly means any adjustment of the biological community in an ecosystem to achieve a desired end. The term has been hijacked by lake restorers to mean alteration of the fish community to increase the numbers of grazer zooplankton, particularly *Daphnia* species [82,192,194].

Husbanding of the superior *Daphnia* species may be done by adding piscivorous fish to reduce the numbers of zooplanktivorous fish [11,12,14,31,32], potentially by changing the hydrology of the system so as to concentrate piscivorous fish into the lake basin [105], or by removing all or most of the fish community [38,59,83,104,113,131,143,207,209]. A mixture of approaches may also be used . The most successful biomanipulations carried out to date have involved exhaustive removal of the entire fish community [177], but this is expensive compared with piscivore stocking (though cheap compared with most other aspects of lake restoration).

Removal of fish may also give indirect benefits through reducing phosphorus transfer from the shallows to the open water. In large lakes, the fish move there as adults and excrete phosphorus in an available form [100].

Piscivore addition

In mainland Europe, two piscivores have been used, the pike (*Esox lucius*)[16,68,78,199] and the zander, or pikeperch (*Stizostedion lucioperca*)[13,14,24] (**Fig.7.1**). The latter is apparently the ideal piscivore as it feeds by pursuit of the shoals of small zooplanktivorous fish such as roach, perch and bream, which are particularly abundant following spawning in May and June. It also tolerates turbid water. The pike is a 'sit and wait' predator which lurks in plant beds for its prey to come near. It is most effective in clear water, however. If the lake lacks extensive plant beds, which it will, of course, in the early stages of a restoration project, then pike will not thrive for lack of habitat.

There is a problem in the UK with use of the zander. It is not a native fish and although it has been introduced and is apparently spreading in the canal system, it is illegal, under the Wildlife and Countryside Act (1981) and its Amendment

Biomanipulation may be the addition of piscivores, potentially by adjustment of seasonal water levels to concentrate piscivores into a lake, or removal of the entire fish community.

Perch

Pike

Fig 7.1 Pike and perch are the main native piscivorous fish in the UK. Perch, however, are also zooplanktivorous in the first two years or so of their lives and pike need weedy habitats to provide the cover in which they lurk and await their prey.

(1985) deliberately to introduce it, without licence, to a new water. Even were it to prove effective under British conditions, it would be difficult therefore to use it. This stricture also applies to other exotic species such as the American large mouthed bass (*Micropterus salmoides*), which are widely used in biomanipulation in North America and of which large numbers can be raised easily in hatcheries.

In any case, piscivore introduction is a less desirable technique than fish removal. This is for several reasons. First, although a tranche of piscivores may be added, they will not survive for very long because, if they are effective, they will exhaust their own food supply, the zooplanktivorous fish. The latter will recover numbers but there is no guarantee that the piscivores will have survived in the interim. The coexistence of any pair of predator and prey is governed by the need for a lot more prey production than predator production (the elementary principle by which food chains

operate) and by the need for prey refuges, if both predator and prey are not to enter into population fluctuations of great amplitude (boom and bust cycles).

Addition of piscivores, though it may have immediate effects, will not have long-lasting effects unless there is renewed stocking every year. Apart from the expense of this, there is the practical problem of obtaining sufficient fish, and the ethical problem of deliberate stocking into a situation where it is known the fish will not survive for very long. In Danish experiments [199], it was found that stocking of pike fingerlings (2-10cm long) was needed at the rate of at least 1000 fish per hectare every year to give noticeable effects on the zooplankton populations.

Water level manipulation

A more acceptable practice would be manipulation of water levels to concentrate piscivores into shallow lakes during summer [105], though it has yet to be used. The principle behind this is that many shallow lakes were formed within river floodplain systems where the winter floods created large sheets of shallow water within the floodplain (Fig.7.2). Many fishes, including pike, moved out into the extended sheet of water and bred there in the late spring, producing a large population of young. As the floods receded in summer the fish concentrated in the permanent basins in the floodplain where the young pike fed upon the young roach and bream, thus reducing their consequent impact on the zooplankton.

Many European floodplains have been drained and the rivers engineered to deeper and straighter channels to prevent flooding but there is now a recognition that this has been a mistake and that floodplains should be reinstated. There thus exists the future possibility of biomanipulating simply by allowing winter flooding and natural summer

Fig 7.2 Part of the Netherlands, showing urban areas (black), floodplain wetlands in the mid nineteenth century (grey) and still extant wetlands and lakes (blue). The marked reduction in such areas and their current discontinuity is clear. (After Klinge et al 1995).

recession. The technique has not yet been used,
but even if it proves impotent alone, it can only
help and will be a highly desirable approach to
stabilising the system (Chapter 8).

Fish-eating birds

There is at least one example where clear water
has accidentally been restored by the
piscivorous activity of cormorants[118]. A single
cormorant is capable of decimating the fish
stock of a hectare of shallow lake in a single
winter if confined to that lake as a food source.
The known example concerned a cormorant
with an accidentally damaged wing, which
could not fly out and which attracted other
cormorants to the lake (**Fig 7.3**). Theoretically it
would be possible to control the fish
populations sufficiently to husband the
zooplankton by using pinioned cormorants,
which could be moved from lake to lake as

**Cormorants are fish feeding birds, whose
behaviour appears to be leading them inland
from the sea to inland waters. A large colony
breeds near the Nardermeer in the
Netherlands.**

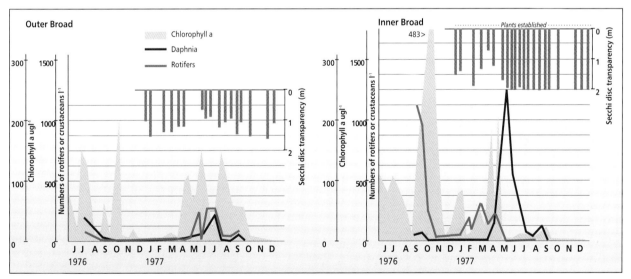

**Fig 7.3 Effects of cormorant predation on the fish of a small lake. The panel (left) shows
development of large algal growths (measured as chlorophyll a) in a small lake which was open to
the nearby river, from which fish could freely move into it. Algal development was high in both
1976 and 1977. The panel (right) shows data from an adjacent lake, about 1 ha in area, which was
isolated from the river and on which a crippled cormorant established itself in the winter of
1976/77. The bird attracted in other cormorants and much of the fish stock was removed and
could not be replaced. *Daphnia* numbers increased to a greater extent than in the 'open' lake (the
outer broad) and persisted for longer. The water cleared (see Secchi disc transparency) and aquatic
plants established. No plants were found in the outer broad. (From Leah et al 1980).**

restorations were completed. There would be legal difficulties to be overcome in that it is illegal to capture cormorants under the Wildlife and Countryside Act, but birds bred from existing captured stock could be used or special licences obtained. There might also be ethical objections. At the very least, the indications are that any removal of piscivorous birds, in the interests of angling, for example, would be a retrograde step.

Fish removal

The second approach to biomanipulation has been to remove all of the fish stock and to maintain it at very low levels against recolonisation for a number of years. Unless fish poisons such as rotenone are used[173,182], this is not as easy as it may sound and is certainly not a casual activity to be carried out on a couple of days! The larger and less isolated the lake, the more difficult it becomes to remove sufficient fish, and prevention of recolonisation poses problems where the lake is interconnected with others and used for a variety of purposes such as navigation - and angling! Rotenone is discouraged in the UK (its use requires special consent from the Environmental Agency) but not in some other European countries. It is a substance originally extracted from the roots of the African derris plant and can be used to kill fish outright, or to anaesthetise them. They can be resuscitated with potassium permanganate but there are usually many deaths.

Transfer of any fish will require a variety of permissions - from the landowner, of course, from the Environment Agency, who have a duty under the Salmon and Freshwater Fisheries Act 1975 (Section 30) to prevent possible transfer of fish parasites, and from English Nature, the Countryside Council for Wales, Scottish Natural Heritage, or other appropriate conservation bodies in other countries if the site has official conservation status.

The easiest case to consider is a small lake, say a few hectares, which can be drawn down by a sluice and completely emptied. The fish can then be concentrated progressively and removed for sale or to other waters. Good organisation is necessary for many fish suffer from prolonged stress and handling. They should be immediately transferred to storage tanks bubbled with air or oxygen. Working across a soft mud flat will not facilitate this. Because it is very difficult to obtain complete information on fish communities, the fish should be identified, weighed and measured, and scale samples taken from a subsample, in the interests of furthering the understanding of fish communities in lakes and the processes which contribute to changes in them - and restoration of them. This will add to the transfer time and must be carefully planned, preferably with Environmental Agency advice.

Fish need careful handling and storage during biomanipulation operations. Storage here is in tanks vigorously bubbled with air, whilst the fish await measurement and eventual removal to a nearby water.

Complete removal of fish needs careful planning and a variety of fishing techniques geared to local conditions and the particular species present.

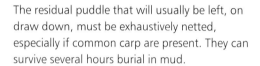

Fishing often carries an eccentric air with it, even when sophisticated electrofishing equipment is being used!

Seine netting is labour intensive, but effective where shores are gently sloping.

The residual puddle that will usually be left, on draw down, must be exhaustively netted, especially if common carp are present. They can survive several hours burial in mud.

In such circumstances, it will probably not be necessary to re-fish the lake for several years, unless there are lakes upstream and interconnecting channels. A sequence of several fish-proof barriers must then be placed across the streams, allowing the passage of water but not of fish. It is desirable that natural populations of piscivores like pike are present in the barred stretches.

Few lakes, however, can be easily or completely drawn down and recourse has to be made to a variety of fishing methods. The first step is to establish as much as possible about the fish community from whatever anecdotal information is available - generally this will be from local anglers fishing the lake rather than from official sources. There may have been some past surveys carried out by the Environment Agency, or as part of research projects. Particularly useful is information on seasonal movements within the lake, and favoured spawning areas. A pilot fishing is desirable to establish what species are present and to help select appropriate fishing methods. Local variants of standard methods, used by

commercial fishermen in some areas, should always be chosen where available. They will have been developed and refined by the experience of many years.

Fishing should be carried out in winter for three reasons. First, there will have been natural mortality during the preceding summer of the small fish hatched that year so that numbers to be handled will be at their minimum for the year; secondly, dissolved oxygen levels in the cold water will be at their highest for the year and stress will be minimised. Thirdly, fishing before the annual spawning is essential because newly hatched fish are very difficult to catch in quantity. They are too small for nets of mesh sizes that can be easily used.

The first step is to place stop nets across outflows and inflows and across any small side channels or drains into which fish may retreat following disturbance in the main basin. In a big lake it is helpful to divide the basin into manageable segments by stop nets but wind and wave action may prevent this, or make it ineffective. The side channels can be fished using electrofishing techniques, which depend on stunning the fish in an electric field. This is potentially hazardous and must only be done by qualified operators who have passed a training course, based on national guidelines.

The appropriate techniques for fishing the main basin will depend on its size. Small lakes may be systematically fished along lanes created by long nets stretched bank to bank and sequentially moved across the lake as fishing progresses. Within the lane, if it is about as wide as the boat used, fish can be taken out by electrofishing. Small fish are less readily caught by electrofishing than large ones and it will never be possible to remove absolutely every one by any netting or electrofishing technique.

Laning techniques are impracticable for lakes greater than about 5-10ha. In larger lakes, repeated gill netting by fleets of nets of many different mesh sizes can be used but there is the objection that such techniques kill the fish and they are discouraged in the UK but not necessarily elsewhere in Europe. Permission to use gill or any other nets in public freshwaters in the UK is required from the Environment Agency. The remaining approaches are then trawling, in larger lakes, and seine netting in all lakes. These are less efficient than gill netting and rotenone and require exhaustive and repeated use if the majority of fish are to be removed. Special non-return traps and fyke nets may also be used for particular species. The total fishing effort is hard to estimate but is likely to be of the order of 5-6 person-weeks per hectare, decreasing per hectare with increasing lake size for the initial fishing.

It will rarely be possible to remove all fish and some will persist to spawn in the late spring. Here a knowledge of favoured spawning grounds is essential, for netting can be placed in the water at these sites, often in the reedswamp fringes, to form a substratum on which the eggs of roach, bream and perch will

---

Table 7.1 Removal techniques that have been used in fish removal in the Norfolk Broads [80]

(i) **Systematic electrofishing**: This has been done from a 'push rowed' 3m rowboat, with a rower and an operator, using a high frequency (to 2000Hz) 300V, 12A system producing pulsed direct current supplied from 1.7 or 3kV generators. The fish are stunned and attracted usually to the hand held anode, and transferred using light weight nets to containers in the boat. The technique is particularly suited to confined spaces (ditches, littoral margins).

(ii) **Electrofishing for isolated large fish or small shoals of such fish**: The fish are chased with a 4m, powered boat with the cathode tied across the bottom of the boat and the anode applied at the bow. This needs calm, clear water conditions and is a subsidiary operation following the effects of systematic fishing.

(iii) **Seine netting**: Nets from 50 to 120m have been used particularly for encircling concentrations of fish. A floating mobile pontoon was used because the Broads lack the sloping edges conventionally used for drawing in the nets.

(iv) **Isolating nets**: Light weight 60m monofilament nets were used, paid out from the back of a rowboat to surround shoals and concentrate them for removal by electrofishing.

(v) **Passive fish traps (fyke nets)**: These nets, which are non-return traps, are conventionally used by eel fishermen and are set for periods of 12 to 24 hours to catch large fish which have evaded other methods. They are set about 5m from the bank or in fleets of five over about 100m.

(vi) **Scare lines and fish traps**: Ropes onto which brightly coloured scraps of cloth are towed through the water by boats. This herds fish into traps made from stop nets, from which the fish are removed by seining.

(vii) **Prevention of successful spawning**: Bream, roach and tench, and perhaps other fish, will readily spawn onto netting if this is placed in traditional spawning areas. The netting can then be removed to dry, thus killing the eggs. Again this is a subsidiary measure, following major systematic removal.

often be laid. The netting can then be removed and air dried to kill the eggs. The spawners can also be readily seined out during spawning if the sites are known. Some young will hatch somewhere, however, and floods may bring in fish from elsewhere the next winter. It is sensible, therefore, to carry out lower intensity fishing operations in subsequent years after the main fishing whilst the restoration is being carried out. Again local knowledge may help for fish often aggregate in particular areas during the winter and these can be more easily surrounded by nets or electrofished.

It may also be useful to employ somewhat unorthodox methods to remove particular stragglers. Large bream often evade nets dragged through the water, but must be removed as they will breed prolifically. In the Norfolk Broads, they have been removed, after the shoals have been visually located, by driving them into waiting nets set in a large V shape using lines of rope to which 'fluttering' pieces of rag have been tied. **Table 7.1** lists the array of methods used in fish removal from the Norfolk Broads, which are small (up to 54 ha in these cases), flat bottomed and shallow (about 1m).

How much needs to be taken out?

The maximum biomass of fish that can be left in a lake whilst still sustaining sufficient *Daphnia* populations to control the phytoplankton is not precisely known. Values quoted in the literature include 2-3, 3-5, 4.5, and 15 grams per square metre[93,96]. In the absence of refuges for the *Daphnia*, such as are provided by aquatic plants, it is likely to be at the lower end of this range, perhaps 1-4 grams fresh weight per metre squared, or 10 to 40 kilograms per hectare. Much will depend on what proportion of this biomass is of zooplanktivorous fish and the ratio of piscivores to zooplanktivores.

The available data suggest that in phytoplankton-dominated lakes, the total fish biomass will be between 200 and 500 kilograms per hectare. Where only half, or even somewhat more of the biomass has been removed, gargantuan though this may seem, there has been no real improvement.

A further uncertainty lies in whether the fishing should be selective and whether piscivores should be returned to the lake. There will be no detriment to doing this and they may help

We do not yet know what biomass of fish it is safe to leave in but it is likely to be 10 - 40 kg per ha or less. We suggest complete removal of all fish species which are zooplanktivorous at some stage of their life history, other than piscivores, and to return the piscivores other than perch.

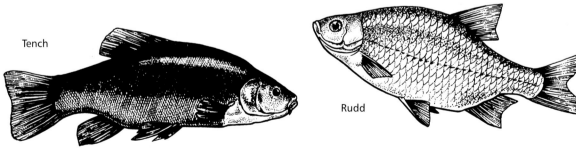

Tench

Rudd

Tench and rudd are more desirable members of a fish community in a shallow lake than carp and bream, despite their consumption of some aquatic plant material. They are not zooplanktivorous for long periods of their lives and, at the densities in which they normally occur, they are not especially destructive.

remove remaining planktivores. If the fishing has been reasonably successful, however, many of the piscivores may starve or be forced into cannibalism and this may seem unacceptable. The best compromise would be to return the piscivores, though not including perch, which, although piscivorous as adults, are zooplanktivorous as juveniles, and to monitor their health after return.

An even greater uncertainty lies in whether or not to return bottom-feeding fish such as tench (*Tinca tinca*) and rudd (*Scardinius erythrophthalmus*), though not common carp which should never be returned. Often when the water has cleared and aquatic plants begin to return, the bottom becomes covered by filamentous or thalloid algae such as *Enteromorpha*, which provide rather little habitat structure and which may suppress growth of more desirable, larger plants. However, this is not necessarily the case[189]. It is possible that the bottom disturbance and direct grazing on filamentous and thalloid algae by some bottom feeding fish may create niches for the higher plants to grow, but there is virtually no certain information on this either.

Where biomanipulation is difficult

There may be a number of circumstances that preclude biomanipulation of the whole lake or make it very difficult, even after all the stages of removing forward switches and nutrient control have been accomplished. The first of these is the difficulty of isolating the lake to prevent recolonisation of fish. This is especially true of lakes connected with substantial river inflows and outflows, that contain fish communities, which it will be impossible to remove. Barriers across such rivers are impracticable for they would impede boat or water movements and devices such as curtains of bubbles to deter fish passage are not certain barriers. It takes only a few fish returning to the lake to spawn to re-establish a sizeable population within a relatively short time.

Keeping fish out of a lake from which they have been removed may pose problems. Alternative strategies may be needed such as artificial zooplankton refuges.

Movement of water, and a portage for boats, can be provided on small streams by pebble barriers that also prevent fish from moving back in during a biomanipulation.

Elaborate devices such as engineered locks, dosed with rotenone at every use are likely to be uneconomic. At Lake Breukelveen in the Netherlands, an electronically controlled netting gate was used which could be lowered temporarily to allow boats to pass [207]. Its effectiveness could not be assessed, however, because the biomanipulation of this lake removed only about 40% of the fish and no improvement was noted as a result of this alone. Where water flow can be diverted and where navigation problems do not occur, isolation by dams is a possible expedient. This was done at Cockshoot Broad in Norfolk and is described in the case studies section (Chapter 10). Where connecting streams are small and boat passage is confined to rowing boats, mounds of pebbles placed across the stream will allow water flow, prevent fish passage and provide portages for the rowboats.

There are two solutions where isolation is impossible. The first is simply to maintain the fishing effort more or less continuously so as to remove fish faster than they recolonise. This will be expensive, but can be partly offset by the sale of the fish for stocking of private waters and may be necessary only for a few years pending reestablishment of plants.

The second is to provide refuges within the lake to simulate the refuges ultimately to be

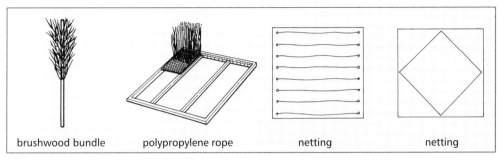

Fig 7.4 Various refuge designs. Brushwood bundles are made from twigs bound around a pole and stuck in the lake bed at densities of one or two per metre squared. Polypropylene rope is woven into fabric mats or frames and laid on the bottom. Fruit cage netting can be suspended in parallel lines or arranged as boxes. The netting has proved poorly effective in pilot plots, the others more effective but not entirely so and expensive. (From Irvine et al 1990).

provided by the aquatic plants when the restoration is complete. A number of experiments have tested possible refuges, including parallel lines of fruit cage netting, forests of polypropylene rope, which floats upwards from the mats, anchored on the bottom, into which it is woven, and bundles of twigs of alder and willow [91] **(Fig.7.4)**. Available data suggest that considerable areas of refuges of these kinds will be necessary if fish have open access to a lake and as much as half of the lake area may need to be covered fairly closely with them. This, however, is a guess because no experiment so far has reached this stage.

Polypropylene rope was found to be effective, but extremely expensive (75 ecu per square metre), dangling netting was ineffective and twig bundles, though initially effective were less so after submergence for more than a year. This was possibly because they acquired a periphyton in some way inimical to the water fleas, or because the pilot plots were too small to deter fish predators attracted to their edges from all over the lake. The labour costs of cutting the twigs and establishing the refuges were also very high and prohibitive for more than a pilot scale experiment. Such refuges would conceivably work if used extensively enough at an economic cost, but the latter is

Construction of a barrier to fish movement in Alderfen Broad. All fish were removed from one side but tench were retained on the other, as part of an experiment.

Experimental fish-free exclosure (about 1ha) constructed in Hoveton Great Broad. The water cleared inside the exclosure, from which the fish were removed, and plants began to colonise. The circular structures are sub-enclosures for investigation of the effects of wave exposure and bird grazing on aquatic plant development.

likely to preclude their use for all but very small lakes.

Enclosure refuges

An alternative is to create fish-free enclosures within lakes, behind fish proof barriers [141]. This has been successfully done in two of the Norfolk Broads, Hoveton Great Broad and Hoveton Little Broad [80]. In principle, once restoration has been shown to be successful in one such enclosure, more enclosures can be built, fished out and joined to the initial enclosure until a substantial proportion of the lake has been covered. The barriers should then be removed and the newly established aquatic plant beds should be able to act as refuges for the entire lake.

There are some problems. One is in the choice of material for the enclosures. It must be

Experimental enclosures in Hoveton Great Broad were made from recycled plastic board supported by wooden uprights. Stainless steel windows of mesh size 1mm were inserted to allow mixing of water and equalising of water levels in this tidal (5-10cm) lake. Such mixing is desirable to minimise stagnation and blue-green algal development. Problems occurred with blockage of the windows by attached algae and marl deposition. The windows had to be cleaned with a wire brush at frequent intervals.

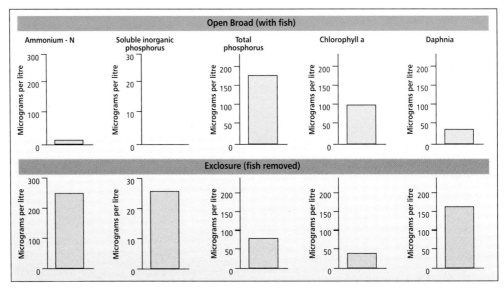

Fig 7.5 The effects of removing fish from within an enclosure in Hoveton Great Broad in 1992. *Daphnia* **has increased and phytoplankton crops have declined, compared with the open broad to which the fish had free access. The enclosure allowed movement in and out of water through stainless steel mesh windows. Nonetheless the chemical effects of the change in grazing regime are still shown. There was more soluble inorganic phosphorus and ammonium in the water when fish were absent. This is because there was less uptake by algae on the one hand and excretion by the** *Daphnia* **of these substances on the other. Total phosphorus was lower in the presence of greater** *Daphnia* **populations. This is probably because some of the phosphorus is lost to the sediments, packaged in** *Daphnia* **faeces.**

fish- (including fish larva) proof whilst allowing passage of water. The enclosure must be able to withstand the undermining effects of water currents, especially if the system is linked with a tidal river and changes of several centimetres regularly occur. Thirdly we do not yet know at what coverage of a lake with such enclosure refuges it will be safe to remove the barriers and allow access to the fish population. The only suggestion that can be made is that patience should prevail and that coverage should be as extensive as possible.

The first two problems were solved in Hoveton Great Broad by using a fence of laminated recycled plastic and wood boards held in slotted wooden uprights and penetrating about a metre into the lake bed. There were 0.5m x 1m windows of 1mm stainless steel mesh at intervals of around 15m to allow water movement to equalise levels and flush out the enclosures. In general, as large a proportion of the barrier as possible should be water-permeable so as to encourage flushing and rapid equilibration of water levels. Where tides are greater, stronger materials such as sheet steel piling may be needed.

Flushing is important because the longer the retention time of the water, the more likely it is that blue green algae will develop in summer. Blue green algae can be controlled by grazers [38] but not always [48,152], especially once substantial populations have been allowed to develop. The colonies or filaments of these organisms are quite large and the latter, especially, readily clog the filtering apparatus of *Daphnia* ; they produce substances which may deter feeding, and offer a relatively poor diet to the animals, so may be avoided. Undermining of the enclosure walls has occurred due to tidal movements, at first helped by clogging of the stainless steel meshes by periphyton. This was alleviated by regular vigorous brushing with a wire brush. Once these problems have been

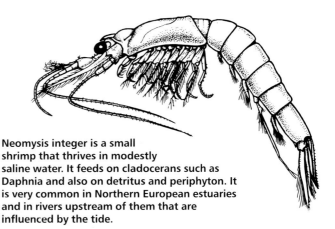

Neomysis integer is a small shrimp that thrives in modestly saline water. It feeds on cladocerans such as Daphnia and also on detritus and periphyton. It is very common in Northern European estuaries and in rivers upstream of them that are influenced by the tide.

overcome the technique has been shown to be eminently successful (**Fig.7.5**).

Complications: invertebrate predators

Another possibility that may occur is that of increase in alternative, invertebrate predators on *Daphnia*, once the fish predators have been removed. Such predators might include other crustaceans such as *Polyphemus* or *Leptodora*, which are normal members of the zooplankton. Their major prey is smaller zooplankters such as the juveniles (nauplii and copepodites) of copepods, rotifers and small species of water fleas such as *Bosmina*. *Daphnia* usually are too big for them to handle and predators capable of handling *Daphnia* such as water beetles and bugs are usually confined to sheltered areas. In general invertebrate predation should not be a problem.

There are two instances where it may be so, however. The first has been in much bigger lakes, in North America, where an introduced cladoceran predator, *Bythrotrephes*, has reduced *Daphnia* populations [119,120]. This is unlikely to be a problem in shallow lakes, however. The second concerns mysid shrimps, particularly of the genera *Mysis* and *Neomysis*, which also eat *Daphnia* and have been shown to reduce its populations, again in large North American lakes [89,114,154,158,212..] The former is

When fish have been removed there may still be problems with invertebrate predation on Daphnia, particularly by mysid shrimps and especially in mildly saline lakes.

characteristic of cold, deep lakes and again an unlikely complication in the restoration of shallow water bodies, but *Neomysis* poses greater danger.

This is particularly so with *Neomysis integer*, a brackish water shrimp, with a tolerance for salinities down to 150 milligrams chloride per litre and possibly lower, though how long it will survive these conditions is not known. *Neomysis integer* appears not to be a problem in brackish lakes where aquatic plant populations are established. It is an omnivore and feeds on periphyton as well as animal prey [89,92].

Where it has been brought into riverine freshwater lakes close to the sea, as a result of high tides that have increased salinities for a time, there is evidence that *Daphnia* populations have been temporarily reduced to a large extent [153]. This problem may particularly affect coastal lakes, polder lakes and lakes associated with lowland floodplain rivers. In these, rising sea levels, flood control works in the lower reaches, and reduced river flows in drier summers and through increased diversion of water upstream for irrigation, may all conspire to increase salinities to levels at which *Neomysis* may persist. At present its sojourn is usually temporary because freshwater inflows eventually reduce salinities to below its tolerance.

Wind induced turbidity

A further complication comes in very large shallow lakes, where wind and wave action may be sufficient to stir up considerable amounts of bottom sediment. Although biomanipulation may then remove algal turbidity there may still be considerable sediment turbidity and the water may not clear. Removal of fish such as bream and carp will help, for these fish greatly disturb the bottom as they forage. These circumstances are dealt with in the next chapter, as they are relevant to establishing plants. The solution to wind and wave disturbance is to provide wave breaks and quiet areas as 'refuges' for the plants in the same way that enclosure refuges may be

provided for *Daphnia*. Indeed both problems may be dealt with by the same enclosures. In small lakes, indentations in the reedswamp fringes may provide some shelter.

Finally, parasites!

One last problem is that there may be problems in moving the fish that have been taken out of the lake if they contain unusual parasites. They may then have to be destroyed. A case occurred at a lake in Llandrindod Wells where carp removed from the lake were infected by a trematode worm that had been recorded only once previously in the UK. It was an Asian/East European species that completed its life history in oligochaete worms. These are normal and very common members of the sediment invertebrate community. Nonetheless, particularly large specimens of such worms are often imported as bait for sale to anglers and this is the route by which the parasite had probably been introduced.

A prognosis for the success of biomanipulation

Dutch scientists have produced a simple questionnaire scheme [84] to allow lake managers to assess the likely success of biomanipulation measures in their particular lake. The scheme **(Table 7.2)** does not assume that nutrient control measures have been put in place and thus may be conservative in predicting success where such measures are being carried out.

A reminder

Finally an important reminder. A major problem with biomanipulation is convincing the local community that it is a wise procedure. Removing fish does not, at first sight, seem to be something that is in the conservation interest. After all, for a long time, it has been perceived that a large fish stock is a sign of a healthy water. Some of these problems have been discussed in Chapter 3 but it must be re-emphasised here that good public relations are an important prelude to biomanipulation. The emphasis should be that although fish are to be removed, this is only an expedient for a few years, after which the fish community will be restored in greater diversity in a more attractive setting. The age structure of the population will also eventually be wider. In phytoplankton dominated lakes, for example, roach that are more than about three years old are unusual because there are insufficient large (plant-associated) invertebrate prey to support them. Some fishing may still be possible (for pike and perhaps tench, if these are left in the lake) even during biomanipulation. It is unlikely that competitive carp anglers will ever be appeased, however.

The usual cause of failure in biomanipulations is simply that of removal of insufficient fish and it is worth restating that taking out of what may seem to be such a high proportion - say a half or two thirds - in the eyes of many people, will be insufficient. Fish are prolific breeders and will repopulate a water to their original numbers within a season if not exhaustively removed. Where anglers have not been fully convinced of the value of what is being done there may be a tendency to put fish back in, illegally, by dead of night. This is unlikely to upset a planned biomanipulation except on a very small lake, but it is nonetheless a symptom of a gap in planning.

Fish removal does not, at first, seem to be in the conservation interest, indeed it may appear ludicrous. Good public relations are a necessary part of any biomanipulation project.

Question	Answer	Go to	Chance of clear water	Score
SECTION 1				
1 Were large Daphnia present previously at >10 per litre?	Yes No	Q2	High	+1
2 Were filamentous blue green algae present previously?	>100000 per ml 50-100000 per ml <50000 per ml	Q3	Low Moderate	-2 0
3 Was Neomysis previously present?	Yes No		Low High	-2 +1
SECTION 2				
4 Had the lake been stocked with >50kg per ha of large bream or common carp in the last five years?	Yes No	Q5	High	+1
5 What is the estimated biomass of bream and common carp?	<50kg/ha 50-150kg/ha >150kg/ha		Low Moderate High	-1 0 +1
SECTION3				
6 Is the risk of resuspension of sediments in the lake low (small, deeper, sheltered lakes)?	Yes No	Q7		-1
7 Is the risk of resuspension of sediments in the lake high (large, shallow, exposed lakes)?	Yes No	Q8 Q9		
8 Is the lake bottom sandy?	Yes No			0 -1
9 Is the risk of resuspension of sediments moderate and the bottom sandy?	Yes No			-1 0

For total scores of lower than -2, the chances for clear water are POOR; for scores of -1 to +1 they are FAIR; and for 2 or more, they are GOOD.

Table 7.2 A scheme [84] for predicting the likely success of biomanipulation, even in the absence of nutrient control, in achieving clear water. The scores obtained in answer to the questions in each section should be added to give the total score, which is a measure of the likely chance of obtaining clear water. Interpretation is given at the foot of the table.

Decision tree for biomanipulation

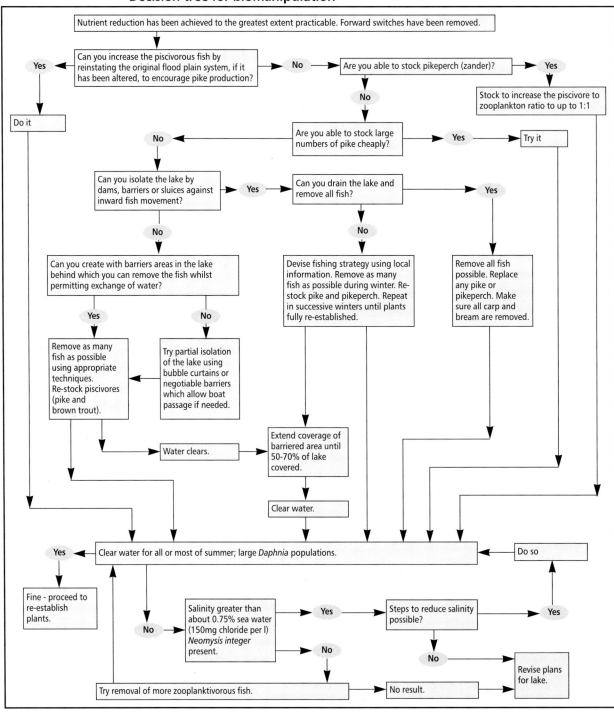

Chapter 8

Steps in the Strategy (4) Re-establishment of Plants

The need for plant refuges

In the early days of biomanipulation, and still to some extent, fish were frequently removed or predators added as a palliative measure to clear the water and remove noxious algal growths [11,12,83,130]. There was perhaps a hope that the effects would be permanent, but a little introspective scrutiny and a review of some basic ecological theory would suggest such permanency to be unlikely and so it has proved. The reason is that it is not possible to maintain an indefinite balance between a predator and its prey (fish and *Daphnia* in this case) unless the prey can retreat to some refuge where it can reproduce, whilst subject to a low risk of being eaten.

In a deep lake, the darker, deeper waters provide such a refuge and the *Daphnia* migrate between the deep waters, where they persist by day, and the surface waters where they feed by night [52,219]. They thus use darkness as a refuge. In shallow lakes darkness is created by the shading of aquatic plants, and a complementary refuge may be created by the chemical and structural conditions in the plant beds, which may impede the feeding of some species of young fish.

Where disturbance of sediment by wind and waves leads to the additional problem of turbidity, plants will also be necessary to stabilise the sediment by absorbing the wave energy, which they do very effectively. To restore a turbid lake permanently, therefore, it is essential to re-establish extensive beds of plants. Fish must not be reintroduced until the plants are well established. Re establishment

of plants, per se, is also a desirable conservation goal.

Problems in the re-establishment of plants

Re-establishment may happen naturally if the switch to turbid conditions happened not too long previously and seeds and other propagules are still present. But often these will have long died or been too deeply buried, and deliberate introductions must be made. Obtaining sufficient material may be difficult, however, and so it is wise to wait a year or more to see if natural recolonisation will occur. If it does not, the following possibilities must be considered:

(i) natural inocula are present but are being prevented from establishment by destruction by birds;

(ii) natural inocula are present but sediment conditions (*inter alia*, their physical nature, degree of disturbance and perhaps chemistry) are preventing their development;

(iii) natural inocula are absent and must be reintroduced.

If, on introduction, there is still failure to grow, problems with birds and sediment must again be considered. Experience so far has been very varied. In many lakes, natural recolonisation has been rapid and trouble free. In the Norfolk Broads, it has been a considerable problem. In one lake, Cockshoot Broad, it occurred naturally in one rather sheltered area but was initially very slow in most of the lake. Where it has been rapid, there have generally been some residual clumps of plants even in the turbid state. Water lilies frequently persist and may act as nurseries, creating quiet conditions around which other plants can grow.

Sediment removal will destroy any residual clumps, and once undertaken may mean that there will be delay in plant establishment. This

Restoration of permanent clear water needs re-establishment of submerged and floating leaved aquatic plant communities. But once plants have disappeared completely, and have to be reintroduced artificially, the costs may be high.

is not a trivial consideration, for once plants have disappeared completely and have to be artificially introduced, the costs are high. Fairly large quantities may be needed, they may require physical protection from bird grazers, labour needs for planting and protection are high, and the structures required for protection are barely aesthetic. When sediment is being removed, lily clumps should be fenced and avoided.

Problems of inimical sediment

If plants do not re-establish naturally, it should first be established that the sediment is not inimical. Although there is evidence that sediment is not always a perfect medium for plant growth - it contains sulphides, high concentrations of iron and manganese in a reduced and potentially toxic form, and has virtually no oxygen - it is also true that aquatic plants have coped with these conditions for several million years. Unless there has been contamination with pollutants such as toxic heavy metals, it is most unlikely that, managed properly, the sediment in a lake will not support plant growth. What may be a problem is that the water depth above the sediment is too low,

leading to excessive movement by water and wind. Plant propagules cannot then become properly rooted before they are buried or otherwise mechanically disturbed, or they may be too exposed to dabbling birds. Removal of sediment to create water depths of a metre or two should obviate these problems. Use of physical structures (wattle fences, for example) may help to quieten the habitat if the water is not being deepened.

Practicalities

There then follow questions of what plants to introduce and in what form, where to obtain them, how much to plant, when and how to do it, and how to protect the plantings.

Aquatic plants comprise a variety of life forms, each with very different characteristics and needs and these should be understood before plants are introduced. First are the emergent species, which are firmly rooted in underwater soils, with their bases underwater in the wetter seasons, but rising above the water surface with stem, leaf and flower structures similar to the land plants from which they have evolved relatively recently. Examples include reed

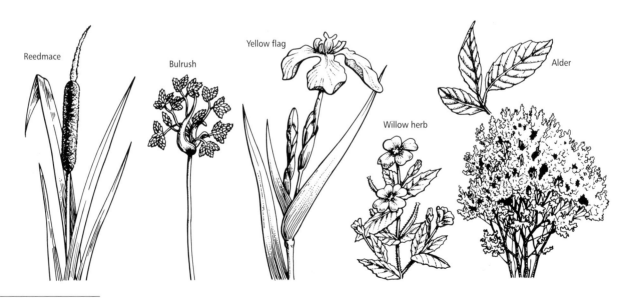

Reedmace

Bulrush

Yellow flag

Willow herb

Alder

(*Phragmites*), reedmace (cattail) (*Typha*), bulrush (*Scirpus* and *Schoenoplectus*), and a variety of other grasses, sedges and tall herbs, most of which are monocotyledonous flowering plants, on the one hand, and a variety of dicotyledonous trees and shrubs on the other. Woody emergents include willows and sallows (*Salix*), and alder (*Alnus*). In general these plants require firm rooting substrata and water tables that are around the substrate surface in summer and not more than about a metre above it (less for woody plants) in winter.

Secondly there are floating-leaved plants, typical of which are the nymphaeids or water lilies. These also are rooted and their inflorescences emerge above the water surface but their leaves typically float at the water surface. They may also have leaves of quite different appearance and anatomy, which remain completely submerged. Both emergents and floating leaved plants are generally confined to shallow waters, down to about 2-3m for the floating leaved plants, but the emergents are more tolerant of drought when water tables fall to below the soil surface. Floating-leaved plants are usually killed by such conditions unless they last for a very short time.

The third functional group includes the totally submerged plants. These also are usually rooted but may not necessarily be so. If they are rooted, the root systems, although functional in uptake of nutrients from the soil or sediment, are not usually extensive. The anchoring and water uptake functions that roots have in terrestrial plants and in emergent plants are less crucial or redundant underwater. The leaves of submerged plants are very different from those of emergent or floating-leaved plants for they are usually thin with very thin cuticles on their surfaces, and sometimes highly dissected. These features appear to be helpful in coping with the major problem for plants growing underwater of low diffusion rates of nutrients and carbon dioxide through the medium[124]. Thinness of leaf minimises the length of the diffusion pathway. It also helps to maximise the availability of light energy to the leaf, for the underwater environment is a shade environment because of the strongly absorptive properties of water, the substances dissolved, and the particles suspended in it.

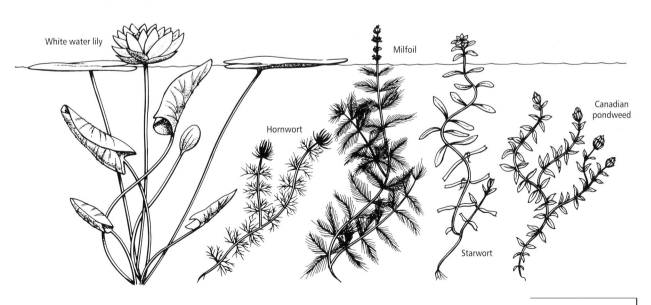

White water lily

Milfoil

Hornwort

Canadian pondweed

Starwort

Finally there are plants like the duckweeds (*Lemna*, *Spirodela*, and *Wolffia)*, and the fern (*Azolla* spp) which float at the water surface, and absorb all their nutrients from the water rather than from the sediment. Availability of light is no problem for them but they are vulnerable to the destructive effects of wave action and thus are confined to sheltered habitats. They are also disadvantaged by their size in the competition for nutrients with phytoplankton in the water. They have the counteradvantage, once their mats have built up, of overlying the phytoplankton and hampering its growth through shading and stilling of the water column.

Many floating and submerged aquatic plants are especially vigorous in their vegetative growth - that is they reproduce and spread by fragments, or contracted shoots called turions, rather than by seed. This is probably an evolutionary consequence of the difficulties of pollination and sexual reproduction underwater, and the need to concentrate scarce energy into means of dispersal safer than seeds in habitats that are vulnerable to drying out or flood. There are two

consequences of this. First, desirable species, once placed in an equable habitat will generally expand their populations quickly. Secondly, so also, indeed more so, will undesirable species, such as certain introduced floating and submerged species, and care must be taken to exclude them. Among floating plants, *Azolla* should never be introduced and inocula of other species should be carefully cleaned of it. The same applies to *Crassula helmsii* and *Lagarosiphon major* among the submerged species. Specialist botanical help should be sought in cases of doubtful identification. Some exotics, like the two species of *Elodea*, *E. canadensis* and *E. nuttallii*, which were once problematic are no longer considered so and have become accepted members of the flora.

What plants to introduce?

There will often be remnants of former emergent and floating leaved communities to give clues about appropriate species if introduction is needed, especially where edges may have been seriously eroded. Historic information may also help. Floating plants need not be actively introduced. They will enter anyway associated with other inocula and at

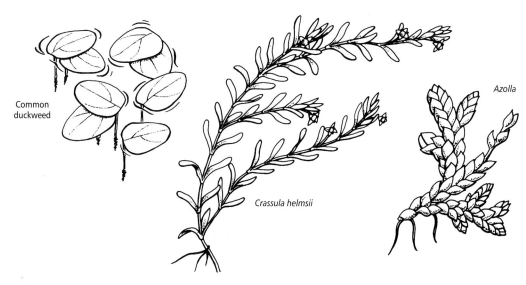

Common duckweed

Crassula helmsii

Azolla

	Emergent species	Submerged, floating leaved and floating species
Suitable only for generally upland or sandy heathland sites with low pH, and very low (<<25 micrograms per litre total phosphorus). Inappropriate for muddy lowland sites with immediately agricultural surroundings.	None	*Sphagnum spp; Potamogeton polygonifolius; Sparganium angustifolium; Juncus bulbosus; Scirpus fluitans; Utricularia minor.*
Likely to survive only at total phosphorus concentrations in the range (<<25-50 micrograms per litre) where alternative phytoplankton dominated communities are unlikely. Severe nutrient control will have had to be provided.	*Eriophorum angustifolium; Sphagnum spp; Carex limosa; Lythrum portula; Baldellia ranunculoides; Carex rostrata; Carex nigra.*	*Subularia aquatica; Utricularia intermedia; Lobelia dortmanna; Isoetes lacustris; Callitriche hamulata; Myriophyllum alterifolium; Nitella spp other than N. flexilis; Utricularia vulgaris; Sparganium minimum; Potamogeton alpinus; Nuphar pumila; Elatine hexandra.*
Likely to survive in moderately nutrient rich waters but not where total phosphorus occurs in winter at concentrations of several hundreds of micrograms per litre.	*Menyanthes trifoliata; Ranunculus flammula; Juncus effusus; Potentilla palustris; Carex lasioscarpa; Carex aquatilis; Agrostis stolonifera; Veronica scutellata; Equisetum fluviatile; Hydrocotyle vulgaris; Equisetum palustre; Eleocharis palustris; Caltha palustris; Phragmites australis; Galium palustre; Scirpus lacustris; Myosotis secunda; Carex vesicaria; Oenantha crocata; Myosotis laxa Mentha aquatica; Phalaris arundinacea; Sparganium erectum; Typha latifolia; Alisma plantago aquatica; Carex elata; Cicuta virosa; Cladium mariscus; Iris pseudacorus; Myosotis scorpiodes; Glyceria maxima; Typha angustifolia; Polygonum hydropiper; Carex pseudocyperus; Apium nodiflorum; Scirpus tabernaemontani; Veronica anagallis-aquatica; Carex paniculata.*	*Fontinalis antipyretica; Glyceria fluitans; Littorella uniflora; Potamogeton natans; Nymphaea alba; Apium inundatum; Potamogeton obtusifolius; P. praelongus; P. perfoliatus; P. berchtoldii; P. gramineus; Hippurus vulgaris; Callitriche stagnalis; Ranunculus peltatus; Callitriche hermaphroditica; most Chara spp; Potomogeton pusillus; P. crispus; Ranunculus trichophyllus; R. aquatilis; R. hederaceus; Callitriche obtusangula; Elodea canadensis; Nuphar lutea; Eleocharis acicualris; Polygonum amphibium; Lemna minor; Sparganium emersum; Elodea nuttallii; Lemna triscula; Ranunculus circinatus; Potamogeton lucens; Stratiotes aloides; Ceratophyllum demersum.*
Likely to survive at the highest nutrient concentrations, other conditions being equable. Most will thrive in much lower nutrient conditions also.	*Carex riparia; Solanum dulcamara; Veronica becabunga; Carex acutiformis; Ranunculus sceceratus; Rumex hydrolapathum; Berula erecta; Carex acuta; Lythrum salicaria; Butomus umbellatus.*	*Potamogeton filiformus; Ranunculus baudotii; Potamogeton pectinatus; Myriophyllum spicatum; Zannichellia palustris; Potamogeton friesii; Oenanthe aquatica; Potamogeton trichoides*

Table 8.1 General guide to likelihood of plant establishment under different nutrient conditions. The lists are given separately for emergent, and then submerged, floating-leaved and floating species. Within each list, plants are recorded in approximate order of tolerance to increasing nutrients. The list is not exhaustive for European waters and is biased somewhat towards northern sites within the UK. (Based on (165) with minor modifications).

least at first should be discouraged as they may compete for establishment with submerged species.

The main decisions that need to be made concern what submerged species to introduce. The choice may be dictated by availability but there is no point in introducing species that have little or no chance of establishing in the prevailing chemical conditions. **Table 8.1** gives some guide to this.

Introductions of plants will generally be in the form of vegetative propagules. This is variously because of low seed production, difficulties of collecting quantities of seed in aquatic situations, and frequent low viability of seed. There is, on the other hand, a general availability of vegetative propagules in the form of rhizomes for emergents and floating leaved species, turions or fragments of shoots for submerged species and whole plants of floating species.

How much should be planted?

For submerged species, as large a quantity as possible is desirable, not because the propagules will grow slowly once established, but because they are vulnerable to destruction by grazing birds such as coot, swans and ducks. This is also true for lilies and other floating leaved species, less so for emergents, which are bulkier. As a very general guide, emergents and floating leaved species should be established at a density of four rhizomes, each containing at least one node with a healthy bud, per metre squared and submerged plants at densities of ten fragments, each about 10cm long, or turions, per metre squared, though these ideals may not be easily achieved. These densities apply to appropriate parts (depths) in the lake in which plants are likely to grow and some simple calculations will reveal the sort of quantities needed.

Where plantings are needed, and the plants cannot be protected, as large a quantity as feasible is desirable, because the propagules are vulnerable to destruction by grazing birds.

Take, for example, a four-hectare lake with a roughly circular outline and a basin sloping down to three metres, with equal areas under <1, 1-2 and 2-3 metres depth. Such a lake would have a diameter of only 230 metres and an area of 23000 square metres under 1m, potentially plantable with emergents. There would be 13000 square metres between 1 and 2 metres depth and plantable with lilies and other floating leaved plants, and a further 4000 square metres under 2m and capable of colonisation by submerged plants. A full planting of this lake would take nearly one hundred thousand rhizome fragments of emergent plants, 16000 lily or other floating plant rhizome fragments and 40000 turions or shoots of submerged plants. And this is for a small lake!

The costs of buying such quantities are astronomical and in any case commercial suppliers should be used with caution (see below). The better strategy is to plant limited areas where the plants have greatest chance of establishment, to protect the plantings carefully, to have patience and to allow spread of plants within the lake by natural means. The general principle of bringing in as much inoculum as possible stands, but practical difficulties will determine the absolute amount in different circumstances. There will also usually be some wastage.

Sources of plants

Sources of plants are not overwhelmingly abundant. The general degradation of lowland habitats, where they might be found, is the reason for the need for shallow lake restoration! The other side of this issue is the inevitable scarcity of sites for obtaining the plants and the need to protect them from damage by plant collection, no matter how worthy the cause. Where plants are abundant, the species available may be the most vigorous and therefore perhaps the least desirable where it is desired to establish a diverse community.

The main sources are where drainage ditches or canals are being cleaned out and plants discarded, or where plants are being thinned to create swims in angling lakes. A network of local intelligence among conservation organisations is necessary to be able to take advantage of opportunities as they arise. Plants must be transferred as quickly as possible. They are not as vulnerable as fish but exposure to air-drying for more than a few hours will reduce viability. Kept wet and cool however, they may survive for days.

The best time for planting in is in late spring, when they can begin growth immediately and establish good overwintering populations by autumn. There is no reason not to transfer them in winter, providing protection is given against bird grazers and wind disturbance. Mid-summer plantings have the disadvantage of a short season for establishment, greater chance of damage in transfer and the risk of transferring attached fish spawn, but lower chance of destruction by bird grazing. In the final analysis, availability will dictate the issue and opportunities must be taken when they occur. You should spurn plant material from lakes contaminated with exotics such as *Crassula helmsii*. Very small fragments can sprout and quickly overrun a small lake.

The temptation to use commercial suppliers will generally be countered by cost. Even with quantity discounts, the expense will be considerable. Commercial suppliers will have at least as difficult a task of obtaining the necessary material as conservation organisations, the care given to the material in transfer will be no better and probably much worse, and the genetic provenance of the material will often be doubtful. Garden suppliers sell many

Fixing of geotextiles on eroded banks to help re-establishment of reed may need use of machinery.

varieties of water lilies, selected for showiness in garden ponds, but which will compete poorly in a natural setting. Some are exotic species which should not legally be released into the wild, and little care is taken by commercial dealers to ensure that undesirable submerged species do not contaminate the supplied plants. *Crassula helmsii*, currently a very noxious weed, introduced from Australia, is currently being spread partly by this means. There is no reason not to use such organisations where they can provide exactly what is required at an acceptable price, but 'Caveat emptor' is very much the approach to be used.

Planting

Plants are more likely to survive if they are planted with care and not simply thrown in! Care, however, is expensive in time and labour. Emergent plants, like *Phragmites* and *Scirpus* are more likely to take, the bigger the rhizome fragment used. Cut sections of *Phragmites* rhizomes may flood and rot if planted underwater. The more securely they are held within or adherent to the sediment, soil or

Commercial sources of plants will be costly; obtain them through liaison with local landowners, internal drainage boards and the British Waterways Board, who clear ditches and canals periodically to maintain drainage and navigation.

Brian Moss

Despite their attractiveness, coot and mute swans can be destructive of aquatic plants, especially when growth is sparse or just beginning. Plantings will need to be protected from such bird damage until the beds are vigorous and can withstand it.

peat, the better. In eroded situations, where there is still some boat disturbance or wave erosion, this latter is particularly crucial.

Varieties of plastic matting, called 'geotextiles' are available which can be spread over an eroding bank and secured in place by metal staples. The rhizome fragments, initially dug into the bank are covered by the mat which has an open weave through which they can grow as they establish. The best are those made from natural fibres such as coir or flax, unless conditions are particularly erosive when a tougher man-made fibre may be preferable. The costs of such techniques are modest for small, relatively sheltered areas, but high for extensive, very exposed ones, for they involve machinery for handling the geotextiles.

In smaller lakes, the same technique as used for lilies and other floating leaved plants can be used. This is to weight the rhizome fragment with part of a building brick (those with holes facilitate attachment with twine) and drop it

onto the bottom. The brick should not be too large as to bury the fragment too deeply, nor so small that the buoyancy of the rhizome (it contains a labyrinth of air spaces) floats it back to the surface. Submerged plants can be planted by sandwiching the shoots between two layers of plastic netting, again weighted with small stones to keep them as a raft on the surface of the sediment. A small piece of brick can also be attached as an anchor to prevent bodily transfer of the sandwich.

Protection during establishment

More difficult is the issue of protecting the plants as they attempt to establish. First, choose sheltered bays or indentations in the lake for planting. Once established, plants will survive a great deal of wave action because of the energy their collective biomass will absorb. Until that mass is in place, they are very vulnerable. Once well-rooted, they will gradually spread to more exposed areas. If this does not occur, fences or barriers can be installed to protect against wave action. Such barriers, made of alder or willow twigs, bound in a frame, wooden lap or wattle fencing, or recycled plastic plaswood, will need to be substantial in order to function, and hence will be comparatively expensive. On a very big lake (100 ha or more) substantial structures of wood or metal could be needed.

Thereafter, the problem is one of protecting the plants, when present at low densities, against bird grazing and incidental damage. Protection may be needed in spring when birds like coot require food and nesting material and supplies are generally short. The birds will collect at sites where material is available, especially since the extensive floodplain wetlands they formerly inhabited, and which spread their populations, have now largely disappeared. There is a high degree of chance as to whether the birds will find the plantings. There is also a vulnerable period in autumn when coot may reduce the overwintering populations from which those of the subsequent spring will develop [166]. Circumstances like extensive and dense plantings and an early, warm spring will favour the plant growth and reduce the risk of destruction. If the birds do discover the plants, however, they may cause havoc! Swans and coot, for example, will bite out the growing points of *Stratiotes* and capsize the floating rosettes.

The plants may be protected by netting cages. These must be such as to prevent birds diving underwater and into them. This is as much to prevent trapping of diving birds as to defend the plants. They must also prevent birds from landing from the air and being unable to take off again due to restricted space. Designs used so far have been largely for experimental purposes and have ranged from metal or plastic meshed cages, hundreds of metres squared in area, to closely spaced wooden slatted structures, only tens of square metres in area, covered with chicken wire. In Denmark, barriers reaching about 1m above the water surface have been effective, even without overall mesh covers. None have been particularly aesthetic and will cause disturbance when they are removed. There is a need to develop a completely submerged, transparent, cheap, biologically degradable grazing shield for this purpose, but this problem has proved intractable. In most restorations, bird damage has been evaded or tolerated, with delays sometimes of several years in plant establishment.

Polygonal 'carousels' have been used in the Norfolk Broads to investigate the effects of grazing birds on aquatic plants established in biomanipulated areas. The sides were made of wooden slats, spaced so closely that coot could not enter, but which allowed water movement. The tops were protected with chicken wire. Vigorous growth was found of aquatic plants planted in the carousels. Here white water lilies (*Nymphaea alba*), water soldier (*Stratiotes aloides*) and hornwort (*Ceratophyllum demersum*) can be seen.

Enclosures to protect plants from bird damage during the early phases of establishment may have to be substantial and are not likely to be particularly aesthetic.

Decision tree for plant establishment

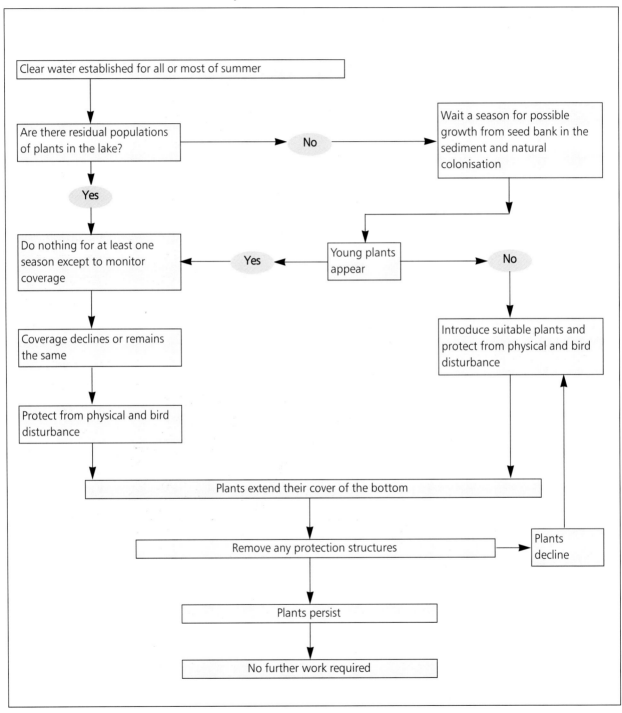

Brian Moss

A well established plant community can withstand moderate impacts without much active management. The greater the impacts, however, the more likely the lake is to revert to plankton dominance.

Chapter 9

Steps in the Strategy (5) Stabilising the System

The most uncertain aspect of restoration programmes on shallow lakes is that of permanency. At what stage is it permissible to remove fish proof fences or artificial refuges? What are the risks that the system will switch back to phytoplankton dominance at particular concentrations of total phosphorus? When should fish be reintroduced and what should the community composition be? The answers to all these questions are difficult, for few programmes are old enough for permanency to be certain. The best that can be offered is a set of guidelines that are likely to be correct.

Some guidelines for establishing permanency of a restoration

These are:

- *that obviously vigorous plant growth should be apparent over all of the bottom shallower than 2m for at least one season before fish removal operations cease and a new fish community is introduced;*
- *that the minimum practicably possible external total phosphorus and nitrogen loadings should be maintained;*
- *that common carp should be permanently excluded, that native piscivores should always be included in the new community and that other fish introduced should be appropriate;*
- *that the state of the lake should be at least minimally monitored for several years following*

Guidelines for establishing permanency of a restoration are that plants should be growing vigorously, that minimal nutrient loadings should be maintained, that common carp should be excluded, that native piscivores and other appropriate fish should form the new fish community and that the situation should be monitored.

completion of restoration (defined by the reintroduction of fish);
and that activities in the catchment should be permanently monitored for changes that might destabilise the restoration.

The new fish community

Some issues from the above list need elaboration. The first is the choice of the new fish community and the practicalities of obtaining the fish. Table 9.1 summarises features of fish species common in the UK in terms of their origin, breeding, feeding, potential for bottom and macrophyte disturbance and likelihood of association with intrusive angling practices such as heavy ground-baiting and intensive approaches likely to lead to local habitat disturbance. High scores are given to features likely to lead to

maintenance of clear water, high plant diversity and biomass, and low phytoplankton biomass in shallow lakes. Summing of the scores thus gives a ranking of desirability of a particular fish species in this respect.

The ranking, from least to most desirable, is: Common carp, bream, tench, roach, crucian carp, rudd, perch, dace, pike, eel, and brown trout. Exotic fish, such as rainbow trout are excluded as undesirable in lakes being restored for conservation purposes. For mainland Europe there are additional species, such as white bream (*Blicca bjoerkna*) and pikeperch (zander) which should be included towards the more desirable end of the list.

Introduction of those fish with the most negative scores should be avoided. Bream should not be introduced if they were not

	Bream	Common carp	Crucian carp	Dace	Eel	Roach	Rudd	Perch	Pike	Tench	Brown trout
Native/Introduced	N	I	(N)[1]	(N)[1]	N	N	N	N	N	N	N
Breeds prolifically	+	-	±	+	++	++	++	++	++	+	+
Disturbs bottom	++	++	+	-	-	-	-	-	-	++	-
Pelagial zooplantivore[3]	++	+	±	-	-	++	+	++	-	-	-
Weed-bed zooplanktivore[3]	-	-	+	-	-	-	+	+	-	-	-
Piscivorous[3]	-	-	-	-	+	-	-	+	++	-	+
Intrusive angling	++	++	-	-	-	-	-	-	-	-	-
Usually abundant	+	++	±	±	++	++	+	++	++	+	±
Destroys plants	-	++	±	-	-	?+	-	-	-	?+[2]	-
Total score*	-7	-23	-2	+20	+28	-3	+1	+5	25	-4	+33

Scoring system
Origin N=5, (N) =0, I=-5; for breeding, -=5, ±=3, +=0,++=-5; for bottom disturbance, ++=-5, +=0, -=5; for zooplanktivory, -=5, ±=-1, +=-3, ++=-5: for piscivory, ++=5, +=3, -=-5; for angling intrusion, -=5, ±=-3, ++=-5; for abundance, ±=0, +=-3, ++=-5; for plant destruction, -=5, ±=-1, +=-3, ++=-5.

[1] Introduced from Southern England. [2] Because of predation on epiphyte eating snails. [3] Post-larval. *Pelagial* means open water, middle of the lake.

Table 9.1 Summary of the characteristics of the most common fish species in lowland Britain in respect of their compatibility with shallow lakes restored to diverse plant communities.

present previously. They are native fish and usually coexist with macrophytes. On the other hand they are also fish that are readily able to take advantage of a renewed forward switch and help stabilise the dominance of phytoplankton. At the other end of the league, stocking of predators such as eel, brown trout and pike should be encouraged. The latter is useful for the control of zooplanktivores, and brown trout, if conditions allow its survival, is prized by anglers and forms some compensation for the removal of common carp. Eels will naturally recolonise a site from which they have been removed because they can move overnight through wet meadows and fens.

Uses and problems

Such a league table provides a general rule of thumb. It is not complete for it is based on British preferences, experience and the rather limited range of fish naturally available in the UK. A major omission is zander, which is native in mainland Europe and which should certainly be included in the Table as a potentially valuable predator, where it is native. The table is, however, a potentially problematic tool for it runs almost diametrically counter to the perception of need by British anglers.

The requirements of anglers are usually for lots of large, hungry fish, which preferably resist capture by fighting. The first three requirements are mutually incompatible but their provision is the underlying theme of traditional fisheries management, which is essentially an 'animal husbandry' activity. The fourth requirement is expressed in the recent widespread interest in carp fishing, particularly by young anglers [134], in the lowlands as a parallel to the perhaps unattainably expensive salmonid fishing of the uplands. The preferences expressed by anglers in a recent survey of 1211 individuals [134] were for carp, roach, bream, tench, chub, pike, barbel and perch.

Fisheries managers have tended to assume that maximum production and high biomass densities of fish must be desirable and that bottom-up processes control the status of aquatic systems. Bottom-up processes are those that determine the status of the photosynthetic communities through nutrients and physical factors and then sequentially have effects up the food web.

The concept that top-down processes (those initiated in the upper parts of the food webs such as predation by birds or fish and working downwards) are important is not yet widely understood. This may perhaps be because a past emphasis on salmonid fisheries, and on large deep lakes and rivers, rightly emphasises bottom-up control in such habitats.

In the UK, the NRA (EA) Fisheries Strategy [156] hints at a change of approach. There is caution about the efficacies of restocking and the need to monitor its effects, and about the introduction of non-native species or strains of fish - albeit with an emphasis on threats to native fish populations rather than habitats. (There is, however, no explicit recognition of common carp as an introduced species). There is also considerable concern for habitat restoration and no indication of support for the removal of predators such as pike, which has been a popular demand of angling clubs in the past.

What is perhaps needed is for better liaison among the various interested bodies so as to agree a common policy of fisheries management in conservation sites *vis a vis* those managed primarily for anglers. In evolving such a policy it must be admitted that the data available are yet few and frequently anecdotal. Is there, for instance, a biomass of carp that is compatible with aquatic plant communities? Carp are native members of mainland European fish communities where such coexistence is sustained. To what extent are the effects of

A problem in re-establishing a fish community is that those fish most sought by anglers may be those least desirable in a stable plant-dominated system.

common carp made worse by the presence of bream - or roach plus bream? Do tench complicate the issue and at what biomass? The uncertainties are endless and unlikely to be resolved without large scale experimentation on a properly replicated pond scale.

The lack of simple population and biomass data for fish communities in most lakes also partly reflects the difficulties of obtaining such data. Fish populations are notoriously difficult to sample on any absolute basis. There is also the problem that because of the influence of weather, reflected in water temperature, on recruitment, stocks of coarse fish naturally vary greatly from time to time. Lack of understanding of this underlies many of the demands made by angling clubs for restocking. However, at present, it is not easy to specify what the natural range of biomass of a given species in a given lake would be. The disturbances due to past restocking and introductions also complicate the issue. It is indeed not yet possible to specify precisely what the 'natural' fish community of any lowland lake in Britain was and, unless the techniques of molecular biology can be used on fossil DNA preserved in the sediments, it may never be possible to be sure.

Procurement of fish for replacement communities

Usually it will not be necessary to restock after biomanipulation, because even the most intensive fish removal operations leave some fish. If some boosting of the community is felt necessary, the practicalities of replacing the fish community are those of obtaining sufficient fish of the required kinds. Liaison with Environment Agency fisheries managers may be helpful, for sometimes landowners decide to remove fish communities from their lakes and restock with particular species for commercial purposes. In some years, with very good recruitment, it may also be possible to remove

fish from an existing lake without jeopardizing its community.

There are also commercial suppliers acting as middlemen in these transactions. In the UK, there are no fish hatcheries specialising in coarse fish, though some exist in mainland Europe, especially for pike. All fish transfers require approval from the Environment Agency under the Salmon and Freshwater Fisheries Act, 1975, and permission will not be given until the fish have been screened for possible infections.

Transport of the fish requires the same care as discussed in Chapter 7 and oxygenated tanks are desirable, indeed essential for more than very short journeys. The numbers that need be added are not large. There should be no attempt to restock to eventually desired levels. There is merit in adding only a few breeding pairs of a range of potentially desirable fish in the first instance and waiting for the community to establish its own structure. Insufficient information is available for this to be planned from the outset. Coarse fish will breed rapidly and the established plant beds will provide refuges for young fish against their own predators during establishment. Fish should be added in the late winter, for reasons of minimising stress to them, and so as to allow a season of reproduction and establishment as soon as possible after addition.

Monitoring

Monitoring the state of the lake after restoration is a further issue needing detailed discussion. Monitoring means recording details of the lake on a systematic basis. It should always be done in the years before, during and following an attempted restoration but it need not be intensive provided it is regular and well planned. Such minimal monitoring will give information as to whether the system is remaining in an acceptable state and warning of whether it may revert to a phytoplankton-dominated state or indeed has reverted.

What it will not do is to tell why the restoration is stable or unstable. A detailed monitoring programme stands a greater chance of doing this but even so a great deal of expense may still leave a lake manager not knowing why something has happened. Only a detailed programme coupled with experimental research will do this. Inevitably such a programme is more expensive, but it is also an investment in the future success of other restoration projects, which might otherwise fail. Research costs are generally recouped in this way. Practical action will always be more expensive than research, and action which fails is a complete loss.

Minimal monitoring

A skeletal monitoring programme need not involve highly trained people and will involve a visit in July or August, taking perhaps a day, with some follow up laboratory work, which can be contracted to an outside agency. The field work should include the mapping of the vegetation in the lake on as small a scale as practicable, and a measure of water transparency using a Secchi disc. It should also involve the taking of a water sample from the middle of the lake and subsequent analysis for chlorophyll a, nitrate and ammonium, soluble reactive phosphorus and total phosphorus. Samples should be stored cool and be analysed within a few hours. The costs of such analyses could be of the order of 100 ecu per sample.

Indications that the lake may need further attention are that the extent and diversity of the plant community is declining, that the Secchi disc is not visible (because of high turbidity) on the bottom in 2m of water when it is lowered from a boat, and that soluble reactive phosphorus is undetectable (because phytoplankton has taken it up). Further indicators are that nitrate is detectable and ammonium present at more than a few tens of micrograms per litre (because plant growth is not coping with the incoming load) and that phytoplankton chlorophyll concentrations are greater than about 20 micrograms per litre. Such indications will suggest that a more detailed monitoring is necessary. Repeat analyses should in any case be made a week or two later. Sometimes short term fluctuations can occur which are not representative of the general state.

More detailed monitoring

A detailed programme should involve at least monthly (and preferably weekly) monitoring

Environment Agency

Continued sampling in the field and analysis in the laboratory are essential during a restoration project. Unexpected events are frequent and they need to be monitored so that lessons can be learned from them to the benefit of future projects.

Monitoring should always be carried out. It need not be intensive as long as it is regular; comprehensive monitoring, with associated research, however, is an investment in the success of future projects.

throughout the year, of inflow and lake water chemistry, phytoplankton populations (as biomass and community composition), and zooplankton community (composition and size range). In mid-summer, aquatic plant communities should be mapped and in early autumn some assessment of the fish stock should be made to establish current species and size ranges. Methods should be standardised from year to year and might include set numbers of seine nettings or the setting of fleets of gill nets. Permission for this may however be difficult to obtain in the UK, though not in mainland Europe. These studies will need supervision and interpretation by trained people, who should be able to give some opinion about obvious changes and reasons for them.

If there is no obvious explanation of any change, a research programme will be needed and, in the nature of the problem, this cannot be specified in advance. The only advice that can be given is that it should be carried out by experienced researchers, with good track records and should be left as open-ended as possible. It may be expensive, for specialist analyses may be needed as well as adequate time. In the end, however, it will pay dividends for future restoration programmes. Indeed the number of remaining uncertainties in our understanding of these shallow systems suggests that continued fundamental research on their functioning is highly desirable, alongside comprehensive monitoring of new restoration schemes.

Monitoring of external change

The final issue is that of monitoring the external changes that can affect a lake. This is a general issue for all involved in conservation management and landscape care. All aspects of use and functioning of the landscape are interlinked. The consequences of a change in farming practice, the establishment of a new housing estate, a new industrial process, climatic changes or even new fashions in recreation, are eventually felt in unexpected directions. A lake manager cannot expect that, once restoration is achieved, the issue can be safely left. There will, barring major changes in emphasis in the ways land is used, generally be a tendency for nutrient loadings to increase and for new forward switch mechanisms to come into play. A regular checking of local planning applications is worthwhile, followed by an alerting of the Environment Agency where there is a likelihood of pollution problems.

Decision tree for stabilising the system

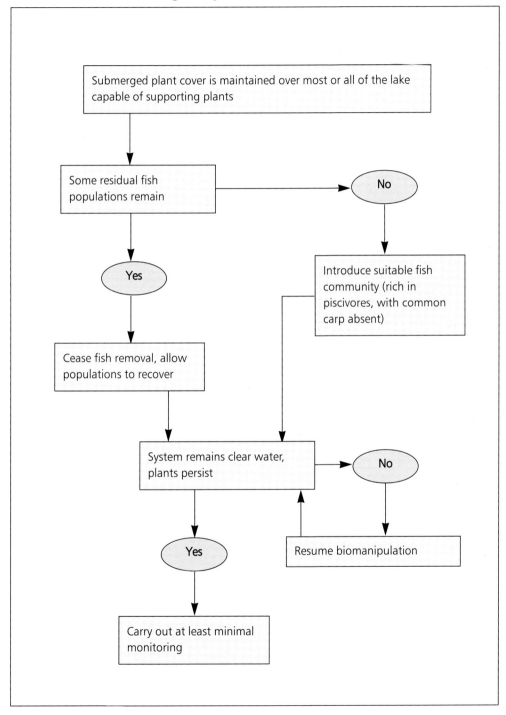

Chapter 10

The Collective Experience - a Compendium of European Case Studies

Much can be learned from the individual experiences of particular projects. There follows a series of accounts of such studies whose salient features are shown in **Table 10.1**.

Cockshoot Broad, UK

What was the problem?

Cockshoot Broad is one of the smaller lakes of the Norfolk Broads. The lakes were formed around the thirteenth century AD as a result of natural flooding of peat pits excavated for fuel over the previous four centuries [62,111,136,137]. The pits were connected to the river system by channels and are close enough to the North Sea to experience physical (and sometimes chemical) tides.

Most have undergone a change [136,140] from former clear water, low nutrient, charophyte-dominated communities. Nutrient loadings and sedimentation rates have increased, due to expansion of the mains sewerage system and intensification of agriculture in the catchments. There is also a boating holiday industry. Forward switch mechanisms in various parts of the system have included increased salinity through deep pumped-drainage of catchments very close to the sea [6], effects of organochlorine pesticides [201] and possibly plant destruction by boats and coypu grazing.

A particular difficulty in restoring the system has been the need to maintain navigation rights and hence the impossibility of isolating individual lakes for fish removal. This was the incentive for exploring various artificial refuge

approaches [91,141]. Cockshoot Broad [147,153] was the exception in that due to its location **(Fig 10.1)** relative to the lower reaches of the River Bure, with water able to enter it from opposing directions, it had accumulated so much sediment that navigation into it had been precluded for many years. It was also relatively inaccessible and so was not fished. Both of these factors helped in obtaining agreement that it should be dammed from the river and biomanipulated.

What was the target for restoration?

Cockshoot Broad (3.3ha, mean depth 1m) was one of a group of Broads to which a variety of restoration techniques were applied during the late 1970s and early 1980s [62,136]. The general target was the re-establishment of clear water and of aquatic higher plant communities. It was accepted that the former diverse charophyte communities probably could not be restored because of the very high background nutrient loads.

What was done?

Initially, the Cockshoot Broad experiment was one of nutrient control alone, and included isolation from external sources by a dam and one-way sluice, that prevented river water, loaded with sewage effluent, from entering **(Fig 10.1)**. The broad then received water only from a stream that passed through wooded wetland and did not contain effluent. There were considerable problems with establishing the dam, which was an earth-filled construction, with rubble and soil held between metal sheets. The foundations initially penetrated only about 2m into the underlying deposits and the tidal difference between the river and broad, although only of the order of 10-20cm, was sufficient to cause bowing and threatened eventual breach.

A replacement dam was made, at much greater expense, with a lighter infill and foundations

Table 10.1 Summary of Case Studies

Site	Country	Area	Cause of Problem		Target	Approach	Current degree of Success
			Forward Switch	Nutrient Sources			
Cockshoot Broad	UK	3.3ha	?Pesticides	Sewage effluent Agriculture (high)	Clear water Submerged plants	Isolation Sediment removal Biomanipulation (fish removal)	High
Lake Vaeng	Denmark	15ha	?	Sewage effluent (moderate)	Clear water Submerged plants	Biomanipulation (fish removal)	High
Zwemlust	Netherlands	1.5ha	Herbicides	Sewage effluent (very severe)	Clear water Submerged plants	Biomanipulation (fish removal and piscivore stocking)	High but deteriorating
Little Mere	UK	2.8ha	Plants initially present	Sewage effluent (very severe)	Removal of high algal growths in downstream lake	Effluent diversion	High
Lake Wolderwijd	Netherlands	2700ha	? Salinity change	Sewage effluent Agriculture (moderate)	Clear water Submerged plants	Biomanipulation (fish removal and piscivore stocking)	Partial
Ormesby Broad	UK	54ha	Plants initially present	Agriculture (moderate)	Charophytes	Biomanipulation (fish removal)	Moderate
Bosherston Lakes	UK	50ha	Plants initially present	Sewage effluent (high)	Charophytes	Effluent diversion in-lake diversion	High
Lake Finjasjon	Sweden	1100ha	?	Sewage effluent (severe)	Clear water Submerged plants	Effluent stripping Sediment removal Biomanipulation (fish removal) Wetlands and buffer zones	High
Barton Broad	UK		? Pesticides and boat damage	Sewage effluent Agriculture (severe)	Clear water Submerged plants	Effluent stripping Sediment removal Biomanipulation	Measures not yet complete

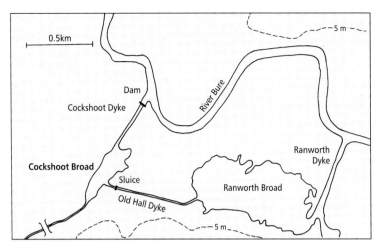

The dam which isolated Cockshoot Broad from the River Bure was constructed from parallel walls of steel sheeting with an infill of earth and gravel.

Fig 10.1 Map of Cockshoot Broad and associated water bodies. The dam was closed in 1982 and the sluice is a one-way sluice which allows water to pass from Cockshoot stream to the river through Ranworth Broad, but which does not allow a reverse flow.

going down to 18m. There have been no problems except that the dam is circumvented by high winter floods which cross the adjoining fen wetland in the very flat landscape. Sediment was removed from most of the basin by suction dredging to a depth of about 1m. The previous water depth had been only about 40cm. Areas to the west of the Broad among islands covered by alder were not dredged. The dyke (the local term for a ditch or channel) **(Fig.10.1)** which formerly connected the Broad with the river, and had had deeper water, was further deepened by a digger. A lagoon was made among alder woodland to the east of the Broad by raising bunds from the peat and the sediment was settled in this. It has since regenerated alder woodland.

Why was it done?

The general view of the functioning of shallow lakes at the time was that nutrient control alone would bring about restoration [140]. This was conditioned by the notable successes hitherto obtained by external nutrient control in deeper lakes. Phosphorus removal, from sewage treatment works in the Norfolk Broads, was seen as necessary but expensive, and political factors confined its installation to another river (see Barton Broad, below). Cockshoot Broad was seen as a relatively low cost project in which the necessity for sediment removal could be tested against another site, Alderfen Broad, where the Broad was isolated but sediment was not removed [147,151,167].

Did it work?

Yes and no! Initially the water cleared and within months of the closure of the dam in April 1982, it appeared that the project was going to be highly successful. Large numbers of *Daphnia magna* appeared and a shoal of large bream could be seen swimming in the very clear water. A small bloom of the flake or 'grass cutting' form of the blue green alga, *Aphanizomenon flos aquae*, appeared but was not seen as a problem because such forms only grow when competition with other algae is minimised by vigorous grazing. By early 1983, vigorous growths of aquatic plants had established, especially in the dyke, from introduced and residual populations of water lilies, *Ceratophyllum demersum, Elodea canadensis*, and *Utricularia vulgaris*. Smaller quantities of other species were present.

The main basin of the broad was slower to colonise but strands of *Ceratophyllum* appeared all over the bottom. Planted lilies fared less well, especially *Nuphar lutea*, which was seen to be attacked by coot.

This situation persisted in 1983 and 1984 with the plant community in the dyke becoming more vigorous though less diverse. Research and monitoring continued and it was noted that *Daphnia magna* was being replaced by *Daphnia hyalina*, a smaller species. In 1985 it became clear that colonisation of the main basin by aquatic plants had failed and that phytoplankton populations were increasing. The water chemistry had not changed except that less of the total phosphorus was available as soluble reactive phosphorus, because of uptake by the phytoplankton **(Fig. 10.2)**. The plant community in the dyke was unaffected and the water lily populations continued to expand during 1986 and 1987. The phytoplankton crop continued to be high and *Daphnia* became increasingly scarce.

Plants eventually disappeared entirely from the main basin but the dyke populations remained vigorous and the water clear. At this stage, sufficient information was accumulating, from experiments in Broadland and elsewhere, to indicate that nutrient control alone was unlikely to lead to restoration of shallow lakes and that top down processes were important. Use of phosphorus removal alone had also failed in the River Ant and at Barton Broad (see below).

The disappearance of *Daphnia*, and experimental fishing which revealed a large fish community in 1985, suggested that the initial apparent success of isolation and sediment removal had been due partly to an inadvertent biomanipulation. The engineering operations had scared most of the fish populations into

Plants colonised early in the long, thin dyke section of Cockshoot Broad and included both water lilies and completely submerged species. Colonisation was much slower in the main basin.

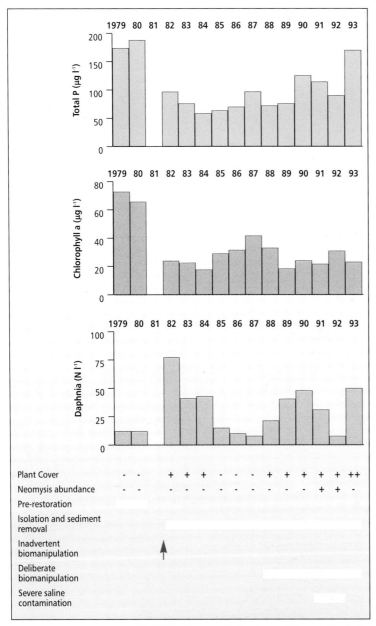

Fig 10.2 Changes in Cockshoot Broad, Norfolk, following isolation from the nutrient rich river, sediment removal, inadvertent biomanipulation and deliberate biomanipulation by fish removal. The effects of import of *Neomysis integer* when severe saline flooding occurred are also shown. (Based on Moss et al 1996).

the main river from whence their return was prevented by the dam. It is also likely that the original fish community was small because of the very shallow water in summer. With time, and with the failure of plants quickly to recolonise the main lake (a failure possibly due to bird damage), the recovering fish community had removed the *Daphnia*, thus returning phytoplankton dominance. The dyke plant community had established early, probably because of the sheltered conditions and the presence of some inocula, and chance escape from bird damage at the crucial earliest stage.

What was then done?
In the winter of 1988/89, an attempt was made to remove all the fish community from the lake. This was done by electrofishing in netted lanes, seining, and provision of netting in the following spring to attract spawn for subsequent removal. The operation was exhaustive, taking over two months with at least three people involved full-time. The fish were weighed and measured which considerably slowed the operation. In subsequent winters there have been supplementary fishing operations to maintain low stocks. Stocks were reduced from about 20 to about 1gram per square metre.

Did it work?
Yes, eventually. There was an immediate return of clear water in summer 1989, a recovery of *Daphnia hyalina* (though not *Daphnia magna*, a species which can barely persist in the face of any fish predation, suggesting that zooplanktivorous fish still remained), and a reduction in phytoplankton chlorophyll. Plants were still slow to colonise and reasonable coverage was not attained (by *Ceratophyllum demersum*) until 1994. Dense beds of *Najas marina* established in 1995 along with *Zannichellia palustris* and *Potamogeton pusillus*. Coverage with the less

desirable thalloid alga, *Enteromorpha*, had occurred in 1989 and 1990. The Broad has now been left and further fishing is being carried out only to keep the zooplanktivore population low. No additional stocking is being made for there is a community already present which is residual and which is supplemented by fish entering in occasional winter floods circumventing the dam. Common carp are not present in the area. The external nutrient loading remains low but there is considerable internal loading of phosphorus from the sediments.

There have been some temporary concerns. A major bed of lilies present in the dyke died back in the early 1990s but lily recruitment has been vigorous in the dyke and this was regarded as a normal cyclic process within the community. More disturbing was a near complete loss of submerged plants from the dyke in 1991 though there was recovery subsequently. This may be attributed to bird damage to overwintering plants in the cold spring of 1991, when growth began late.

The early 1990s also were very dry years and stream and river flows were low. Tidal water penetrates further upriver in such circumstances. Floods from the tidal lower River Bure, with high salinity, normally enter the Broad in winter but are readily flushed out by the incoming stream water. In 1991 and 1992 they were not flushed out very rapidly by the reduced freshwater flow. In 1992, the floods brought in *Neomysis integer*, which persisted in water with only 150 milligrams per litre of chloride (0.8% of sea water) for much of the summer. *Daphnia* populations declined and phytoplankton increased. The set back was temporary but salutary in an area where sea levels are rising and river flows declining due to irrigation use. There has been a steady rise in salinity in the adjacent river since the 1950s, when records began, by about 20%.

What lessons were learned?

The Cockshoot restoration took place over the period when understanding of processes in shallow lakes was increasing apace and research on the Broad was important in this. The key findings were that control of external nutrient loads alone, although quite severe in this case, was not sufficient for restoration of plants; that sediment removal (though in this case it was necessary to establish a reasonable water depth) is probably irrelevant to establishment of suitable water quality; that complete fish removal is probably impossible and that supplementary fishing is needed even in a small lake; that bird damage may be crucial in delaying plant establishment; that setbacks due to weather conditions must be expected; and that climatic changes in the future may threaten the system and so additional precautions against winter flooding will be needed.

Lake Vaeng, Denmark

What was the problem and what was the target for restoration?

Vaeng is a small (15ha) lake, polluted by sewage effluent until 1981 and lacking aquatic plants, despite its shallow water (mean depth 1.2m). It was intended as a demonstration project with the intention of restoring clear water and aquatic plants. The lake had the advantage of a short retention time of its water mass (2-3 weeks) and, apart from a source of sewage effluent, which was diverted in 1981, is supplied by inflow from seepage and springs. Its value as a case study lay in the high chance of a successful restoration (though this was seen in retrospect) and lies in the immediate and continuing success of restoration following biomanipulation, when only a modicum of fish was removed [93,96,115,116,200]. It is also significant in the comparative research done on it and other Danish lakes, which gives guidance about where these techniques are most likely to work [96].

What was done and why?

Diversion of sewage effluent did not restore the lake, though it reduced the annual nutrient loading from 4 to 1.5 grams of total phosphorus per square metre. The total nitrogen loading was reduced only from 78 to 71 grams. This would potentially have reduced the total phosphorus concentration to about 60 micrograms per litre and total nitrogen to a maximal 2.7 milligrams per litre, values that lie at the lower end of the range capable of allowing aquatic plants to persist. There was some release from the sediments, which increased the total phosphorus concentrations in summer to 130 micrograms per litre, whilst internal lake processes kept the total nitrogen to 1 milligram per litre. Again, these are relatively low values for shallow lakes.

Nonetheless, the lake remained dominated by phytoplankton, including small diatoms and blue green algae and had virtually no submerged plants. The Secchi disc depth was around 0.6 to 1m. In October 1986 and spring 1987, about half the zooplanktivorous fish stock, mostly of roach and bream, was removed by gill, fyke and pound (seine) netting and electrofishing. Expressing the removal as a percentage is not as helpful, however, as giving it on an absolute basis. The initial stock was about 30 grams live weight per square metre. This was reduced by 16 in 1987 and a further 6 in 1988, leaving a total of about 8 grams per square metre. There has been no subsequent fish removal and the stocks of zooplanktivorous fish have not returned to their former levels.

What happened?

There was an increase in Secchi disc depth from 0.6 to 1.8m over the next two years. The zooplankton community acquired *Daphnia* species, whereas it was formerly dominated by rotifers, and the phytoplankton community changed to dominance by large diatoms, green algae and a group of flagellates called cryptomonads. It lost its blue green algae. There was a halving in total phosphorus and total nitrogen concentrations to around 50 micrograms per litre and 0.5 milligrams per litre respectively. This latter is not uncommon during biomanipulation and is thought to result from packaging of nutrients into

Lake Vaeng, in Denmark, has been restored by simple biomanipulation.

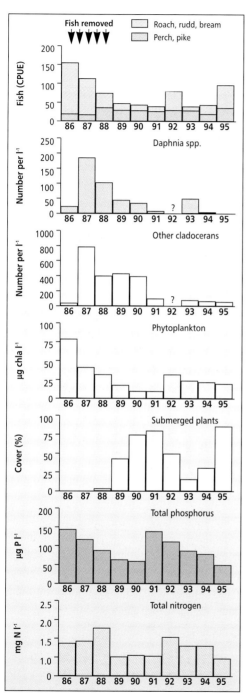

Changes in phytoplankton, zooplankton and fish in Lake Vaeng, following biomanipulation. (Courtesy of Erik Jeppesen).

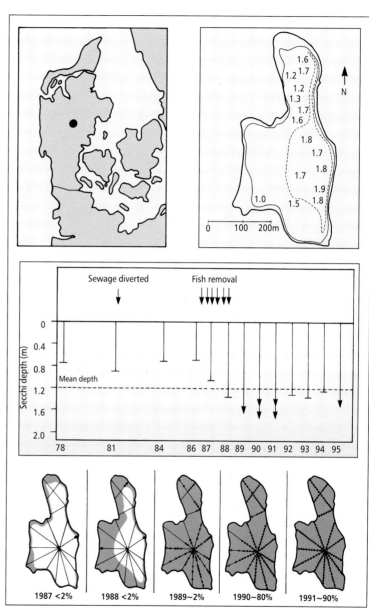

Fig 10.3 Lake Vaeng, Denmark. Upper panels show a map of the lake, with depths in metres, and changes in Secchi disc transparency following sewage diversion (from septic tanks) and then biomanipulation by removal of a significant fraction of the fish stock. Arrows show occasions when the Secchi depth was greater than the lake depth. Bottom panels show progressive colonisation by *Elodea canadensis*, one of several plants which began to spread following biomanipulation, and the area (in green) potentially colonisable by plants in 1987-1991. The area actually colonised (as a percentage of the lake bottom) is also shown. (From Lauridsen *et al* 1993, 1994, Jeppesen et al 1990b).

zooplankton faeces, which sink rapidly, and enhanced retention by the sediments to which they fall.

Plants did not recover quickly **(Fig 10.3)** though experiments in pots showed nothing detrimental about the sediments. There was less than 2% coverage of the lake bottom in 1987 and 1988, but a surge to 50% in 1989 and 80-90% in 1990 and 1991, a situation which has been sustained. Filamentous algae were the first colonisers, then *Potamogeton crispus*. The lake is now dominated by *Elodea canadensis* and both the succession and delay are attributed to coot activity [115,116].

The colonisation of plants began in a part of the lake where wind exposure was greatest and where the sediments were least favourable to plant growth. It was also the part of the lake least favoured by coots for the same reason of exposure. Experiments in bird-proof enclosures showed that *Potamogeton crispus* grew more than six times as well when protected from birds as when exposed to them. However, plants did establish in the lake, over three years, without special protection from birds. As the *Potamogeton* established, more birds were attracted in and the replacement of *Potamogeton* by *Elodea* is attributed to the differential effects of grazing on these plants.

What lessons were learned?
The key issue here, apart from the familiar failure of nutrient control alone to restore aquatic plants, is that a switch back to plant dominance was catalysed despite a substantial residual fish stock. Comparison with experimental restoration attempted in two other Danish lakes and with data from a much wider range of lakes suggests that conditions were especially favourable in Lake Vaeng.

First it is small and shallow. The zooplankton production, which is ultimately dependent,

through production of its algal food, on the light entering on an areal basis, is concentrated into a smaller volume than in a deeper lake. This gives increased grazing effectiveness. Secondly the nutrient concentrations were at the lower, more favourable end of the range over which alternative states can exist. Thirdly, the initial content of blue green algae in the phytoplankton was modest, though not insignificant, and this may be linked with the fourth factor, the high flushing rate. And lastly, following biomanipulation, a high ratio of piscivorous fish (pike and perch) to zooplanktivorous fish was established within the range that can be naturally maintained.

In contrast, in the Frederiksborg Castle lake [96], from which nearly 80% of the fish were removed, leaving about as much (7 grams per square metre) as in Lake Vaeng, and in which piscivorous perch were stocked, there were few changes. There were no attempts at nutrient control. The lake has a very long retention time (4-18 years), favouring blue green algae, is relatively deep (max 8m, mean 3m), becomes thermally layered in summer, which also favours blue green algae, and has high nutrient concentrations (total phosphorus 300-700 micrograms per litre, total nitrogen 2-4 milligrams per litre). The water did not clear and aquatic plants did not establish.

In Lake Søbygård, a 40ha, shallow (max depth 2m) lake with a short retention time (2-3 weeks) [96,97], there was both nutrient control, by treatment of the effluent that entered the lake, and biomanipulation. External phosphorus loading was reduced annually from about 30 to about 6 grams per square metre. The degree of fish removal was modest, for the initial stock was 63 grams per square metre and only about 10 grams were removed per square metre. However, much of the stock was of large, old fish eating bottom organisms rather than zooplankton. The high phytoplankton productivity had kept the pH values at 10.5 to 11 during the preceding years and spawning had been inhibited by this.

Following fish removal and sewage treatment, there was an increase in the *Daphnia* population and a proportionately marked decline in phytoplankton - by about tenfold. The total phosphorus concentrations had been huge, however, around 700 micrograms per litre, and remained between 500 and 600 micrograms per litre whilst the phytoplankton declined from 900 micrograms of chlorophyll a per litre to a still considerable 100 to 200 micrograms per litre, too high to establish enough water clarity for aquatic plants to grow. It is possible that a more severe biomanipulation with more fish removed or a greater reduction in nutrients could have completed the restoration.

Studies on a wide range of Danish lakes[94] (Fig.10.4) have shown an association between low piscivore to zooplanktivore ratios and total phosphorus concentrations above about 200 micrograms per litre. What is of particular interest in Lake Søbygaard is that even at very high nutrient levels, there was considerable control of the phytoplankton, which was dominated at all stages not by blue green algae but by the more edible green algae. Again wide surveys (Fig.10.4) have shown that blue green algae tend to be most dominant in summer at intermediately high phosphorus concentrations, 200 to 1000 micrograms per litre, and are replaced by green algae at higher levels and a mixture of algae at lower.

The implications are that biomanipulation is more likely to be successful, other things being equal, at low and at very high phosphorus concentrations, though in the latter case not successful enough for water to be sufficiently clarified to encourage plant growth.

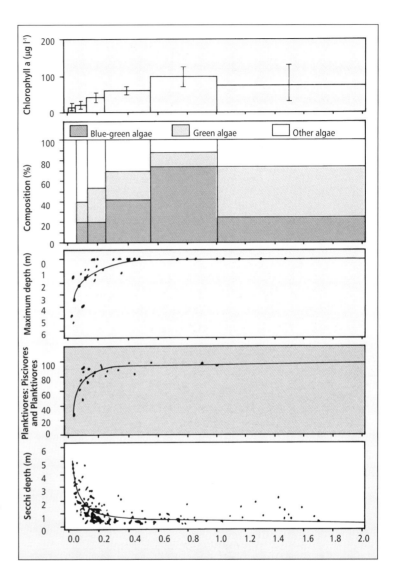

Fig 10.4 Data from a large sample of Danish lakes showing links between phytoplankton populations, maximum depth of colonisation of plants, planktivorous to piscivorous fish ratios and Secchi disc depths in relation to total phosphorus concentrations. As the latter increase, phytoplankton tends to increase and become dominated first by blue-green algae then by green algae. Depth of colonisation of plants declines as does Secchi disc depth, whilst the ratio of zooplanktivores to piscivores among the fish community increases. (From Jeppesen et al 1991).

Little Mere, UK

What was the problem and the target for restoration?

Little Mere is apparently an example of inadvertent restoration of a shallow lake due to nutrient control alone. It thus potentially challenges the hypothesis of alternative stable states and the complex strategy for their restoration on which this book is based! It is small (2.8ha) and shallow (max depth 2.6m, mean 0.7). It lies at the middle of a chain of three lakes, Mere Mere, Little Mere and Rostherne Mere in Cheshire, UK (Fig. 10.5) and until 1981 directly received sewage effluent from more than 3000 people. In 1981, the sewage works was closed and the sewage diverted for treatment at another works,

outside the catchment. This was partly because the works was overloaded and partly to attempt restoration of the deep Rostherne Mere, which lies downstream in a National Nature Reserve and was thought to be eutrophicated by the effluent. It has large blooms of blue green algae and some cattle deaths have been attributed to their drinking bloom-bearing water. Little Mere lies in a Site of Special Scientific Interest but was not a specified target for restoration.

What was done?

Other than diversion of the sewage, nothing was done.

What was the previous state of the lake?

Before diversion of the effluent, Little Mere had water that was dominated by sewage effluent especially in summer. Its range of total phosphorus concentrations was 310-5340 micrograms per litre (mean 2484), much of which was in available form. Ammonium concentrations were equally high (0.8 - 9.6 milligrams per litre, mean 4.6), but nitrate was low, because of the intense denitrification capacity of the deoxygenated sediments. With such high phosphorus and ammonium concentrations, the mere had enormous potential capacity for phytoplankton growth and indeed for a very short period in spring, biomasses of over 300 micrograms per litre of chlorophyll a were found.

At all other times of year, however, the water was very clear [34]. Extensive beds of water lilies were found, covering about 40% of the area and there were some clumps of *Elodea canadensis*, *Potamogeton berchtoldii* and *Nitella flexilis*. It was thus effectively a plant-dominated system even before nutrient diversion.

The reason for the clear water and the plant-dominated state was that the effluent

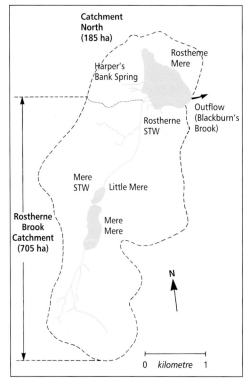

Fig 10.5 Catchment map showing the location of Little Mere.

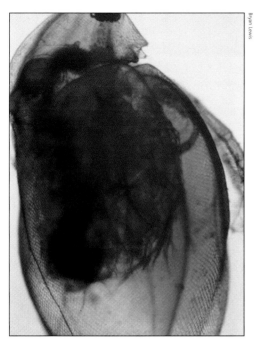

Bryan Lewis

Until 1991, the water of Little Mere was clear despite huge loadings of nutrients from a sewage treatment works. The effluent was deoxygenating and prevented fish survival. _Daphnia magna_, however, thrived in this fish free environment to graze the phytoplankton and keep the water clear. Its large store of haemoglobin, a red pigment which stores oxygen, allowed it to tolerate water that was close to anaerobic at dawn. This animal was about 3mm long.

was of poor quality and deoxygenated the system. Fish could freely enter from upstream where normal populations exist in Mere Mere, but did not survive very long in water that could have only 10% oxygen saturation or lower, even at midday in summer and was probably completely deoxygenated at night. There were very large swarms of the big-bodied _Daphnia magna_ in the lake, with the animals bright cherry red in colour, due to haemoglobin production, a device to enhance oxygen storage. _Daphnia magna_ is so large and visible that it cannot withstand even light fish predation. The algae were thus prevented from

developing by _Daphnia_ grazing, the low oxygen concentrations providing the prime refuge against fish predation on the _Daphnia_.

With diversion of the effluent it was expected that nutrient concentrations would decrease though still remain comparatively high due to release from the sediments, that oxygen concentrations would increase and that fish would recolonise from the upstream Mere Mere. Two scenarios were then possible. The first was that the aquatic plants would expand in area or that even at their existing coverage they would provide sufficient refuge for _Daphnia_ to maintain the system in plant dominance. The second was that the invasion of fish, and the changing chemistry of the water, would simultaneously produce a phytoplankton dominated by inedible blue green algae and a depleted _Daphnia_ population that would be unable to cope with the algae. The lake would then become phytoplankton dominated.

The expectation that blue green algae would come to dominate was because they are abundant, naturally, in the immediately upstream Mere Mere, which is a nitrogen-limited water, and which would determine the nature of Little Mere water soon after effluent diversion from Little Mere. Low nitrogen to phosphorus ratios tend to favour blue green algae, as does a high pH [193]. It was also expected that pH would increase greatly in Little Mere as the residual organic matter from the effluent completely decomposed thus reducing the rate of carbon dioxide production in the lake. Removal of carbon dioxide affects chemical equilibria in the water, causing an increase in the proportion of bicarbonate ions and in pH. Such conditions also favour blue-green algal growth.

What happened?

The nutrient concentrations fell markedly [35,148] **(Fig.10.6)**, the oxygen concentrations

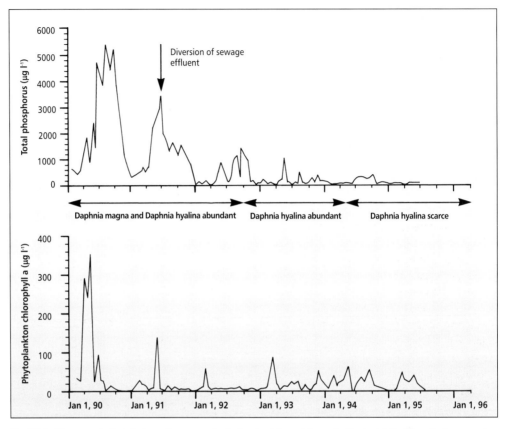

Fig 10.6 Changes in total phosphorus and phytoplankton chlorophyll a in Little Mere before and after the diversion of sewage effluent from the mere. Changes in ammonium ions, which had been very abundant prior to effluent diversion, paralleled those of phosphorus. The water was clear even before diversion because of an absence of fish and the abundance of *Daphnia magna*. When fish returned, the *D. magna* was replaced by *D. hyalina*, and the plant cover increased. Currently the water remains clear, *Daphnia* is scarce and plants cover all of the bottom. (Based on Moss et al 1996).

increased, fish recolonised, the pH increased a little, the *Daphnia magna* disappeared, and the smaller *Daphnia hyalina* increased in numbers. The submerged plant populations expanded to cover the remainder of the lake that was not occupied by lilies, and the phytoplankton did not increase. Nor did blue green algae increase their proportion in the phytoplankton. The size of the spring peak of phytoplankton (largely diatom) biomass has decreased with the decreased nutrient concentrations. In the early years after diversion, (1992-1994)

Potamogeton berchtoldii became the predominant submerged plant, but in 1995, *Callitriche* sp took over. As the plant cover has increased and the beds are dense, *Daphnia* has declined, though the water remains clear [148].

What was learned?

First it was learned that a plant-dominated state with clear water can exist at exceptionally high nutrient concentrations, stabilised by zooplankton grazing, though the deoxygenation refuge is an extremely powerful and unusual one. Secondly the alternative states hypothesis is not challenged by this example. There was not a restoration of aquatic plants - they were already present, because no forward switch mechanism had removed them - but probably an increased stability of the plant-dominated state as the nutrient concentrations were decreased. And thirdly it has become clear that *Daphnia* is not essential to maintain the plant-dominated state because it is now scarce in the lake. The buffer mechanism, which now appears to have taken over, is competition between the plants and algae for nitrogen. *Daphnia* is important in helping switch shallow lake systems back from phytoplankton to plant dominance and perhaps in stabilising the plant-dominated system at high nutrient concentrations, but becomes unimportant at low concentrations. It is also possible that grazing by plant-associated Cladocera of other genera is important in such systems and this is under investigation.

Zwemlust, The Netherlands

What was the problem and what was the target for restoration?

In the early 1980s, the Dutch government created a regulation that the Secchi disc transparency of water bodies used for public swimming should be at least 1m. Zwemlust, a small and sheltered lake (1.5ha, 1.5m mean depth, 2.5m max depth), used for organised bathing, had a Secchi disc transparency of 0.1 to 0.3m. It lies 50m from the River Vecht, from which it derives, by seepage, extremely nutrient rich water. Until 1968 it had clear water and was dominated by aquatic plants. The plants interfered with the swimming so a herbicide (diuron) was applied in that year, resulting in an almost immediate switch to phytoplankton dominance. After nineteen years of dense algal growths, the target for restoration was to

Zwemlust, in the Netherlands, is a lake intensively used for swimming.

restore clear water with a secondary requirement that the lake should not become impossible for swimming due to excessive plant growth.

What was done?

In March 1987, the lake was completely drained by pumping out the water[208,209]. The entire fish community (70-100 grams per square metre) was removed by seine and electrofishing during this process. Pike were to be reintroduced to control any fish that entered subsequently and rudd were also to be introduced to form a reserve food for the pike. Consequently, 170 bundles of willow twigs were fixed to the bottom to form spawning sites for the pike and refuges for zooplankton and newly spawned rudd. About 200 plants of

yellow water lily were also introduced, together with about 1kg wet weight of *Daphnia magna* and *Daphnia hyalina*. Finally, after the lake re-filled by seepage over three days, the pike (1600 newly spawned and artificially propagated, each about 4cm long) and rudd (140 fish, 9-13 cm long) were added. No nutrient control was attempted - the seepage source from the river makes this impossible on a local basis.

What happened?

After the biomanipulation, the phosphorus content of the water remained high with maximal concentrations above one milligram per litre. Ammonium plus nitrate concentrations were similar, giving low nitrogen to phosphorus ratios both before and after biomanipulation, and fell to near indetectability

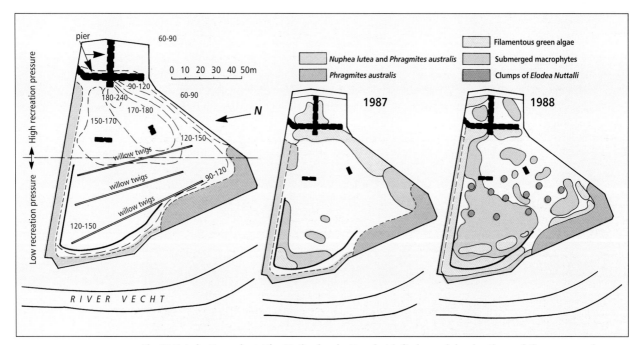

Fig 10.7 Lake Zwemlust, The Netherlands. Panel at left shows lake depths and the area used particularly for swimming. Following biomanipulation, willow twig refuges for young rudd, which were to act as prey for pike, were placed in the lake and existing emergent and floating leaved plants were left. The growth of submerged plants following biomanipulation is shown in the two smaller panels. (From Van Donk et al 1989).

in the summer of 1988 and succeeding years. Secchi disc transparency increased to 2.5 m (lake bottom visible) after the silt, disturbed by refilling, had settled (in four weeks) and the water remained transparent in succeeding years. The former blooms of the blue green alga, *Microcystis aeruginosa* disappeared and the residual phytoplankton was dominated by green algae.

Chlorophyll a concentrations fell from summer maxima of over 200 micrograms per litre to generally less than 10 as *Daphnia* numbers increased in summer to several hundreds per litre. Submerged plants, previously nearly absent in 1986, were still scarce (5% bottom coverage) in 1987. There was a major expansion in 1988 (Fig.10.8), however, with 50-60% coverage by *Chara globularis*, *Potamogeton crispus*, *P. berchtoldii*, *Elodea canadensis* and *Elodea nuttallii*, whilst the planted lilies also thrived [164,210].

There was a problem, however, in that the removal of fish, such as adult tench and roach, that had fed on snails and other bottom invertebrates, led to large densities of these animals. In one way this was helpful for it must have increased grazing on periphyton and promoted plant growth, but in another, the snail *Lymnaea peregra* was found to be infected with the larvae of the parasitic flatworm, *Trichobilharzia ocellata*. The adults of this worm live in the blood vessels of water birds, and snails act as intermediate hosts. Larvae released by the snails infect the birds by penetrating their skin. They may also attempt to penetrate human skin, and although failing, cause dermatitis (swimmer's itch). About 40% of bathers were affected in July 1988. Furthermore, the aquatic plant biomass also interfered with the swimming.

The pike did not establish as large and vigorous a population as anticipated, perhaps because of the delay in establishment of suitable habitat

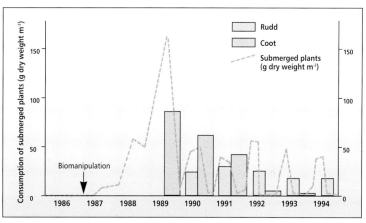

Fig 10.8 **Changes in the biomass of submerged aquatic plants in Lake Zwemlust, following biomanipulation and amounts of grazing made by coot and rudd in the lake. Grazing was associated with a change in dominance by different plant species (En, *Elodea nuttallii*; Cd, *Ceratophyllum demersum*; Pb, *Potamogeton berchtoldii*) and eventually (1994/5), phytoplankton dominance was reasserted. (From Van Donk & Gulati 1995).**

among the plants. Nor did the rudd, whose food supply, the zooplankton, was scarce by 1988 when the large aquatic plant growths seem to have disfavoured *Daphnia* development. It is thought that the phytoplankton was controlled by the *Daphnia* in the first year after biomanipulation and subsequently by competition with the plants for nitrogen. The rudd, however, did subsequently increase, in 1990, to about 40 grams per square metre, a substantial population, which was evidently not severely controlled by the introduced pike, despite further stockings.

Plant dominance persisted for a further three years but in 1992-1994, there was a return to phytoplankton dominance. Experiments with caged and unprotected plants [206] have suggested that this was partly because of grazing by the introduced rudd but mainly because the lake attracted a large population of coot (ca 100 per hectare) whose grazing became devastating (Fig.10.8).

The plant biomass started to decline in 1990 when *Ceratophyllum demersum* became the most prominent plant. It too declined in 1991 leaving only *Potamogeton berchtoldii*, which became heavily burdened by periphyton which retarded its growth. The experiments suggested that the species changes in the aquatic plant community were greatly affected by both coot and rudd but that most of the decline in biomass was due to coot grazing. The blue green alga, *Microcystis aeruginosa* returned in late summer 1992 and subsequently, with chlorophyll a concentrations of 60 to 240 micrograms per litre.

What was learned?

The restoration of Zwemlust has clearly not been stable and there are two reasons for this. The first is that its nutrient concentrations are very high and the mechanism which controlled phytoplankton in the second to the fourth years after biomanipulation was competition for nitrogen. Extra stress on the plants posed by coot grazing would thus have easily undermined the stability by a positive feedback effect.

The second is that, in common with most restoration attempts, that at Zwemlust was carried out in isolation. Formerly the lake would have been part of a greater floodplain system with many lakes and pools among which bird populations would distribute. Provision of a concentrated source of food in the one remaining lake in the area, now that others have been removed through drainage operations, inevitably attracted and concentrated the bird population to levels where they constituted a forward switch mechanism. The only solution to this, other than the culling of birds, is restoration of additional habitats in the area so that the coot population is limited not by food but by other mechanisms.

Again, as in most attempts at restoration with these relatively recently developed techniques,

Zwemlust was a pilot experiment, in which procedures might be changed if it were done subsequently. It was probably a mistake to introduce pike and rudd so early. Delay until the plants had established might have permitted a larger population, of bigger pike, to persist. This might have reduced the coot problem also, for pike take the young chicks of water birds [63] and might have allowed a more diverse community of fish, including tench to be reintroduced.

The carrying out of several procedures at once - refuge provision by willow twigs, biomanipulation, pike introduction, rudd introduction - prevents separation of the individual effect of each of these. This is a common problem where research investigations and management needs are mixed together. The management objective is urgent and particular. The research need takes longer and addresses the fundamental, underlying questions so that general principles may emerge that are applicable elsewhere. Patience is, indeed, a virtue.

In the final analysis, the problem with Zwemlust is that it contains several mutually incompatible features:

(i) locally uncontrollable nutrient loadings;

(ii) a need for clear water for swimming that is unsustainable without persistent aquatic plants to create such conditions;

(iii) an incompatibility between the open water needed for swimming and the presence of plants;

and (iv) the isolation of the basin in cultivated and urban land remote from similar inter connected semi-natural habitat.

Lake Wolderwijd, The Netherlands

What was the problem and target for restoration?

Not all shallow lakes are small. Some are substantial and pose particular problems for restoration when they have become turbid. Lake Wolderwijd is one such and illustrates some of the problems of attempting to restore, in this case, a lake of 2700ha and a mean depth of 1.5m. Wolderwijd is a polder lake, created in 1968 to take drainage water for subsequent controlled release to the sea. The water was clear for two years and aquatic plants were abundant but the lake became turbid, for unknown reasons, in 1970 and has since remained so, with Secchi disc depths of 25cm, high total phosphorus concentrations of around 100 to 200 micrograms per litre and chlorophyll a concentrations in summer of around 200 micrograms per litre. The target for restoration was creation of clear water as a demonstration that this was possible by biomanipulation of such a large lake[129,132].

What was done?

From 1990 to June 1991 the initial fish stock of 200kg per hectare was reduced to 45 kg per ha by removal of 425 tonnes of fish, mainly bream, roach and ruffe. Large seine nets, trawls and fykes were deployed by commercial fishermen. In May 1991, 575000 small pike (3-4 cm length) were added with the intention of their ultimately controlling the young-of-the-year of the remaining fish. The zooplank-tivorous fish stock was reduced from 87 to 20kg per ha. The ratio of piscivorous fish to zooplanktivorous fish was increased from 1 to 50 to 1 to 10, but this is still comparatively low. No nutrient control was attempted.

What happened?

In May 1991, the water became very clear and *Daphnia* were abundant. However, at this time of year prior to biomanipulation, *Daphnia* were

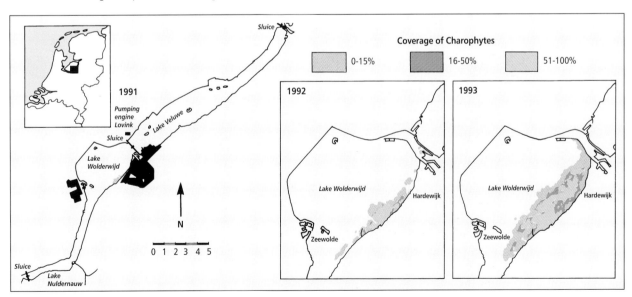

Fig 10.9 Lake Wolderwijd is a man made lake created in the Netherlands as part of a scheme to convert a major inlet of the sea into land. Biomanipulation has not entirely restored the lake to clear water but has led to an extension of Chara beds among what otherwise remains very turbid water. (Based on Meijer & Hosper 1997).

equally abundant. Total phosphorus concentrations were also reduced to around 70 micrograms per litre compared with 140 the previous year and there was a similar reduction in total nitrogen (2.2 to 1.3 milligrams per litre). But again this result is confounded by the fact that the lake had been more than usually well flushed with low phosphorus water in the previous winter. There was some reduction in the proportion of blue green algae in the phytoplankton but they were still predominant.

The *Daphnia* population collapsed in July 1991 and the lake returned to turbid conditions though Secchi disc depths were greater (40-50 cm) than in previous years. In August, the mysid shrimp, *Neomysis integer* increased to apparently greater numbers than in previous years (500 cf 30 individuals per square metre). This was attributed to the removal of perch, its main predator. About half of the predation on *Daphnia* was caused by *Neomysis*, the remainder by fish [127]. There was no increase in the area of coverage of aquatic plants, which had been 35% before biomanipulation, with *Potamogeton pectinatus* and *P. perfoliatus*. *Chara* (*C. contraria* and *C.. vulgaris*) started to replace the *Potamogeton*, and in recent years quite large areas of the most tolerant *Chara* species have grown, with clear water among them surrounded by a sea of turbid water (**Fig 10.9**). The fish biomass increased from 45 kg per ha to 115 kg per ha in the summer of 1991.

What lessons were learned?

The most important lesson learned was that it is possible to remove a significant proportion of the fish stock from a large lake, but clearly this was insufficient to bring about an unequivocal improvement. The residual stock was about 4 grams per square metre, several times higher than that which was effective in Cockshoot Broad, though lower than that effective in Lake Vaeng. An important issue is the composition of the stock. A single biomass value is not informative enough; what matters is the biomass of zooplanktivorous fish and the ratio of piscivores to zooplanktivores. The latter remained low. We cannot yet be precise about these values and we need also to be able to quantify the effect of piscivorous birds, which may take more prey than piscivorous fish. In this lake they probably took about 15 kilograms per hectare each year, including some of the piscivorous fish.

It is thought that a more selective removal of fish might have prevented the *Neomysis* from increasing and decimating the *Daphnia* in summer 1991. This may be true but it is difficult, on present information, to predict the effects of retaining perch on *Daphnia* and *Neomysis*. It eats both. *Neomysis* may have increased also because more inflow water, perhaps of relatively high salinity, entered the lake in the 1990/1991 winter. Chloride concentrations in the lake reached 140 mg per litre and although this is comparatively low for an estuarine mysid. *Neomysis* can probably reproduce at such levels.

The replacement of higher aquatic plants by charophytes is of interest in view of the still high phosphorus concentrations (up to 100 micrograms per litre in summer) though the *Chara* species that are growing are among the more tolerant. There is some evidence that charophytes, through inhibition of phytoplankton by the secretion of organic substances (allelopathy) may be particularly potent in clearing the water [19,20,21,218] and it is possible that, once started, the present spread of charophytes may continue. What is not yet clear is whether the charophyte increase is linked with the biomanipulation or with some other change.

The additional problem in this study is a general problem in studying large lakes. The logistics of fish removal are complicated and costly. The operations in 1990/91 cost about 2 million Dutch Guilders (0.84M ecu). Ideally they should have been continued in 1991/92 and 1992/1993 to keep the fish stock down and to allow pike biomass to build up. Continued

fishing has been recommended [129] but not carried out. This was an ambitious project, but unfortunately perhaps not ambitious enough to repay the initial investment.

Ormesby Broad, UK

Ormesby Broad, at 54 ha, is one of the larger of the Norfolk Broads, though it is as shallow as the smaller ones (average just over 1m). It is one of a group of Broads, the Trinity Broads, that lie along a tributary of the River Bure, called the Muck Fleet, quite low down the valley of this tidal river. Tidal back flow, however, and hence effluent-rich main river water, have been prevented from entering the system by a one-way sluice, close to the river, since 1868. The Trinity Broads are surrounded by agricultural land with some possibility of septic tank and stock effluent entering them, but compared with the other Broads they are comparatively nutrient poor. Though occasional peaks in total phosphorus above 100 micrograms per litre may occur, the usual mean is around 50 micrograms per litre. Inorganic nitrogen concentrations are also modest with

Ormesby Broad. The waterworks, which has benefited from clarification of the water by biomanipulation, is in the right foreground.

winter maxima around 1 milligram N per litre. A range of experiments in 1987/88 [69] showed severe summer phosphorus limitation in Ormesby Broad. Spring and autumn phytoplankton chlorophyll a peaks were about 50 micrograms per litre with summer levels less than half of this.

In recent years, there has generally been an aquatic plant community in the Broad. A vigorous reed fringe remains and the floating leaved and submerged plant communities have been relatively rich in species. These have included *Chara globularis* var *globularis*, *Chara vulgaris* var *contraria*, *Zannichellia palustris, Elodea canadensis, Enteromorpha* sp, *Potamogeton friesii, P. pusillus, P. crispus, P. pectinatus, P .trichoides Myriophyllum spicatum, Ranunculus circinatus, Ceratophyllum demersum, Lemna minor, Fontinalis antipyretica, Hippuris vulgaris, Nuphar lutea, Nymphaea alba,* and *Polygonum amphibium* [101,102].

There might seem to be little problem with the Broad therefore. It is certainly in a better state than most of the other lakes in the area. However, the plant biomass has not been great in recent years and appeared to have dwindled even more in 1993. Palaeolimnological work[69] showed a lake dominated by charophytes until the mid nineteenth century, after which they became scarcer, whilst other plants remained. The lake is also used for water supply by Essex and Suffolk Water, which has experienced difficulties with treatment in recent years.

Hameed [69] demonstrated an inverse relationship between *Daphnia* numbers and chlorophyll a in Ormesby Broad and from time to time the water has cleared dramatically [39] probably in years when fish recruitment has been poor and *Daphnia* has flourished. In spring, 200 animals per litre were not uncommon but numbers dwindled as the young-of-the-year fish moved to feed on them. Because most of the nutrient supply is from diffuse sources and not easy to control, Ormesby Broad offered the prospect of restoration, by biomanipulation alone, of a more stable plant community, with perhaps greater representation of charophytes, inocula of which were already present. This would be in a context where water supply might also benefit and in which the water company would have an incentive to bear future costs of management.

What was done?

A barrier was placed across the outflow stream to the Broad in early 1995. Fishing operations began with removal of fish by netting and electrofishing from the many ditches feeding the Broad, where many fish aggregate in winter [123]. This obviated intensive fishing in the main body of the lake, though shoals of large bream were removed using scare lines in the open water later in the year. Some bream remained free to spawn in late spring. The fish community was dominated by small roach, bream and perch, but ruff, pike, eel, gudgeon, tench and rudd were also recorded. Over 300 thousand fish were removed with a biomass of 8.2 tonnes (153 kg per ha). Of these, eels (79kg), pike (166kg) and tench (33kg) were returned to the Broad. The remaining fish were transported elsewhere. About one tonne of small bream was removed in August at the barrier isolating the Broad. The fish accumulated there following a decline in water level . A follow-up fish removal was carried out in the winter of 1995/96 when a small number of zooplanktivores and the bulk of the remaining bream have been removed.

Nothing else was done. Nutrient control was infeasible and no attempt was made to protect the naturally present plant inocula fom birds. This would have been impracticable on any significant scale.

What happened?

Matters of sociological consequence and ecological interest! Decisions concerning the restoration of the broad had had to be taken at short notice and there had not been sufficient time to inform the public widely before the barrier was set up on the outflow, and fishing operations had begun. There was thus protest from local anglers and among people who had rights by custom to operate rowing boats on the broad. The barrier prevented movement of the boats. The project had temporarily to be stopped on 24 February, soon after it had begun. Two public meetings were held in the area, attended by 280 people at the first and 100 at the second. For a rural area these are substantial numbers. The aims of the project were fully explained and a liaison committee of twenty local representatives was formed. The barrier at the outflow was redesigned as a low mound of pebbles, through which water, but not fish could pass and over which boats could be portaged.

In early summer, *Daphnia* populations were large, but numerically lower than in previous years (April-Sept mean 1993, 131 per litre; 1994, 105; 1995, 44[123] but included a substantial proportion of the large *D. magna*, which had not been a common member of the community previously. *Daphnia cucullata* and *D. longispina/hyalina* were also present. The water became very clear in June and early July and the aquatic plant biomass was considerable. Charophytes formed dense beds in the gravelly margins whilst the remainder had a dense cover of *Potamogeton* species and *Zannichellia palustris*. However, the remaining large bream in the broad evidently spawned. Predation by their young removed the *Daphnia magna* populations in late July and for the rest of the summer, as in the pre-biomanipulation years. Consequently chlorophyll a levels increased to give turbid water again. The April-September

Public relations are important in all restoration programmes.

mean chlorophyll a concentration, however, was lower (17.5 micrograms per litre) than in the previous two years (1993, 34.3; 1994, 35.6) and there was no significant change in nutrient concentrations [96]

What was learned?

Apart from the lessons concerning the need for early and comprehensive public relations, the findings from Ormesby Broad are of interest in two respects. First, charophyte abundance, if not dominance was established at comparatively high (about 50 micrograms per litre) initial phosphorus concentrations, without external nutrient control. The starting concentrations were nonetheless within the expected range (just) in which charophytes thrive. Secondly, despite the increased plant biomass, there was a mid-summer decline in daphnids. This is not unexpected at high plant densities, when nutrient, especially nitrogen limitation may begin to control the algal biomass. In addition the water company had the benefit of water with low algal concentrations for much of the summer and are now keen to look at similar biomanipulation treatment of the several other lakes connected with Ormesby Broad.

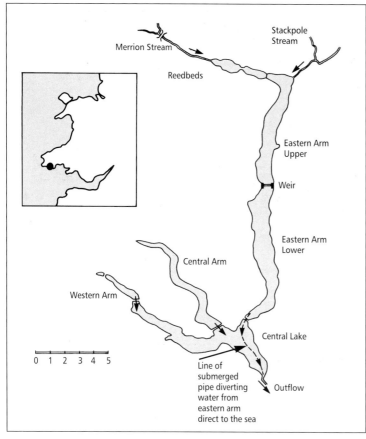

Fig 10.10 Map of the Bosherston Lily Ponds, Pembrokeshire.

Bosherston Lakes, Wales, UK

Bosherston Lakes[53,75,172] were elevated to this title when they were designated as a Site of Special Scientific Interest. They are more usually known locally as Bosherston Lily Ponds, a name which conveys a lot more information. Post cards show a mass of white water lilies in narrow valleys clothed with oak woodland. There are effectively four basins (**Fig.10.10**), three of them the dammed tributaries of a higher order stream which discharged to the sea. The system was progressively dammed from 1780 onwards as an amenity for the Cawdor estate, which owned the area.

Stone-wall causeways with sluices were built across the three tributaries, called the western, central and eastern arms, thus minimising water exchange between them through the wider central lake into which they discharge. The catchment geology is largely of limestone and the lakes, particularly the central arm, are partly fed by springs. Until the 1970s the western arm was dominated by water lilies, and the central arm by charophytes. The central lake was very clear also with a mixed community of plants in which charophytes (*Chara hispida*) were prominent. The eastern arm already had some problems, for although it had an aquatic plant community of pondweeds, it bore obvious blue-green algal blooms.

Through it came the main inflow stream to the system, into which, rather distantly, was discharged sewage effluent from an army range and more immediately from the village of Stackpole. A further set of dams in the upper reaches of the eastern arm had filled in with sediment and were colonised by reedswamp. This probably mitigated the residual effects of the army sewage effluent, but that from Stackpole was increasing in volume. The intensity of farming in the catchment had also increased. In the 1970s and 1980s, there were noticeable increases in the algal biomasses in the eastern arm, western arm and central lake. There was a notable decline in aquatic plants in the latter. Charophyte cover diminished, and was replaced by thalloid algae and pondweeds. The central, spring fed arm, with a small catchment and low intensity agriculture, remained apparently unchanged.

The problem was then not one of restoring a plant community but of reducing nutrients sufficiently to restore the particularly valued charophyte communities to the western arm and central lake, and, if possible to the eastern arm.

What was done?

The effluent from the Stackpole sewage treatment works was diverted directly to the sea in 1984. Slurry-handling facilities were upgraded on nearby farms. This, however, did not have much immediate effect partly because some nutrient input from the army range remained, partly because the agricultural background was now high and partly because of internal release of phosphorus from the sediments. It was then decided to protect the central lake by diverting the water from the eastern arm direct to the sea.

This was preferable to removal of sediments from the eastern arm because in the steeply surrounding topography there was nowhere to dump the sediments which would not also have conflicted with the high conservation value of the surrounding area. The lakes lie in a National Nature Reserve, and the costs and

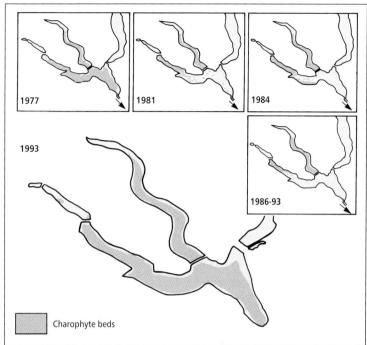

Recovery of charophytes in the Bosherston Lakes. The diversion pipe was installed in 1992. (From Moore 1993).

In Bosherston Lake, a plastic water pipe, sleeved with concrete weights, was sunk to the lake bed and used to divert nutrient rich water directly to the sea.

disturbance of taking the sediments (perhaps 46000 cubic metres) elsewhere for disposal would have been considerable. Old ponds on the inlet stream to the eastern arm which had filled with sediment have been reexcavated to act as traps for new sediment.

A 56-cm diameter polyethylene pipe was fitted (cost about 163000 ecu) to the sluice in the causeway that divided the eastern arm from the central lake. It was sleeved with concrete annuli to weight it and directed to the outlet of the central lake, 400m away, where it was fitted to a sluice. These operations were facilitated by keeping the pipe air-filled during construction. Finally the pipe was filled with water and sunk into the sandy bed. Water is not diverted through the pipe at all times so as not to reduce the retention time of the central lake significantly. In winter the sluice is overtopped and eastern arm water flows directly into the central lake.

But in late spring and summer when nutrient levels in the eastern arm are high, the sluices to the pipe are opened and the central lake is by-passed. There has been substantial recovery of the charophytes in the central lake.

The eastern arm retains considerable pondweed populations and an attempt is being made to reduce the nutrient stocks in this arm by removal of vegetation at the point of its senescence in late summer. The 70 to 100 tonnes (wet weight) removed probably account for about 30-40% of the annual external phosphorus load. The upper parts of the plants are cut, at a depth of one metre, from a flat bottomed punt by a reciprocating blade and the cut material is drawn onto the boat by a rotating wire mesh belt. The cost is about 3000 ecu per year. There has been some reduction in algal growth and extension of *Chara*. Weed cutting, however, is unlikely to remove much nutrient, compared with the sediment reserve. Much of the nutrient uptake of aquatic plants comes from the sediment and the amount stored even in the top ten centimetres will be enough to sustain plant and algal crops for many decades or centuries. Plant removal, even in autumn, when the propagules which initiate the following spring growth are being formed, could induce a forward switch by mechanical plant loss in this arm. An alternative approach might now be biomanipulation to improve the water and habitat quality. An objection to biomanipulation might be its possible influence on otter populations which frequent the lake. This could be minimised by retaining eels, which are the major fish food of otters and which are not zooplanktivorous.

What was learned?

The lesson of this case study is that charophyte communities can be restored if conditions are particularly favourable. In this case a balance could be struck between a water supply of very high quality (coming through the central and western arms) and the poor quality water of the eastern arm. The case also shows that 'hard' engineering can be sensitively used through the use of a comparatively cheap pipeline, which involves very little recurrent cost. An insensitive approach to this site would have been sediment dredging, which would have involved building a road to tanker out the sediment or an ugly and prominent lagoon somewhere in a nature reserve.

Finjasjön, Sweden

What was the problem and what was done?

Lake Finjasjön, in Scania, Southern Sweden[4,71] is typical of many lowland lakes in Europe. It is substantial enough (1100ha in area; mean depth 3m; maximum depth 13m) to have attracted a sizeable community, in the town of Hassleholm, and thereby acquired a problem of eutrophication, first from sewage, then after 1949, from conventionally treated sewage effluent. In the 1920s the water was clear with a Secchi disc depth of around 2m, but the blue green alga, *Gloeotrichia echinulata* became abundant in the 1940s. The sewage treatment works discharged directly to the lake although it would have been more convenient to

discharge to the outflow. This was apparently due to a policy decision by the Swedish government that any pollution problem should be experienced at the point of origin and not exported to some other community.

Blooms developed, particularly those of the blue green alga, *Microcystis aeruginosa*, in the 1960s and 1970s. They were potentially linked to symptoms of skin rashes among swimmers. This led to installation of phosphorus stripping at the treatment works in 1977. The external phosphorus load was reduced from 65 to 5 tonnes per year.

The blooms did not diminish, though there was some response in the nature of the diatom species which formed the spring growth. Though the inflow then had about

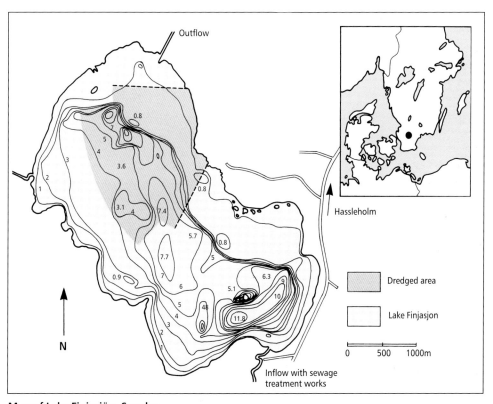

Map of Lake Finjasjön, Sweden.

40 micrograms of total phosphorus per litre, the lake had concentrations of around 100 in winter and 300 to 500 in summer. Chlorophyll a concentrations were up to 200 micrograms per litre. Although more phosphorus was leaving the lake by the outflow than entered it in the now reduced external load, enough internal loading was taking place to maintain the very high concentrations. More than half of the lake was covered by organic sediments to thicknesses of 3m. The lake had some aquatic plants but they were confined to shallow water at the edge and grew poorly. The mean depth is about 3m.

What was then done?

Sweden pioneered techniques of lake restoration by sediment removal[17] and it was logical to try this at Finjasjön, beginning in 1987. The costs per year proved astronomical (about 1.25 million ecu) but suction dredging was stopped in 1991 after five years, when 25% of the area had been dredged because the dredged areas continued to release phosphorus at rates comparable with the undredged areas. The large growths of *Microcystis* continued in summer.

There is an interesting parallel at Lake Brabrand, near the town of Aarhus in Denmark. This is a smaller (153ha), shallower (1.1m) lake, with a short water retention time (5-20 days) and a higher phosphorus load (20 tonnes per year) even after phosphorus stripping at the local

Fish were removed from Lake Finjasjon by trawling a net from two powered boats.

sewage treatment works. It was formerly a clear water plant-dominated lake. No improvement followed stripping and so a Mud-Cat suction dredger was purchased following a decision to remove 400000 cubic metres of black phosphorus-rich sediment to depths of 30 to 90 cm in various targeted parts of the lake. Dredging started in 1989, and is still not complete (1996). There has been no improvement in water quality. The cost of dredging is likely to be about 3.5 million ecu.

What was then done at Finjasjön?

Following pilot fisheries surveys, a decision was made to biomanipulate Lake Finjasjön in 1992. Gill nets were used but most of the removal was by trawling using paired small boats. Between October 1992 and summer 1993, a modified herring trawl removed 186 tonnes of mainly small bream and roach, the predominant fish in the lake. Calculations based on the catch and the fishing effort suggested that the total initial stock had been about 500 tonnes and so fishing continued in winter 1993/94. About 430 tonnes of fish have been removed and the ratio of piscivores to zooplanktivorous fish has been increased from 1 to 10-20 to 1 to1. A constructed wetland of 30 ha was also made to polish the quality of the sewage effluent and buffer zones alongside the inflow streams were also established. The wetland is intended to retain effluent for 5-6 days and is calculated to be able to remove 50% of the phosphorus load, through harvesting of the plants (*Phragmites australis, Typha latifolia, Elodea canadensis*) every second year and 30% of the combined nitrogen through denitrification[5]. The emerging concentration of total nitrogen will still be around 15mg l[-1], however, and that of phosphorus, 0.1mgl[-1], which are still substantial amounts. The buffer zones are comparatively thin (about 5m) and were attained by negotiation with the farmers.

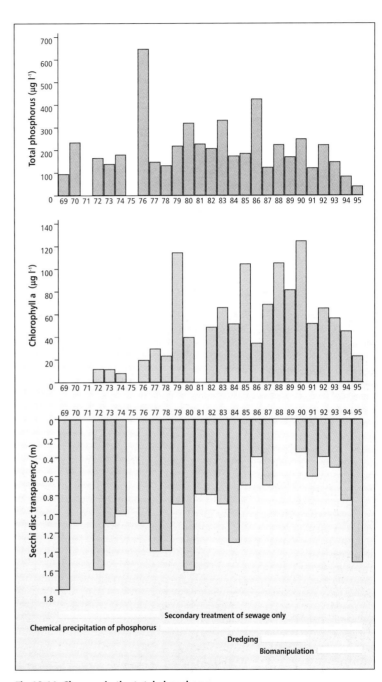

Fig 10.11 Changes in the total phosphorus concentrations and algal chlorophyll a concentrations during the sequence of attempts to restore Lake Finjasjön to clear water. (Data courtesy of Helene Annadotter).

In 1994 and 1995 (Fig 10.11), following biomanipulation, the transparency of the water increased, the phytoplankton biomass was reduced and the monoculture of *Microcystis aeruginosa* was replaced by a more diverse phytoplankton community. There has been an extension of the coverage of submerged plants, including *Myriophyllum* and *Potamogeton* in the lake.

What is being learned?

Some hard lessons about the frustrations and costs of restoring even moderately large lakes. The projected cost of sediment dredging, had it been continued was 13 million ecu; 5 million ecu were actually spent. In contrast, the biomanipulation has cost 0.63 million ecu, the wetland and associated engineering a further 0.75 million ecu and the annual running costs for the wetland are about 0.125 million ecu.

The lesson, in hindsight, is that the funds spent on a fruitless suction dredging (the lake is not shallow enough to justify dredging merely to create depth) would have been better invested in an earlier intensive fishing. However, mistakes seen in hindsight are the fodder of increased understanding. While the improved scientific knowledge is of global value, it is, however, only a consolation prize to the locality and its funding bodies!

Despite the lake's large size, biomanipulation appears to have been successful, though, as in other cases the long term outcome cannot yet be known. Indeed, every basic technique available for lake restoration is being applied to the lake; if this collection is unsuccessful, the outlook for the restoration of large shallow lakes is not hopeful.

Barton Broad, UK

What is the problem?

Barton Broad was the first of the fifty or so Norfolk Broads on which restoration was attempted. Some of the earliest detailed limnological work in the Norfolk Broads was carried out on it [135,160,161,162,163].

As a result of this, a nutrient budget was produced that showed that the bulk of the external load to what was very much a blue green algal-dominated, extremely eutrophicated Broad came from two sewage treatment works. There was also considerable internal loading. Palaeolimnological work established a former *Chara* dominance and anecdotal accounts from the 1950s and 1960s were of strong dominance by water lilies and submerged plants.

Barton Broad was chosen as the subject of the first restoration attempt because detailed data

Barton Broad in the 1950s. Remains of the peat peninsulas used originally for transporting peat from the pits can be seen as parallel islands, whose angle changes on either side of a Parish boundary. Turkey Broad is the area at the foot of the picture. There is also much evidence of marginal plant beds.

existed for it, as the result of the historical accident that a graduate student, Patrick Osborne, in consultation with two of the present authors, chose it as most resembling other hypertrophic lakes he had previously worked on in the then Rhodesia, when selecting a site for his doctoral research! In practice it is perhaps the most difficult site in Broadland to restore. This is because of its size (67ha), its high nutrient loading, its tidal nature and the fact that the navigable River Ant now runs directly through it, so that isolation is not possible. Formerly the basin was set to one side of the river, but the latter was diverted in the eighteenth century to reduce the navigation distance for commercial boats.

What was done?

The details of its history as revealed in sediment cores **(Figs 10.12 and 10.13)** were informative enough to persuade the then Water Authority (Anglian Water) to install phosphate stripping at one of the two sewage treatment works

(Stalham) and to divert the effluent from a more distant one (North Walsham) to the sea. This was, in any case, a cheap alternative to rebuilding of a works that was seriously overloaded and functioning poorly. At the time, with the successes of nutrient control in the restoration of deep lakes much to the fore, it was believed that similar control would be effective for the shallow Barton Broad.

What happened?

The nutrient removal and diversion, plus control of a food factory effluent were completed by 1981 and had some effect on the phytoplankton populations of the broad, but the water remained very turbid and plants did not re-establish. The total phosphorus concentrations were maintained at high level by internal loading and the buffer mechanisms that stabilise phytoplankton dominance could be seen to be operating powerfully. This situation has continued until the present **(see Fig.2.5)**.

Barton Broad in 1996. Most of the islands have been eroded away by boat movements and wave action following loss of aquatic plants from the Broad.

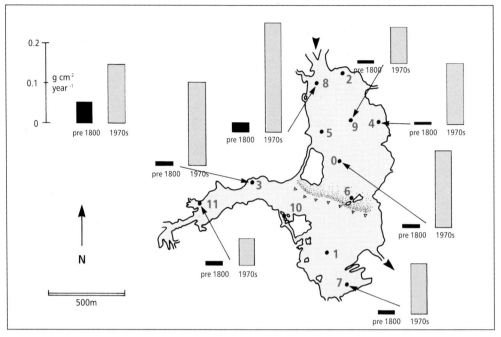

Fig 10.12 The black tongue. Sediment cores from Barton Broad taken in the late 1970s showed distinctive layering of the sediment (Fig 10.13). In the northern part of the broad extending from the main inflow, the River Ant, the sediment at the surface was black and plotting of the data synoptically suggested a tongue of sulphide rich sediment, probably originating from sewage effluent, coming down river. The cores were dated using lead 210 dating and the sedimentation rates calculated. Because the water content varies, these are best expressed as amount of dry material laid down per square metre per year. Rates have clearly increased in the twentieth century. Linear rates of sedimentation are now about one centimetre per year. Numbers refer to the cores illlustrated in Fig 10.13. (Data based on Moss 1980).

What is being done now?

The broad is important for holiday boating, lying at the heart of the network of broads and rivers; it is also shallowing rapidly as sediment is being laid down at the rate of about one centimetre each year. A sub-basin to the south, once probably a separate peat pit, called Turkey Broad, is shallowing more rapidly than the rest as it is distant to the scouring action of the river running through. There have been concerns that boating and sailing will become impossible over much of Barton Broad.

Barton Broad is a major sailing centre. The Broads Authority has thus conceived a plan to remove sediment from the Broad by suction dredging over the next five years and to reinstate a former large peat island that has become eroded by boats, in the absence of the protection offered by submerged plants and lilies. It will also biomanipulate Turkey Broad, which can be isolated by a reed barrier, with a boat pass, from the remainder once it has been dredged. It is not expected that the aquatic plants will be restored by the sediment dredging alone (see the cases of Finjasjön and Lake Brabrand above). This is unlikely to occur without biomanipulation but will be possible in the isolated Turkey Broad. Because of the cost and scale of the project, this is an important message for the public relations element of the

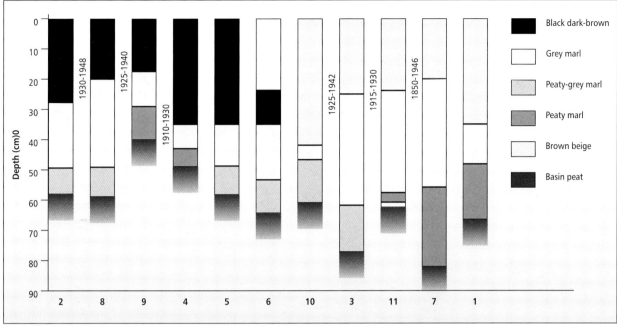

Fig 10.13   Details of the sediment cores taken to construct Fig 10.12. Grey sediments are associated with early plant dominance, Brown beige sediments in the southern part of the broad are associated with plankton dominance, and black dark- brown sediments with plankton dominance and ingress of organic rich sediment, later to be stained with sulphide, from the sewage effluent. (From Moss 1980).

project. The nutrient control at the sewage treatment works will continue, for this will expedite the recovery of Turkey Broad and eventually the remainder of the basin. Statutory consents are now in place requiring the operators of the relevant sewage treatment works to meet a 1mg per litre standard for their effluents and new equipment is being installed.

Detailed planning

Suction dredging of a large water body needs detailed planning and this alone has taken over three years since May 1992. The intention is to take out only the most phosphorus-rich sediment and to dispose of it on agricultural land to the west of the lake. Part of the early planning was a contemporary depth survey, coupled with some analysis of sediment cores to determine both how much sediment should

be removed, its heavy metal content and the feasibility of disposing of it to the land available. A sympathetic land owner was identified and the Agricultural Development and Advisory Service carried out topographic and soil surveys, provided advice on the working of the fields and topsoil conservation and the construction of bunds from the topsoil to keep the sediment from running off. Legal agreements concerning compensation for land agents fees, legal fees, and compensation for crop losses and loss of shooting income were negotiated. It was established that the bunds did not require planning permission but that associated access tracks and ditchwork did.

In late1993, a civil engineer was engaged to draw up tender documents for the suction dredging and conduct studies on the relative costs of having the work done by an outside contractor or by the Broads Authority's own field staff.

The contract documents identified the constraints but did not stipulate how the job should be done. Tenderers for the work were asked to submit a plan of how they would do the work. This placed liability on the eventual contractor in the event of any failure of the structures, such as sediment lagoon bunds. The successful contractor was also chosen for his sympathetic and sensitive works plan, as well as on price.

The National Rivers Authority (now the Environment Agency), who are co-operating in the endeavour, agreed to continue monitoring the Broad.

In February 1994, a dredging trial was carried out over a hectare of broad with the sediment disposed to a 20m x 20m bund to establish settling and drying times. Within six months the sediment had been reduced to a third of its former volume. The contract for suction dredging was then advertised in an international dredging journal (*Dredging and Port Construction*) and locally. There were sixteen expressions of interest from British and Dutch concerns, which the engineer assessed for technical capability, experience and financial soundness. In July 1994, eight companies were invited to tender for the work and a tender was accepted in September 1995.

Finally in November 1995, work began with the construction of an access track to the disposal site and the widening of a ditch at its base to carry run off water. Bunds were made at close intervals across the fields concerned, with the topsoil being lifted by an excavator to form the bunds which contain the lagoons. The top soil was not compacted in doing this (as it would have been if a bulldozer or scraper had been used) and it will be redistributed as top soil at the end of the project. A total area of 21 ha is being used for settlement of sediment derived from 60 ha of Broad.

During the five years of the project the compliance of the contractor will be carefully monitored by measures of the volume of sediment removed and the depth dredged (overdredging is not paid for under the terms of the contract). Dredging depth can now be carefully controlled using computerised sensors. Safety measures have also been put in place to minimise the risk of boat collision with the dredger and of trespassers entering the lagoon site. Working hours have been limited to 0800-2000, Monday to Saturday and reed-filled ditches are being used to reduce the turbidity of the run off water which will re-enter the Broad.

A programme of special open days and activities for the public has been instituted and media interest encouraged. Finally very detailed communication is being maintained by the project engineer and the project manager, who are Broads Authority appointees and the contractors on a weekly basis. Local people and users of the broad will also be involved. Funding for the project, which is likely to cost 1.6 million ecu is guaranteed by the Authority, but is being sought elsewhere to as large an extent possible. The Soap and Detergent Industry Association Environment Trust is a current sponsor.

Removal of sediment to be deposited in these lagoons from Barton Broad, will recreate sufficient depth for recreation and navigation. Subsequent biomanipulation should re-establish clear water and conservation value.

Chapter 11

Expectations and the Future

'Blessed are the meek: for they shall inherit the earth'.
Matthew 5,4.

'Only when we are straight in our own heads, and have structured societies that are able to override their own innate tendency to be overtaken by hawks and hawkishness, can we hope to create the kind of world that can be sustained, for only the meek can inherit the earth'.
Colin Tudge, 1994, 'The Engineer in the Garden'.

It is presently more than usually difficult to predict the future. The world is changing rapidly and we seem poised between two contrasting directions. First there is a general tendency to continue exploiting natural resources to an extent that must have profound consequences for human comfort in the future. As more countries industrialise and existing industrial nations are forced to compete, we might expect this trend to accelerate.

On the other hand, there is an increasing realisation that this trend cannot go on indefi-nitely and that resource consumption has to be made sustainable - we replace what we use. This realisation is unlikely to be politically popular as it implies a substantial change in life style, though it contains the essence of the main difference between ourselves and other animals, the ability to plan far ahead. The realisation of a sustainable approach to our environment is the challenge we now face.

The causes of problems in lakes, as in all other natural and semi-natural habitats include the immediate or proximate and the ultimate. Most

of this book has been concerned with diagnosing and remedying the former - increased nutrient loading, forward switches. But the ultimate causes - the current mores of society, the choice between exploitation and sustainability- are more important for they may undermine in general what is being attempted in particular.

Recognition of some of these ideas is starting to come to the fore in some of our legislation. The 1995 Environment Act states that the Environment Agency's principal aim is'....to protect or enhance the environment taken as a whole ... to make the contribution towards attaining the objective of achieving sustainable development...' There has perhaps never been a better time to begin the task of restoring some of our damaged lakes using the holistic approaches set out in this handbook. Some will question the wisdom of such approaches. Will it work? Is it cost-effective? What might be the effect on our rural communities? These are questions that must be dealt with if a restoration project is to find the support that it will need to be successfully completed.

Finding answers will not be easy, but, even when the difficulties seem huge, it will always be better to be ambitious, to attempt large projects (if they are at least feasible) rather than small ones, for the rewards will be greater. To confine action to the small is to undermine the strength of the argument for conservation. If little is asked, less will be given. It will also be sensible to take calculated risks - that a restoration may not be successful, for example - for confinement to the certain also trivialises the endeavour and prevents new and useful knowledge being learned.

We are an immensely rich society. Many things are possible. It is simply a matter of collective choice as to how the richness is used. An ethic of restoration and repair must inherently be superior to one of consumption and destruction. That is the ultimate reason for lake and other restoration programmes. They paint a red cross on a field still flayed by the hawks to no final good.

References

1. **Andersson,G., Bergren,H., Cronberg,G., & Gelin,C.** (1978) Effects of planktivorous and benthivorous fish on organisms and water chemistry in eutrophic lakes. *Hydrobiologia*, **59**, 9-15.

2. **Andersson,G., Berggren,H. & Hamrin,S.** (1975) Lake Trummen restoration project III Zooplankton, macrobenthos and fish. *Verhandlungen internationale der Vereinigung theoretische und angewande Limnologie* **19**, 1097-1106.

3. **Andersson,G., Blindow,I, Hargeby,A. & Johansson,S.** (1990) The recovery of Lake Krankesjön. *Anser* **29**, 53-62 (Swedish, English summary.)

4. **Annadotter,H., Cronberg,G., Aagren,R., Jönsson,L., Lundstedt,B., Nilsson,P-A & Ströbeck,S.** (1997) Multiple techniques for the restoration of a hypertrophic lake. In Harper,D., Brierley, W., Phillips,G. & Ferguson,A. (eds) *The Ecological Basis for Lake and Reservoir Management.* Wiley, Chichester, in press.

5. **Annadotter,H., Nilsson,P.A., Lundstedt,B. & Ströbäck,S.** (1995) Ny vatmarksanlägning för kombinerad reduktion av fosfor och kväve. (A new constructed wetland for combined reduction of phosphorus and nitrogen.) *Vatten* **51**, 103-106.

6. **Bales,M., Moss,B., Phillips,G., Irvine,K. & Stansfield,J.** (1993) The changing ecosystem of a shallow, brackish lake, Hickling Broad, Norfolk.II Long term changes in water chemistry and ecology and their implications for restoration of the lake. *Freshwater Biology* **29**, 141-165.

7. **Balls, H.R., Moss,B., & Irvine,K.** (1989) The loss of submerged plants with eutrophication I Experimental design, water chemistry, aquatic plant and phytoplankton biomass in experiments carried out in ponds in the Norfolk Broadland. *Freshwater Biology* **22**, 71-87.

8. **Battarbee,R.W., Mason,J., Renberg,I. & Talling,J.F.** (1990) *Palaeolimnology and Lake Acidification.* The Royal Society, London.

9. **Beklioglu,M. & Moss,B.** (1995) The impact of pH on interactions among phytoplankton algae, zooplankton and perch (*Perca fluviatilis*) in a shallow, fertile lake. *Freshwater Biology* **33**, 497-509.

10. **Bengtsson,L, Fleischer,S., Lindmark,G. & Ripl,W.** (1975) Lake Trummen restoration project.I Water and sediment chemistry. *Verhandlungen der internationale Vereinigung theoretische und angewandte Limnologie* **19**, 1080-1087.

11. **Benndorf,J.** (1987) Food web manipulation without nutrient control: A useful strategy in lake restoration? *Schweizerische Zhurnal der Hydrologie* **49**, 237-248.

12. **Benndorf,J.** (1988) Objectives and unsolved problems in echotechnology and biomanipulation:a preface. *Limnologica (Berlin)* **19**, 5-8.

13. **Benndorf,J., Kneschke,H., Kossatz,K. & Penz,E.** (1984) Manipulation of the pelagic food web by stocking with predacious fishes. *Internationale Revue der gesamten Hydrobiologie* **69**, 407-428.

14. **Benndorf, J., Schultz,H., Benndorf,A., Unger,R., Penz,E., Kneschke,H., Kossatz,K., Dumke,R., Hornig,U., Kruspe,R. & Reichel,S.** (1988) Food web manipulation by enhancement of piscivorous fish stocks: long term effects in the hypertrophic Bautzen reservoir. *Limnologica* **19**, 97-110.

15. **Bennion,H.** (1994) A diatom-phosphorus transfer function for shallow, eutrophic ponds in southeast England. *Hydrobiologia* **275/276**, 391-410.

16. **Berg,S., Jeppesen,E. & Søndergaard,M.** (1997) Pike (*Esox lucius* L.) stocking as a biomanipulation tool. 1. Effects on the fish population in Lake Lyng (Denmark). *Hydrobiologia* (in press).

17. **Bjørk,S.** (1972) Swedish lake restoration program gets results. *Ambio* **1**, 153-165.

18. **Bjørk,S.** (1994) Restoration of lakes through sediment removal - Lake Trummen, Sweden. 130-140 in Eiseltova, M. (Editor) *Restoration of Lake Ecosystems, a Holistic approach.* International Waterfowl and Wetlands Research Bureau, Publication **32**, Slimbridge.

19. **Blindow,I.** (1991) *Interactions between submerged macrophytes and microalgae in shallow lakes.* Doctoral Dissertation, University of Lund, Sweden.

20. **Blindow,I.** (1992) Long and short term dynamics of submerged macrophytes in two shallow lakes. *Freshwater Biology* **28**, 15-27.

21. **Blindow,I., Andersson,A., Hargeby,A., & Hansson,S.** (1993) Long-term pattern of alternative stable states in two shallow eutrophic lakes. *Freshwater Biology* **30**, 159-167.

22. **Boar,R.R., Crook,C.E. & Moss,B.** (1989) Regression of *Phragmites australis* reedswamps and recent changes of water chemistry in the Norfolk Broadland, England. *Aquatic Botany* **35**, 41-55.

23. **Boorman,L.A. & Fuller,R.M.** (1981) The changing status of reedswamp in the Norfolk Broads. *Journal of Applied Ecology* **18**, 241-269.

24. **Brabrand,Å. & Faafeng,B.A.** (1993) Habitat shift in roach (*Rutilus rutilus*) induced by pikeperch (*Stizostedion lucioperca*) introduction:predation versus pelagic behaviour. *Oecologia* **95**, 38-46.

25. **Breukelaar,A.W., Lammens,E.H.R.R., Klein Breteler,J.G.P. & Tatrai,I.** (1994) Effects of benthivorous bream (*Abramis brama*) and carp (*Cyprinus carpio*) on sediment resuspension and concentrations of nutrients and chlorophyll a. *Freshwater Biology* **32**, 113-121.

26. **Brönmark,C.** (1989) Interactions between epiphytes, macrophytes and freshwater snails: a review. *Journal of Molluscan Studies* **55**, 299-311.

27. Brönmark,C., Klosiewski,S.P. & Stein,R.A. (1992) Indirect effects of predation in a freshwater, benthic food chain. *Ecology* 73, 1662-1674.

28. Brönmark,C. & Weisner,S.E.B. (1992) Indirect effects of fish community structure on submerged vegetation in shallow, eutrophic lakes: an alternative mechanism. *Hydrobiologia* 243/244, 293-301.

28a Brooks,J.L. & Dodson,S.I. (1965) Predation, body size and composition of plankton. *Science* 150, 28-35.

29. Cahn,A.R. (1929) The effect of carp on a small lake: the carp as a dominant. *Ecology* 10, 271-274.

30. Canfield,D.E. Jr, Shireman,J.V., Colle,D.E., Haller,W.T., Watkins,C.E.II & Maceina,M.J. (1984) Prediction of chlorophyll a concentrations in Florida lakes:importance of aquatic macrophytes. *Canadian Journal of Fisheries and Aquatic Sciences* 41, 497-501,

31. Carpenter,S.R. (1988) *Complex Interactions in Lake Communities.* Springer Verlag, New York.

32. Carpenter,S.R., Christensen,D.L., Cole,J.C., Cottingham,K.L., He,X., Hodgson,J.R., Kitchell,J.F., Knight,S.E., Pace,M.L., Post,D.M., Schindler,D.E. & Voichick, N. (1995) Biological control of eutrophication in lakes. *Environmental Science & Technology* 29, 784-786.

33. Carpenter,S.R. & Kitchell,J.F. (eds) (1994) *The Trophic Cascade in Lakes.* Cambridge University Press, Cambridge.

34. Carvalho,L. (1994) Top-down control of phytoplankton in a shallow hypertrophic lake: Little Mere, (England). *Hydrobiologia* 275/276, 53-63.

35. Carvalho,L., Beklioglu,M. & Moss,B. (1995) Changes in Rostherne Mere following sewage diversion - a challenge to the orthodoxy of external phosphorus control as a restoration strategy. *Freshwater Biology* 34, 399-410.

36. Carvalho,L. & Moss,B. (1995) The current status of a sample of English Sites of Special Scientific Interest subject to eutrophication. *Aquatic Conservation* 5, 191-204.

37. Chescheir,G.M., Skaggs,R.W. & Gilliam,J.W. (1992) Evaluation of wetland buffer areas for treatment of pumped agricultural drainage water. *Transactions of the American Society of Agricultural Engineers* 35, 175-182.

38. Christoffersen,K., Reimann,B., Klysner,A.K. & Søndergaard,M. (1993) Potential role of fish predation and natural populations of zooplankton in structuring a plankton community in eutrophic water. *Limnology and Oceanography* 38, 561-573.

39. Clarke,K.B. (1973) The unusual clarity of the Ormesby Broads during 1971. *Transactions of the Norfolk & Norwich Naturalists Society,* 22, 254-260.

40. Cooke,G.D., Welch,E.B., Peterson,S.A. & Newroth,P.R. (1993) *Restoration and Management of Lakes and reservoirs..* Lewis publishers, Ann Arbor, Michigan.

41. Cranswick,P.A., Waters,R.J., Evans,J., Pollitt,M.S. & Stroud,D.A. (1995) *The Wetland Bird Survey 1993-94: Wildfowl and Wader Counts.* BTO/WWT/RSPB/JNCC, Slimbridge.

42. Crivelli, A.J. (1983) The destruction of aquatic vegetation by carp. *Hydrobiologia* 106, 37-41.

43. Cronberg,G. (1982) Phytoplankton changes in Lake Trummen induced by restoration. *Folia Limnologica Scandinavica,* 18, 1-119.

44. Cronberg,G. (1996). Personal communication.

45. Cronberg,G., Gelin,C. & Larsson,K. (1975) Lake Trummen restoration project II Bacteria, phytoplankton and zooplankton productivity. *Verhandlungen internationale der Vereinigung theoretische und angewandte Limnologie* 19, 1088-1096.

46. Crowder,A. & Painter,D.S. (1991) Submerged macrophytes in Lake Ontario: current knowledge, importance, threats to stability and needed studies. *Canadian Journal of Fisheries and Aquatic Sciences* 48, 1539-1545.

47. Daldorph,P. & Price,R. (1994) Long term phosphorus control at three eutrophic reservoirs in south-eastern England. *Archiv für Hydrobiologie Beih.* 40, 231-243.

48. De Bernardi,R. & Giussani,G. (1990) Are blue green algae a suitable food for zooplankton? An overview. *Hydrobiologia* 200/201, 29-44.

49. De Nie,H.W. (1987) The decrease of aquatic vegetation in Europe and its consequence for fish populations. EIFAC/CECP Occasional paper 19.

50. Dillaha,T.A., Reneau,R.B., Mostaghimi,S. & Lee,D. (1989) Vegetative filter strips for agricultural non-point source control.*Transactions of the American Society of Agricultural Engineers* 32, 513-519.

51. Dillon,P.J. & Rigler,F.H. (1974) The phosphorus-chlorophyll relationship in lakes. *Limnology & Oceanography* 19, 767-773.

52. Dini,M.L. & Carpenter,S.R. (1991) The effects of whole lake fish community manipulations on *Daphnia* migratory behaviour. *Limnology and Oceanography* 36, 370-377.

53. Duigan,C. & Haycock,B (1995) Reserve focus-The Bosherston lakes. *British Wildlife* 6, 231-234.

54. Eaton,J.W., Best,M.A., Staples,J.A. & O'Hara,K. (1992) *Grass Carp For Aquatic Weed Control. A User's Manual.* National Rivers Authority, Bristol.

55. Eiseltova, M. (Editor) (1994) *Restoration of Lake Ecosystems, a Holistic Approach.* International Waterfowl and Wetlands Research Bureau, Publication 32, Slimbridge.

56. Ellis,E.A. (1965) *The Broads.* Collins, London.

57. ENDS (Environmental data services) (1996) Eutrophication threat from agricultural sources. No 254, 12-13.

58. ENTEC UK Ltd (1995) *A Review of Eutrophication-Related Legislation in England and Wales.* National Rivers Authority, Peterborough.

59. Faafeng,B.A. & Brabrand,Å. (1990) Biomanipulation of a small, urban lake - removal of fish excludes blue green algal blooms. *Verhandlungen internationale der Vereinigung theoretische und angewandte Limnologie* **24**, 597-602.

60. Fletcher,A.R., Morison,A.K., & Hulme, D.J. (1985) Effects of carp, *Cyprinus carpio* L. on communities of aquatic vegetation and turbidity of water bodies in the lower Goulburn river basin. *Australian Journal of Marine and Freshwater Research* **36**, 311-327.

60a. Foy,R.H. & Withers,P.J.A. (1995) The contribution of agricultural phosphorus to eutrophication. *Proceedings of the Fertilizer Society* **365**, 1-32.

60b Foy,R.H., Smith,R.V., Jordan,C. & Lennox,S.D. (1995) Upward trend in soluble phosphorus loadings to Lough Neagh despite phosphorus reduction at sewage treatment works. *Water Research* **29**, 1051-1063.

61. Gehrels,J. & Mulamootill,G. (1989) The transformation and export of phosphorus from wetlands. *Hydrological Processes* **3**, 365-370.

62. George,M. (1992) *The Land Use, Ecology and Conservation of Broadland.* Packard Publishing, Chichester.

63. Giles,N. (1992) *Wildlife after Gravel: Twenty Years of Practical Research by the Game Conservancy and ARC.* Game Conservancy, Fordingbridge.

64. Gliwicz,Z.M.(1975) Effect of zooplankton grazing on photosynthetic activity and composition of phytoplankton. *Verhandlungen internationale der Vereinigung theoretische und angewandte Limnologie* **19**, 1490-1497.

65. Gliwicz,Z.M. (1990) Why do cladocerans fail to control algal blooms? *Hydrobiologia* **200/201**, 83-97.

66. Gosling,L.M. (1972) The coypu in East Anglia. *Transactions of the Norfolk and Norwich Naturalists Society* **23**, 49-59.

67. Grimble,P. (1994) Water quality and agriculture: pollution and nitrate leaching. Agricultural Development and Advisory Service, Norwich, UK.

68. Grimm,M.P. (1989) Northern pike (*Esox lucius* L.) and aquatic vegetation, tools in the management of fisheries and water quality in shallow waters. *Hydrobiological Bulletin,* **23**, 59-65.

69. Hameed,H.A. (1989) *Studies on the Limnology of the Trinity Broads, Norfolk.* PhD Thesis, University of East Anglia, Norwich.

70. Hammer,D.A. (Ed) (1989) *Constructed Wetlands for Wastewater Treatment.* Lewis Publishers, Chelsea, Michigan.

71. Hamrin,S.F., Annadotter,H., Linge,H., Persson,A., Romare, P. Soler,T. & Strand,J. (1993) *Sjörestaurering genom mörtfiskreduktion: en förstudie.* (English translation available by R.Aagren, Dept of Limnology, Lund & Inst of Freshwater Research of the Swedish National Board of Fisheries, Lund and Drottningholm).

72. Harper,D. & Pacini,N. (1995) *Practical Manual of Eutrophication Control Methodologies.* National Rivers Authority, Peterborough.

73. Hasler,A.D. (1947) Eutrophication of lakes by domestic drainage. *Ecology* **28**, 383-395.

74. Hawke,C.J. & José,P.V. (1996) *Reedbed Management for Commercial & Wildlife Interests.* Royal Society for the Protection of Birds, Sandy.

75. Haycock,B. & Duigan,C. (1994) Saving stoneworts at Bosherston. *Enact* **2**, 21-23.

76. He,X., Scheurell,D., Soranno,P.A. & Wright,R.A. (1994) Recurrent response patterns of a zooplankton community to whole lake fish manipulation. *Freshwater Biology* **32**, 61-72.

77. Hedley,M.J., Mortvedt,J.J., Bolan,N.S. & Syers,J.K. (1995) Phosphorus fertility management in agroecosystems. 59-92 in H.Tiessen (editor) *Phosphorus in the Global Environment,* J.Wiley, Chichester.

78. Hessen,D. (1986) Introduction of pike (*Esox lucius)* to a small pond: effects on planktivorous fish, zooplankton and algae. *Fauna* **36**, 119-124.

79. Holdway,P.A., Watson,R.A. & Moss,B. (1978) Aspects of the ecology of *Prymnesium parvum* (Haptophyta) and water chemistry in the Norfolk Broads, England. *Freshwater Biology* **8**, 295-311.

80. Holzer,T.J. & Perrow,M.R. (1996). *Practical Methods for Broads Restoration.* LIFE report, Vol 6, Broads Authority, Norwich.

81. Horppila,J. & Kairesalo,T. (1992) Impacts of bleak (*Alburnus alburnus*) and roach (*Rutilus rutilus*) on water quality, sedimentation and internal nutrient loading. *Hydrobiologia* **243/244**, 323-331.

82. Hosper,H. (1989) Biomanipulation, a new perspective for restoring shallow, eutrophic lakes in the Netherlands. *Hydrobiological Bulletin* **23**, 11-19.

83. Hosper,S.H. & Jagtman,E. (1990) Biomanipulation additional to nutrient control for restoration of shallow lakes in the Netherlands. *Hydrobiologia* **200/201**, 523-534.

84. Hosper,H. & Meijer,M.L. (1993) Biomanipulation, will it work for your lake? A simple test for the assessment of chances for clear water, following drastic fish-stock reduction in shallow, eutrophic lakes. *Ecological Engineering* **2**, 63-72.

85. Howard Williams,C. (1981) Studies on the ability of a *Potamogeton pectinatus* community to remove dissolved nitrogen and phosphorus compounds from the water. *Journal of Applied Ecology* **18**, 619-637.

86. Hrbacek,J., Dvorakova,M., Korinek,V., & Prochazkova,L. (1961) Demonstration of the effect of the fish stock on the species composition of zooplankton and the intensity of metabolism of the whole plankton association. *Verhandlungen internationale der Vereinigung theoretische und angewandte Limnologie* **14**, 192-195.

87. Irvine,K., Bales,M., Moss,B. & Snook,D. (1993) Trophic relationships in the ecosystem of a shallow, brackish lake - Hickling Broad, Norfolk, with special reference to the role of *Neomysis integer* Leach. *Freshwater Biology* **29**, 119-139.

88. Irvine,K. Balls,H., & Moss, B. (1990) The entomostracan and rotifer communities associated with submerged plants in the Norfolk Broadland - effects of plant biomass and species composition. *Internationale Revue der gesamten Hydrobiologie* **75**, 121-141.

89. Irvine, K., Moss,B., Bales,M.T. & Snook, D. (1993) The changing ecosystem of a shallow brackish lake, Hickling Broad, Norfolk, U.K. I Trophic relationships with special reference to the role of *Neomysis integer* (Leach). *Freshwater Biology* **29**, 119-139.

90. Irvine, K., Moss,B., & Balls,H.R. (1989) The loss of submerged plants with eutrophication II Relationships between fish and zooplankton in a set of experimental ponds, and conclusions. *Freshwater Biology* **22**, 89-107.

91. Irvine,K., Moss,B. & Stansfield,J. (1990) The potential of artificial refugia for maintaining a community of large-bodied Cladocera against fish predation in a shallow eutrophic lake. *Hydrobiologia* **200/201**, 379-389.

92. Irvine,K., Snook,D. & Moss,B. (1995) Life histories of *Neomysis integer*, and its copepod prey, *Eurytemora affinis*, in a eutrophic and brackish shallow lake. *Hydrobiologia* **304**, 59-76.

93. Jeppesen,E., Jensen,J.P., Kristensen,P., Søndergaard,M., Mortensen,E., Sortkjaer,O. & Olrik,K. (1990a) Fish manipulation as a lake restoration tool in shallow, eutrophic, temperate lakes 2: threshold levels, long-term stability and conclusions. *Hydrobiologia* **200/201**, 219-227.

94. Jeppesen,E., Kristensen,P., Jensen,J.P., Søndergaard,M., Mortensen,E. & Lauridsen,T. (1991) Recovery resilience following a reduction in external phosphorus loading of shallow, eutrophic Danish lakes: duration, regulating factors and methods for overcoming resilience. *Memoria del Istituto Italiano di Idrobiologica* **48**, 127-148.

95. Jeppesen,E., Søndergaard,M., Kanstrup,E., Eriksen,R.B., Hammershoj, M., Petersen,B., Mortensen,E., Jensen,J.P., & Have, A. (1994) Does the impact of nutrients on the biological structure and function of brackish and freshwater lakes differ? *Hydrobiologia* **275/276**, 15-30.

96. Jeppesen,E., Søndergaard,M., Mortensen,E., Kristensen,P., Riemann,B., Jensen,H.J., Müller,J.P., Sortkjaer,O., Jensen,J.P., Christoffersen,K., Bosselmann,S. & Dall,E. (1990b) Fish manipulation as a lake restoration tool in shallow, eutrophic temperate lakes 1: cross-analysis of three Danish case studies. *Hydrobiologia* **200/201**, 205-218.

97. Jeppesen,E., Søndergaard,M., Sortkjaer,O., Mortensen,E., & Kristensen,P. (1990c) Interactions between phytoplankton, zooplankton and fish in a shallow, hypertrophic lake: a study of phytoplankton collapses in Lake Sobygård, Denmark. *Hydrobiologia* **191**, 149-164.

98. Johnes,P.J. (1996) Evaluation and management of the impact of land use change on the nitrogen and phosphorus load delivered to surface waters: the export coefficient modelling approach. *Journal of Hydrology*, **183**,323-349.

99. Johnes,P.J., Moss,B. & Phillips,G. (1996) The determination of total nitrogen and total phosphorus concentrations in freshwaters from land use, stock headage and population data-testing of a model for use in conservation and water quality management. *Freshwater Biology* **36**, 451-473.

100. Kairesalo,T., Horppila,J, Luokkanen,E., Malinen,T. & Peltonen,H. (1997) Direct and indirect mechanisms behind a successful biomanipulation of Lake Vesijärvi. In Harper,D., Brierley,W., Phillips,G. & Ferguson,A. *The Ecological Basis for Lake and Reservoir Management.* Wiley, Chichester, in press.

101. Kennison,G.C.B. (1990) *Aquatic macrophyte surveys of the Norfolk Broads 1989.* Broads Authority, Norwich.

102. Kennison,G.C.B. & Prigmore,D. (1994) *Aquatic macrophyte surveys of the Norfolk Broads 1993.* Broads Authority, Norwich.

103. Keskitalo,J. (1990) Occurrence of vegetated buffer zones along brooks in the catchment area of Lake Tuusulanjärvi, South Finland. *Aqua Fennica* **20**, 55-64.

104. Keto,J. & Sammalkorpi,I. (1988) A fading recovery: a conceptual model for Lake Vesijarvi management and research. *Aqua Fennica* **18**, 193-204.

105. Klinge, M., Grimm,M.P. & Hosper,S.H. (1995) Eutrophication and ecological rehabilitation of Dutch lakes:presentation of a new conceptual framework. *Water Science & Technology,* **31**, 207-218.

106. Klötzli, F. (1971) Biogenous influence on aquatic macrophytes especially *Phragmites communis. Hidrobiologia* **12**, 107-111.

107. Klötzli,F. & Zust,S. (1973) Nitrogen regime in reed beds. *Polske Archivum Hydrobiologie* **20**, 131-136.

108. Kornijow,R., Gulati,R.D. & Ozimek,T. (1995) Food preference of freshwater invertebrates: comparing fresh and decomposed angiosperm and a filamentous alga. *Freshwater Biology* **33**, 205-212.

109. Kristensen,P. & Hansen,H.O. (eds) *European Rivers and Lakes. Assessment of their Environmental State.* European Environmental Agency, Environmental Monographs 1. Copenhagen.

109a. Krug,A. (1993) Drainage history and land use pattern of a Swedish river system- their importance for understanding nitrogen and phosphorus load. *Hydrobiologia* **251**, 285-296.

110. Lamarra,V.A. (1975) Digestive activities of carp as a major contributor to the nutrient loading of lakes. *Verhandlungen der internationale Vereinigung theoretische und angewandte Limnologie* **19**, 2461-2468.

111. Lambert,J.M., Jennings,J.N., Smith,C.T. & Hutchinson,J.N. (1960) *The Making of the Broads: a reconstruction of their origin in the light of new evidence.* Royal Geographical Society, London.

112. Lammens,E.H.R.R. (1988) Trophic interactions in the hypertrophic lake Tjeukermeer; top-down and bottom-up effects in relation to hydrology, predation and bioturbation during the period 1974-1985. *Limnologica (Berlin)* **19**, 81-85.

113. Lammens,E.H.R.R., Gulati,R.D., Meijer,M.L. & Van Donk,E. (1990) The first biomanipulation conference: a synthesis. *Hydrobiologia* **200/201**, 619-628.

114. Lasenby,D.C., Northcote,T.G. & Furst,M (1986) Theory, practice and effects of *Mysis relicta* introductions to North American and Scandinavian lakes. *Canadian Journal of Fisheries and Aquatic Sciences* **43**, 1277-1284.

115. Lauridsen,T.L., Jeppesen,E. & Østergaard Andersen,F. (1993) Colonization of submerged macrophytes in shallow fish manipulated Lake Vaeng: impact of sediment composition and waterfowl grazing. *Aquatic Botany* **46**, 1-15.

116. Lauridsen,T., Jeppesen,E. & Søndergaard,M. (1994) Colonisation and succession of submerged macrophytes in shallow Lake Vaeng during the first five years following fish manipulation. *Hydrobiologia* **275/276**, 233-242.

117. Leah,R.T., Moss,B. & Forrest,D.E. (1978) Experiments with large enclosures in a fertile, shallow brackish lake, Hickling Broad, United Kingdom. *Internationale Revue der gesamten Hydrobiologie* **63**, 291-310.

118. Leah,R.T., Moss,B. & Forrest,D.E. (1980) The role of predation in causing major changes in the limnology of a hyper-eutrophic lake. *Internationale Revue der gesamten Hydrobiologie* **65**, 223-247.

119. Lehman,J.T. (1991) Causes and consequences of Cladocera dynamics in Lake Michigan: implications of species invasion by *Bythrotrephes*. *Journal of Great Lakes Research* **17**, 437-445.

120. Lehman,J.T. & Caceres,C.E. (1993) Food-web responses to species invasion by a predatory invertebrate: *Bythrotrephes* in Lake Michigan. *Limnology and Oceanography* **38**, 879-891.

121. Lowrance,R. (1991) Effects of buffer systems on the movement of N and P from agriculture to streams. pp 87-96 in *International Conference on N,P and Organic Matter. Contributions by Invited International Experts*, Ministry of the Environment, Copenhagen, Denmark.

122. Lynch,M. & Shapiro,J.H. (1981) Predation, enrichment and phytoplankton community structure. *Limnology & Oceanography* **26**, 86-102.

123. Madgwick,F.J. & Phillips,G.L. (1996) *Restoration of the Norfolk Broads. Final Report* Project No LIFE 92-3/UK/031. Broads Authority and National Rivers Authority.

124. Madsen,T.V. & Sand-Jensen, K. (1991) Photosynthetic carbon assimilation in aquatic macrophytes. *Aquatic Botany* **41**, 5-40.

125.Markstein,B. & Sukopp,H. (1980). The waterside vegetation of the Berlin havel. *Garten und Landschaft* **1/80**, 30-36.

126. Marsden,M.W. (1989) Lake restoration by reducing external phosphorus loading: the influence of sediment release. *Freshwater Biology* **21**, 139-162.

127. Meijer,M.-L. (1996) Personal communication.

128. Meijer,M.L., De Haan, M.W., Breukelaar, A.W & Buitenveld,H. (1990) Is reduction of the benthivorous fish an important cause of high transparency following biomanipulation in shallow lakes? *Hydrobiologia* **200/201**, 303-315.

129. Meijer,M.L. & Hosper,H. (1997) Effects of biomanipulation in the large and shallow Lake Wolderwijd, the Netherlands. *Hydrobiologia* (in press).

130. Meijer,M.L., Jeppesen,E., van Donk,E., Moss,B., Scheffer,M., Lammens,E., van Nes,E., van Berkum,J.A., de Jong,G.J. Faafeng,B.A., & Jensen,J.P. (1994a) Long term responses to fish-stock reduction in small shallow lakes: interpretation of five-year results of four biomanipulation cases in The Netherlands and Denmark. *Hydrobiologia* **275/276**, 457-466.

131. Meijer, M.-L., Raat, A.J.P. & Doef, R.W. (1989) Restoration by biomanipulation of the Dutch shallow, eutrophic Lake Bleiswijkse Zoom: first results. *Hydrobiological Bulletin* **23**, 49-57.

132. Meijer,M.L., van Nes,E.H., Lammens,E.H.R.R., Gulati,R.D., Grimm,M.P., Backx,J., Hollebeek,P., Blaauw,E.M. & Breukelaar,A.W. (1994b) The consquences of a drastic fish stock reduction in the large and shallow Lake Wolderwijd, the Netherlands. Can we understand what happened?. *Hydrobiologia* **275/276**, 31-42.

133. Merritt,A. (1994) *Wetlands, Industry and Wildlife.* Wildfowl & Wetlands Trust, Gloucester.

134. Moon,N. & Souter,G. (1994) *Socio-Economic Review of Angling 1994.* National Rivers Authority R & D Note 385.

134a. Moore,J. (1993) *Report on a re-survey of Charophyte beds in Bosherston Lakes, Stackpole NNR, on September 8th 1993.* Field Studies Council Research Centre, Pembroke.

135. Moss,B. (1980) Further studies on the palaeolimnology and changes in the phosphorus budget of Barton Broad, Norfolk. *Freshwater Biology* **10**, 261-279.

136. Moss, B. (1983) The Norfolk Broadland: Experiments in the restoration of a complex wetland. *Biological Reviews* **58**, 521-561.

137. Moss, B. (1987) The Broads. *Biologist* **34**, 7-13.

138. Moss,B. (1988a) The palaeolimnology of Hoveton Great Broad, Norfolk: clues to the spoiling and restoration of Broadland. *Symposia of the Association for Environmental Archaeology, 7, The Exploitation of Wetlands*, 163-191.

139. **Moss,B.** (1988) *Ecology of Freshwaters, Second edition, Man and Medium.* Blackwell Scientific, Oxford.

140. **Moss,B.** (1989) Water pollution and the management of ecosystems: a case study of science and scientist. 401-422 in *Toward a More Exact Ecology.* (Ed by P.J. Grubb and R.H. Whittaker) Thirtieth Symposium of the British Ecological Society. Blackwell Scientific, Oxford.

141. **Moss,B.** (1990) Engineering and biological approaches to the restoration from eutrophication of shallow lakes in which aquatic plant communities are important components. *Hydrobiologia* 200/201, 367-377.

142. **Moss,B.** (1991) The role of nutrients in determining the structure of lake ecosystems and implications for the restoring of submerged plant communities to lakes which have lost them. pp 75-86 in *International Conference on N,P and Organic Matter. Contributions by Invited International Experts,* Ministry of the Environment, Copenhagen, Denmark.

143. **Moss, B.** (1992) The scope for biomanipulation in improving water quality. 73-81 in D.W. Sutcliffe & J.G. Jones (Eds) *Eutrophication: Research and application to water supply.* Freshwater Biological Association, Ambleside.

144. **Moss,B.** (1994) Brackish and freshwater shallow lakes - different systems or variations on the same theme? *Hydrobiologia* 275/276, 1-14.

145. **Moss,B.** (1995) The microwaterscape - a four dimensional view of interactions among water chemistry, phytoplankton, periphyton, macrophytes, animals and ourselves. *Water Science & Technology* 32, 105-116.

146. **Moss,B. & Balls,H.** (1989) Phytoplankton distribution in a floodplain lake and river system II Seasonal changes in the phytoplankton communities and their control by hydrology and nutrient availability *Journal of Plankton Research* 11, 839-867.

147. **Moss, B., Balls,H.R., Irvine,K. & Stansfield,J.** (1986) Restoration of two lowland lakes by isolation from nutrient-rich water sources with and without removal of sediment. *Journal of Applied Ecology* 23, 391-414.

148. **Moss,B., Beklioglu,M., Carvalho,L., Kilinc,S., McGowan,S. & Stephen,D.** (1997) Vertically challenged limnology; contrasts between deep and shallow lakes. *Hydrobiologia* (in press).

149. **Moss,B. & Leah,R.T.** (1982) Changes in the ecosystem of a guanotrophic and brackish shallow lake in eastern England: potential problems in its restoration. *Internationale Revue der gesamten Hydrobiologie* 67, 635-659.

150. **Moss,B., McGowan,S. & Carvalho,L.** (1994) Determination of phytoplankton crops by top-down and bottom-up mechanisms in a group of English lakes, the West Midland Meres. *Limnology & Oceanography* 39, 1020-1030.

151. **Moss,B., Stansfield, J. & Irvine,K.** (1990) Problems in the restoration of a hypertrophic lake by diversion of a nutrient rich inflow. *Verhandlungen der internationale Vereinigung theoretische und angewandte Limnologie* 24, 568-572.

152. **Moss,B., Stansfield, J. & Irvine,K.** (1991) Development of daphnid communities in diatom- and cyanophyte- dominated lakes and their relevance to lake restoration by biomanipulation. *Journal of Applied Ecology* 28, 586-602.

153. **Moss, B., Stansfield,J., Irvine,K., Perrow,M. & Phillips,G.** (1996) Progressive restoration of a shallow lake - a twelve-year experiment in isolation, sediment removal and biomanipulation. *Journal of Applied Ecology* 33, 71-86.

154. **Murtaugh,P.A.** (1981) Selective predation by *Neomysis mercedis* in Lake Washington. *Ecology* 62, 894-900.

155. **National Rivers Authority** (1990) *Toxic Blue Green Algae.* Water Quality Series 2. National Rivers Authority, HMSO, London.

156. **National Rivers Authority** (1993) *Fisheries Strategy.* NRA, Bristol.

157. **National Rivers Authority** (1995) *Pesticides in the Aquatic Environment.* Water Quality Series 26, HMSO, London.

158. **Nero,R.W. & Sprules,W.G.** (1986) Zooplankton species abundance and biomass in relation to occurrence of *Mysis relicta* (Malacostraca; Mysidacea). *Canadian Journal of Fisheries and Aquatic Sciences* 43, 420-434.

159. **Organisation for Economic Cooperation and Development** (1982) *Eutrophication of Waters: Monitoring, Assessment and Control.* OECD, Paris.

160. **Osborne,P.L.** (1980) Prediction of phosphorus and nitrogen concentrations in lakes from both internal and external loading rates. *Hydrobiologia* 69, 229-233.

161. **Osborne,P.L.** (1981) Phosphorus and nitrogen budgets of Barton Broad and predicted effects of a reduction in nutrient loading on phytoplankton biomass in Barton, Sutton and Stalham Broads, Norfolk, United Kingdom. *Internationale Revue der gesamten Hydrobiologie* 66, 171-202.

162. **Osborne,P.L. & Moss,B.** (1977) Palaeolimnology and trends in the phosphorus and iron budgets of an old man-made lake, Barton Broad, Norfolk. *Freshwater Biology* 7, 213-233.

163. **Osborne,P.L. & Phillips,G.L.** (1978) Evidence for nutrient release from the sediments of two shallow and productive lakes. *Verhandlungen internationale der Vereinigung theoretische und angewandte Limnologie* 20, 654-658.

164. **Ozimek,T., Gulati,R.D. & van Donk,E.** (1990) Can macrophytes be useful in biomanipulation of lakes? The Lake Zwemlust example. *Hydrobiologia* 200/201, 399-407.

165. **Palmer,M.A., Bell,S.L. & Butterfield,I.** (1992) A botanical classification of standing waters in Britain:applications for conservation and monitoring. *Aquatic Conservation* 2, 125-144.

166. **Perrow,M.** (1996) in Madgwick,F.J. & Phillips,G.L. (Eds) *Restoration of the Norfolk Broads. Final Report* Project No LIFE 92-3/UK/301. Broads Authority and National Rivers Authority.

167. Perrow,M.R., Moss,B. & Stansfield,J.H. (1994) Trophic interactions in a shallow lake following a reduction in nutrient loading: a long term study. *Hydrobiologia* **275/276**, 43-52.

168. Phillips,G.L. (1977) The mineral nutrient levels in three Norfolk Broads differing in trophic status and an annual mineral content budget for one of them. *Journal of Ecology* **65**,447-474.

169. Phillips,G.L., Eminson,D.F. & Moss,B. (1978) A mechanism to account for macrophyte decline in progressively eutrophicated freshwaters. *Aquatic Botany* **4**, 103-126.

170. Phillips,G. & Moss,B. (1994) *Is biomanipulation a useful technique in lake management?* National Rivers Authority R & D Note 276, Peterborough.

171. Phillips,G.L., Perrow,M. & Stansfield,J. (1996) Manipulating the fish-zooplankton interaction in shallow lakes: a tool for restoration. pp 174-183 in *Aquatic Predators and their Prey*, ed by S.P.R. Greenstreet and M.L. Tasker. Blackwell Science, Oxford.

172. Rees,A.W.G., Hinton,G.C.F., Johnson, F.G., & O'Sullivan,P.E. (1991) The sediment column as a record of trophic status: Examples from Bosherston Lakes, SW Wales. *Hydrobiologia* **214**, 171-180.

173. Reinertsen,H., Jensen,A., Koksvik,J.I., Langeland, A. & Olsen,Y. (1990) Effects of fish removal on the limnetic ecosystem of a eutrophic lake. *Canadian Journal of Fisheries and Aquatic Sciences* **47**, 166-173.

174. Reynolds, C. S. (1971) The ecology of the planktonic blue green algae in the North Shropshire meres, England. *Field Studies* **3**, 409 -432.

175. Reynolds C.S. (1979) The limnology of the eutrophic meres of the Shropshire -Cheshire plain - a review. *Field Studies* **5**, 93-173.

176. Reynolds, C. S. & Bellinger, E. G. (1992) Patterns of abundance and dominance of the phytoplankton of Rostherne Mere, England: evidence from an 18-year data set. *Aquatic Sciences* **54**, 10-36.

177. Reynolds,C.S. (1994) The ecological basis for the successful biomanipulation of aquatic communities. *Archiv für Hydrobiologie* **130**, 1-33.

178. Ripl,W. (1976) Biochemical oxidation of polluted lake sediment with nitrate. A new restoration method. *Ambio* **5**, 312-315.

179. Royal Society (1983) *The Nitrogen Cycle of the United Kingdom*. Royal Society, London.

180. Ryding,S.-O. & Rast,W. (1989) (Editors) *The Control of Eutrophication of Lakes and Reservoirs*. Man & Biosphere Series Vol **1**. UNESCO, Paris & Parthenon Publishing, Carnforth.

181. Sanders,H.O. & Cope,O.B. (1968) Toxicity of several pesticides to two species of cladocerans. *Transactions of the American Fisheries Society* **95**, 165-169.

182. Sanni,S. & Waervågen,S.B. (1990) Oligotrophication as a result of planktivorous fish removal with rotenone in the small, eutrophic Lake Mosvatn, Norway. *Hydrobiologia* **200/201**, 263-274.

183. Sas,H. (1989) *Lake restoration by reduction of nutrient loadings: expectations, experiences, extrapolations*. Academia Verlag Richarz, Sant Augustin.

184. Scheffer, M., Hosper,S.H., Meijer,M.L., Moss,B. & Jeppesen,E. (1993) Alternative equilibria in shallow lakes. *Trends in Ecology and Evolution* **8**, 275-279.

185. Schindler,D.W. (1977) Evolution of phosphorus limitation in lakes. *Science* **195**, 260-262.

186. Schindler,D.W. (1978) Factors regulating phytoplankton production and standing crop in the world's freshwaters. *Limnology and Oceanography* **23**, 478-486.

187. Schriver,P., Bøgestrand,J., Jeppesen,E. & Søndergaard,M. (1995) Impact of submerged macrophytes on fish-zooplankton-phytoplankton interactions:large scale enclosure experiments in a shallow eutrophic lake. *Freshwater Biology* **33**, 255-270.

188. Schröder,R. (1979) Decline of reedswamps in Lake Constance. *Symposia Biologiae Hungaricae* **19**,43-48.

189. Schutten,H.(1996) in Madgwick,F.J. & Phillips,G.L. (Eds) *Restoration of the Norfolk Broads. Final Report* Project No LIFE 92-3/UK/301. Broads Authority and National Rivers Authority.

190. Sears,J. & Hunt,A. (1991) Lead poisoning in mute swans, *Cygnus olor*, in England. In Sears,J. & Bacon,P.J. (eds) *Proceedings of the Third IWRB International Swan Symposium, Oxford 1989. Wildfowl Supplement No 1*.

191. Serafy,J.E. & Harrell,R.M. (1993) Behavioural response of fishes to increasing pH and dissolved oxygen: field and laboratory observations. *Freshwater Biology* **30**,53-61.

192. Shapiro,J. (1990) Biomanipulation:the next phase - making it stable. *Hydrobiologia* **200/201**, 13-27.

193. Shapiro,J. (1990) Current beliefs regarding dominance by blue-greens: the case for the importance of CO_2 and pH. *Verhandlungen internationale der Vereinigung theoretische und angewandte Limnologie* **24**, 38-54.

194. Shapiro,J., Lamarra, V. & Lynch,M. (1975) Biomanipulation: an ecosystem approach to lake restoration. 85-96. In Brezonik,P.L & Fox,J.L. (eds) *Water Quality Management through Biological Control*. Report Env 07-75-1, Univ of Florida, Gainsville.

195. Shapiro,J. & Wright,D.J. (1984) Lake restoration by biomanipulation:Round lake, Minnesota, the first two years. *Freshwater Biology* **14**, 371-383.

196. Sharpley,A.N., Hedley,M.J., Sibbesen,E., Hillbricht-Ilkowska,A., House,W.A. & Ryszkowski,L. (1995) Phosphorus transfers from terrestrial to aquatic ecosystems. 171-200 in H.Tiessen (editor) *Phosphorus in the Global Environment*, J.Wiley, Chichester.

196a Sharpley,A.N., Chapra,S.C., Wedephol,R., Sims,J.T., Daniel,T.C. & Reddy,K.R. (1994) Managing agricultural phosphorus for protection of surface waters: issues and options. *Journal of Environmental Quality* 23, 437-451.

197. Simons,J., Ohm,M., Daalder,R., Boers,P. & Rip,W. (1994) Restoration of Botshol (The Netherlands) by reduction of external nutrient load: recovery of a characean community with *Chara connivens*. *Hydrobiologia* **275/276**, 243-253.

198. Smith,S. (1995) The coypu in Britain. *British Wildlife* 6, 279-285.

199. Søndergaard,M., Jeppesen,E. & Berg,S. (1997) Pike (*Esox lucius* L.) stocking as a biomanipulation tool 2. Effects on lower trophic levels in Lake Lyng (Denmark). *Hydrobiologia* (in press).

200. Søndergaard,M., Jeppesen,E., Mortensen,E., Dall,E., Kristensen,P., & Sortkjaer,O. (1990) Phytoplankton biomass reduction after planktivorous fish reduction in a shallow, eutrophic lake; a combined effect of reduced internal P-loading and increased zooplankton grazing. *Hydrobiologia* **200/201**, 229-240.

201. Stansfield,J.H., Moss,B. & Irvine,K. (1989) The loss of submerged plants with eutrophication III Potential role of organochlorine pesticides: a palaeoecological study. *Freshwater Biology* 22, 109-132.

202. Stephen,D., Moss,B. & Phillips,G.L (1997) Do rooted macrophytes increase sediment phosphorus release. Hydrobiologia (in press).

203. Stevenson,A.C., Juggins,S., Birks,H.J.B., Anderson,D.S., Anderson,N.J., Battarbee,R.W., Berge,F., Davis,R.B., Flower,R.J., Haworth,E.Y., Jones,V.J., Kingston,J.C., Kreiser,A.M., Line,J.M., Munro,M.A.R. & Renberg,I. (1991) *The Surface Waters Acidification Project Palaeolimnology Programme: Modern Diatom/Lake-water Chemistry Data-sets.* ENSIS Ltd., London.

204. Timms,R.M. & Moss, B. (1984) Prevention of growth of potentially dense phytoplankton populations by zooplankton grazing, in the presence of zooplanktivorous fish, in a shallow wetland ecosystem. *Limnology & Oceanography* 29, 472-486.

205. Ulrich,K.E. & Burton,T.M. (1985) The effects of nitrate, phosphate and potassium fertilization on growth and nutrient uptake patterns of *Phragmites australis* (Cav.) Trin. ex Steudel. *Aquatic Botany* 21, 53-62.

206. Van Donk,E., De Deckere,E., Klein Breteler,G.P., & Meulemans,J.T. (1994) Herbivory by waterfowl and fish on macrophytes in a biomanipulated lake:effects on long term recovery. *Verhandlungen internationale der Vereinigung theoretische und angewandte Limnologie*, 25, 2139-2143.

207. Van Donk,E., Grimm,M.P., Gulati,R.D., Heuts,P.G.M., De Kloet, W.A. & van Liere,L. (1990) First attempt to apply whole lake food-web manipulation on a large scale in the Netherlands. *Hydrobiologia* **200/201**, 291-301.

208. Van Donk,E. & Gulati,R.D (1995) Transition of a lake to turbid state six years after biomanipulation: mechanisms and pathways. *Water Science & Technology* 32, 197-206.

209. Van Donk,E., Gulati,R.D. & Grimm,M.P. (1989) Food web manipulation in Lake Zwemlust:positive and negative effects during the first two years. *Hydrobiological Bulletin* 23, 19-34.

210. Van Donk,E., Gulati,R.D., Iedema,A. & Meulemans,J.T. (1993) Macrophyte-related shifts in the nitrogen and phosphorus contents of the different trophic levels in a biomanipulated shallow lake. *Hydrobiologia* 251, 19-26.

211. Venugopal, M.N. & Winfield,I.J. (1993) The distribution of juvenile fishes in a hypereutrophic pond: can macrophytes potentially offer a refuge for zooplankton? *Journal of Freshwater Biology* 8, 389-396.

212. Vijverberg,J. (1982) Production, population biology and diet of *Neomysis integer* (Leach) in a shallow Frisian lake (The Netherlands). *Hydrobiologia* **93**, 41-51.

213. Vollenweider,R.A. (1968) *The scientific basis of lake and stream eutrophication, with particular reference to phosphorus and nitrogen as eutrophication factors.* Technical Report of the OECD, Paris DAS/CSI 68.

214. Vought,L.B.-M., Dahj,J., Lauge Pedersen,J. & Lacoursiere,C. (1994) Nutrient retention in riparian ecotones. *Ambio* 23, 342-348.

215. Vought,L.B.-M., Pinay,G., Fuglsang,A. & Ruffinoni,C. (1995) Structure and function of buffer strips from a water quality perspective in agricultural landscapes. *Landscape & Urban Planning* 31, 323-331.

216. Wilson,H.M., O'Sullivan,P.E. & Gibson,M.T. (1995) Analysis of current policies and alternative strategies for the reduction of nutrient loads on eutrophicated lakes:the example of Slapton Ley, Devon. *Aquatic Conservation* 3, 239-252.

217. Winfield,I.J. (1990) Predation from above: observations on the activities of piscivorous birds at a shallow eutrophic lake. *Hydrobiologia* 191, 223-231.

218. Wium-Andersen,S.U., Anthoni,C., Cristophersen,C. & Houen,G. (1982) Allelopathic effects on phytoplankton by substances isolated from aquatic macrophytes (Charales). *Oikos* 39, 187-190.

219. Zaret,T.M. & Suffern,J.S. (1976) Vertical migration in zooplankton as a predator avoidance mechanism. *Limnology and Oceanography* 21, 804-813.

Index and Glossary of Terms

Agricultural Development and Advisory Service 61,90,155

Agriculture 16,40

-Act 60

-Code of Good Agricultural Practice 41,76,77

-consequences of intensive 40,41

-and eutrophication 16,40,41

-traditional methods 77

Alder 101,109

Algae 16,17, 21, 32, 114, 133

A general term applied to photosynthetic organisms that are generally aquatic, may be microscopic or very large (seaweeds), may have a bacteria-like cell structure, or one like all other organisms, contain chlorophyll a and often a variety of other pigments that give them characteristic colours (blue-green, red, green, yellow-green etc, and which, when they reproduce sexually, produce sex cells in structures that are not bounded by sterile (non-reproducing) cells. They evolved early, but are incorrectly described as 'simple, or primitive plants'.

-blooms 17, 39

A much misused term. Blooms are surface scums of blue-green algae (q.v.) which accumulate under calm weather conditions from populations that were previously distributed through the water. They are formed only by those blue green algae that have mechanisms that give them positive buoyancy and the bloom may be a reflection of breakdown of a mechanism that otherwise maintains these algae at depths optimal for their growth. However, the term has been much used to describe any large growth of algae, and, increasingly, any, even moderate, growth of almost any microorganism in waters. It is thus rapidly becoming meaningless.

-blue green 17, 73, 74, 90, 126, 130, 135, 139, 140, 149, 152

A group of largely microscopic, photosynthetic organisms with a bacterial structure (prokaryote), but containing chlorophyll a and a photosynthesis biochemistry unlike other bacteria but similar to that of other algae and higher plants. Alternative names are blue-green bacteria, cyanophytes, cyanobacteria, or, probably the most suitable, cyanoprokaryotes. Blue and red pigments, contained within them, give an often characteristic colour.

-dominance in shallow lakes 43,44, 45

-filamentous 52,100

-thalloid 100,128, 146

Forming three dimensional structures usually easily visible to the naked eye.

-toxic 16, 42, 49, 54

Allelopathy 31, 45

Production of substances by one organism that inhibit the growth, activity or reproduction of another.

Alternative stable states 18, 19, 44, 45, 47, 91, 137

Potential existence of markedly different biological communities under the same external environmental conditions.

-buffers 45, 47

-role of nutrients 45, 62-64

-switches 46,47, 50

Alum 85

American large-mouthed bass 94

Amino acids 22

Components of proteins. They are soluble in water and contain an amino (NH_2) group.

Ammonium 22, 29, 30, 40, 73, 82, 102, 121, 134, 136, 138

Anaerobiosis 29, 30

Absence of oxygen

Anecdotal evidence 55

Aquatic plants 26, 15, 19, 20, 34, 42, 47

-emergent 108, 109, 112, 113, 138

-floating 110, 112

-floating leaved 47, 109, 110, 112, 138

-links with other organisms 31, 34

-loss of 15, 17, 47

-planting 112-114

-protection of inocula against birds 63, 114, 115

-re-establishment 63, 64, 107, 111

-refuges for zooplankters 33, 43, 107

-reproduction 110

-sediment stabilisation 34, 44

-submerged 47, 109, 112, 114, 126, 131, 132, 139, 144, 152

-supply 112, 113

-vulnerability 26,27

Bacteria 29, 39

Barton Broad 44, 89, 90, 125, 152-155, 157

BATNEEC 76

An approach to pollution control where the Best Available Technology, Not Entailing Excessive Cost is used to minimise pollution of the environment as a whole having regard to the best practicable environmental option available (BPEO). The term is defined in the Environmental Protection Act 1990 in relation to discharge made from the more polluting industries under Integrated Pollution Control (IPC). A useful approach when it is necessary to minimise the input of a pollutant to the environment, rather than achieve a set standard by dilution, dispersion and natural degradation in the environment.

Biodiversity 58,60

The array of different living organisms. The simpler term 'diversity' served perfectly well until recently.

-action plan 54

Biomanipulation 19, 47, 50, 63, 64, 90, 93, 148

Deliberate alteration of the biological community to achieve a desirable and planned change in environment.

-addition of piscivores 93,94

-by drawdown 94, 96, 97, 138

-degree necessary 99

-in enclosures 102, 103

-inadvertent 95, 127, 90, 91

-fish removal 96, 128, 130, 141

-partial fish removal 93, 98, 99

-prognosis for success 104,105

-public relations 104, 145

Birds 35

-components of ecosystem 35

-grazing 129, 132, 139

-piscivorous 35,95, 96

-removal 70, 71

Bladderwort 46

Bog 36,37

A plant community that occurs in acid, waterlogged onditions.

-succession to 37

Bottom-up effects 119

Mechanisms by which organisms at the lower (photosynthetic) levels of food webs determine the nature and production of those in the intermediate and upper levels.

Bream 35, 44, 93, 98, 119, 120, 141, 151

-common 118, 144

-white 118

British Trust for Ornithology 71

Broads 18, 25, 51, 52, 55, 56, 71, 76, 88, 98, 99, 124, 143, 144, 152

"The Broads" is a major wetland in eastern England of national park status. The term includes the Broads Authority executive area - a mosaic of marshes, fens, carr woodland, interconnected rivers and around 40 shallow lakes. These lakes or "broads" were formed by the digging of peat between the ninth and thirteenth centuries.

Broads Authority 156

Broads Environmentally Sensitive Area 84

Buffer mechanisms 19, 153

Devices which tend to preserve one of a series of alternative stable states against the action of switches (q.v.) tending to change the present state to an alternative one.

-phytoplankton dominance 43-45

-plant dominance 31-34, 45

Buffer zones 79-81, 84, 151

Areas of natural, semi-natural or uncultivated vegetation bordering streams, rivers or lakes or otherwise intercepting water being delivered from the catchment to the water body.

Bulrush 109

Bythrotrephes 103

Carp 54, 55, 60, 68, 104, 105

-Chinese grass 48, 54, 67

-common 47, 48, 63, 67, 69, 100, 118, 129

-Crucian 118

-damage caused by 69, 70

-fishing attractions 119

Catchment area 21, 24

The land (and including the streams, rivers, wetlands and lakes) from which water runs off to supply a particular location in a freshwater system. One might thus talk of the catchment of a particular point along a river, or at its mouth, or of a particular lake. In North America, the term watershed is often used instead of catchment area. In the UK, watershed means the line separating two adjacent catchments.

-role of geology 24

Chaos 35, 36

Chara 59, 134, 141, 142, 144, 146, 148, 152

Charophytes 45, 57, 58, 62, 88, 124, 142, 144, 145, 146

A group of green algae, visible to the naked eye, with a characteristic structure in which the 'stems' are very large single cells, from which whorls of similarly constructed branches emerge. Charophytes are anchored in sediments by branching cellular systems, not roots. They often deposit marl (calcium carbonate) giving them a rough texture and the common name of 'stoneworts', though not all do this. They also have a characteristic smell, which some people describe as 'garlicy'.

Chemistry 21

-sediment 29, 30, 42, 43, 84-87

-soil 82

-water 21-23, 45, 73, 74

Chlorophyll a 41, 43, 121, 134, 145, 149, 151

The major photosynthetic pigment of algae and plants. Often used as a measure of the biomass of the former.

-measure of amount of phytoplankton 41

-phosphorus relation 43

Cladocera 32, 34, 47

Water fleas. A group of crustaceans up to a few mm long, which either filter particles from water for food or grasp larger particles such as smaller animals. The best known genus is Daphnia.

Clays 22

Cockshoot Broad 100, 107, 124-128, 142

Code of Good Agricultural Practice 76-78, 83

Colloids 22

Common reed 51, 108

Conductivity 66

A measure of the total dissolved ionic content of water, reflected in its ability to conduct electricity.

Constructed wetlands 80, 81, 89, 151

Artificial swampy habitats designed to improve the quality of water passed through them.

Coot 35, 112, 114, 127, 132, 134, 140

Copepodites (see Copepods)

The penultimate five, out of a total of twelve, life history stages of copepods.

Copepods 32

A group of crustaceans more diverse in the sea than freshwaters. Some species filter particles for food, others grasp larger particles such as smaller animals. The life history comprises six successively larger naupliar and then five copepodite stages before the sexually reproducing adults are formed as the twelfth stage.

Cormorant 35, 95

Coypu 48, 51, 66

Crustacea 31, 56

One of the several jointed-legged groups of animals that comprise the Arthropoda. Crustaceans have no particular set body pattern, as do the insects and spiders, often form a shell or carapace rich in calcium and are predominantly aquatic. They include the water fleas, copepods and mysids.

Cryptomonads 130

A group of brown coloured flagellate algae, very common in the phytoplankton.

Dace 118

Daphnia 32, 33, 35, 47, 49, 66, 67, 93, 99, 102, 103, 104, 107, 132, 133, 137, 139, 142, 145

D.hyalina 127, 128, 136, 138, 145

D.magna 126, 127, 128, 135, 136, 138, 145

Denitrification 23, 29, 34

Conversion by bacteria of nitrate ions to nitrogen gas. The nitrate is used as an oxidising agent to release energy from organic matter.

Detergents 77, 78

Diatoms 56, 88, 130, 149

A group of algae, brown or yellow coloured, that is very common in natural waters. The cell wall is made of polymerised silicate, forming a sort of glass and is readily preserved in sediments, when the organic part of the organisms decays. Because of a long interest in this group by naturalists, its ecology is reasonably well known and diatoms in fossil deposits can be used to interpret changes in past environments.

Dicotyledons 109

One of two main groups of flowering plants, producing two first leaves (cotyledons) on seed germination and generally a plant that has broad, net-veined leaves, thereafter.

Diffuse sources 77, 78, 82

Supplies of nutrients or other pollutants that come from a myriad of small-sized locations (e.g the land surface) as opposed to a clearly located source (e.g. a sewage treatment works) that is individually usually comparatively large.

Discharge 61

The amount of water delivered by a stream or catchment in a given time.

Diversity

See 'Biodiversity'.

DNA 120

Deoxyribosenucleic acid, the chemical component of genes.

Duck 55, 67, 70, 112

Duckweed 50, 110

Dyke 126, 127, 129

Local term in Eastern England for a ditch, small stream or artificial channel.

Eel 118, 119, 144

Electrofishing 97, 98, 128, 144

Use of an electric field created in freshwaters to stun and catch fish.

English Nature 54,71

Statutory body responsible for nature conservation in England.

Environment Act 70, 158

Environment Agency 15, 22, 62, 67, 70, 85, 89, 90, 96, 121, 156, 158

Environmental Quality Standard 75, 76

The concentration of a substance designated to protect an identified 'use' or aspect of a water body.

Environmentally Sensitive Areas 68, 69, 81

Euphotic zone 26

The part of a water body in which net growth of photosynthetic organisms is not limited by light availability.

European Environment Agency 115

European Union

-Dangerous Substances Directive 85

Ecological Quality of Waters Directive 76

-Habitats Directive 54

-Nitrates Directive 83,84

-Urban Wastewater Treatment Directive 75, 76, 78, 88

Eutrophication 15, 16, 41, 73, 84

The process in which there is an increase in the rate of addition of substances of nitrogen and phosphorus to a natural system, usually aquatic. The term is currently being used by some people rather more loosely to emphasise the problematic consequences of this process. However, although there are always at least subtle biological consequences of addition of even small quantities of nutrients, this may not result necessarily in a perceived problem.

-agriculture 15, 16, 40-42

-consequences 16, 17

-disturbance of catchment 46

-sewage effluent 15, 16, 39-41

Exotic species 110, 119

Species introduced by humans, deliberately or accidentally, into an area where they are not native. Often, lacking the native predators, parasites and other constraints that controlled their populations within their natural range, they may increase in numbers and cause severe problems.

Export Coefficient Modelling 42, 61, 62

A technique for calculating nutrient loadings and concentrations in a stream or lake from a knowledge of land use, numbers of stock and number of people in the catchment, stream discharge and the rates at which the nutrients are leached or excreted from the various sources.

Fish 32, 33

-barriers 100-103

-direct damage to plants 47, 48

-farms 78, 79

-feeding on *Daphnia 32, 33*

-feeding on zooplankton 32

-handling 96,120

-kills 49, 90, 91

-ponds 69

-recycling of nutrients 33

-removal 93, 96-99

Fisheries management strategies 119

Floodplain wetlands 94

Areas of marsh, swamp, wet grassland and open water, maintained by the rise and fall of a river as it rises from its dry-season or summer channel to occupy the full width of its natural bed, its floodplain.

-loss of 94

Flushing 103

Replacement of the water in a lake by incoming stream, river or ground water.

Frogbit 46

Fyke nets 98, 130, 141

Non-return traps for fish curious enough to enter them.

Geese 35, 51, 70

-Canada 48, 70, 71

-Egyptian 67

-Greylag 48, 67, 70, 71

Geotextiles 113, 114

Open weaved matting made from natural, or more usually man-made fibres, laid and pegged down to stabilise eroding banks.

Gill nets 98, 122, 130

Fine nets suspended passively in the water into which fish swim and become trapped as their heads pass through. The body is wider and cannot pass and the fish cannot extricate itself because the gill covers catch on the netting as it attempts to move backwards. Most fish are lethally damaged.

Grazing

-on periphyton 31

-on phytoplankton 31, 32

-on plants 34, 35

Guanotrophy 74

Eutrophication (q.v.) by the excreta of birds which feed outside the lake but excrete into it when they rest or roost.

Gudgeon 144

Haemoglobin 135

Iron-containing protein pigment capable of storing oxygen.

Herbicides 47, 48, 66

Substances used to kill plants.

Hickling Broad 49, 56, 67, 68

Hollyweed 45, 109

Hornwort 115

Hover 151

Term used locally in Eastern England for floating mats of reedswamp.

Hoveton Great Broad 57, 101-103

-diatom diagram 58

-sediment core 57

Inflorescence 109

The flower or massed group of flowers of a higher plant.

Iron dosing 85, 86

Addition of iron compounds to lake water or sedment to precipitate phosphorus compounds.

Lake

-Bosherston 125, 146-148

-Brabrant 90,150

-Breukelveen 100

-Finjasjön 125, 149-152

-Frederiksborg Castle 132

-Krankesjön 65, 66

-Lillesjön 86

-Little Mere 125, 134-136

-Søbygaard 132, 133

-Trejkanten 86

-Trummen 89-91

-Vaeng 125, 134-136

-Wolderwijd 141-143

-Zwemlust 125, 137-140

Lakes 15, 17

-Cumbrian 24, 25

-deep 24

-eutrophic 24

A term impossible to define precisely, but conveying the sense of high fertility and productivity.

-glacial 17, 24

-human damage to 15, 39

-human use of 53-55

-man-made 25

-mesotrophic 24

A term impossible to define precisely, but conveying the sense of modest fertility and productivity.

-morphometry 24, 25

-oligotrophic 24

A term impossible to define precisely, but conveying the sense of low fertility and productivity.

-origin 24, 25

-shallow 15, 18, 30

-trophic state 24

A term generally describing the degree of fertility or productivity of a lake.

Legislation 67, 69, 71, 75, 76, 77, 81, 82, 83, 85, 89, 93, 96, 120, 158

Leptodora 163

Light absorption in water 26, 27 109

Limestone 146

Littoral zone 27, 28

The part of a lake which is shallow enough for sufficient light to penetrate to the bottom to support growth of bottom-living algae or larger plants. It includes not only the bottom itself but also the overlying water.

Loading 19, 42, 61, 140

The amount of nutrient supplied to a water body in a given time (e.g. kg nitrogen per year). It may also be expressed per unit area (e.g. kg phosphorus per metre squared per year) and may be attributed to a particular source (e.g effluent loading) as well used for the total supply.

-external 42, 61-63, 91, 132

Loading from the catchment area

-internal 62, 63, 84, 90, 91

Redistribution of nutrients within the lake itself, usually from stores in the sediments to the overlying water.

Marl 26, 102

Complex mixture of mostly calcium carbonate, other inorganic precipitates and organic matter deposited on a leaf surface as a result of the chemical changes caused by the leaf during photosynthesis. The basis of these is that as the leaf takes up carbon dioxide or bicarbonate ions, increases in local pH occur, which favour carbonate formation. In calcium rich waters, the carbonate then precipitates onto the leaf. Eventually the precipitate may form a marl sediment when the plant dies.

Mere Mere 134, 135

A not unattractive small lake in Cheshire, UK.

Methane 30

Ministry of Agriculture, Fisheries and Food 76, 83

Monitoring 170, 120, 122

-detailed 121

-minimal 121

Monocotyledons 109

One of two main groups of flowering plants, producing a single first leaf (cotyledon) on seed germination and generally a plant that has narrow, parallel-veined leaves, thereafter. Includes grasses, sedges and rushes.

Morphometry 24, 26

The physical features (area, depth, shape, profile) of a lake basin.

Mysid shrimps 103

A group of crustaceans found mostly in the sea. A few species occur in freshwaters.

Mysis 103

National Nature Reserve 134, 147

An area designated by the statutory conservation agencies in the UK as representative of a major ecosystem type and of considerable conservation importance. It is given special legal protection.

National Rivers Authority 76, 156

Agency responsible in England and Wales , until 1996, for the regulation of water use. It was combined that year with the Pollution Inspectorate and the Waste Disposal agencies to form a single Environment Agency (q.v.).

Nature conservation 54, 58, 119

Nauplii (See Copepod)

Early life history stages of copepods (q.v.).

Neomysis integer 103, 104, 129, 142

Niche 28

The position occupied by a species in a community. 'Position' includes not only the physical location but the activity of the species (as predator, prey, parasite or scavenger) and its links with other species in any other way.

Nitrate 16, 22, 29, 40, 73, 86, 121, 134, 138

-Sensitive areas 84

-Vulnerable Zones 83, 84

Nitrilotriacetic acid 78

Nitrogen 16, 21, 22, 34, 39, 41, 61, 74, 79, 82, 145

-agriculture 16

-compounds 22

-dissolved 22

-fixation 73

Conversion of atmospheric or dissolved nitrogen gas to combined form (usually as amino groups (see amino acid) by specific bacteria and blue green algae, either free living or in physical association with larger species (e.g the root nodules of leguminous plants).

-fixing blue-green algae 73

-fixing bacteria 22

-limitation 41

-particulate 22

-total 22, 57, 90, 117, 151

-transfer between land and water 23, 61, 83

-volatilisation from stock units 82

Norfolk Broads (see Broads)

North West Midland Meres 24, 25

Nucleic acids 22

Substances containing genetic information in organisms or used in transferring this information within the cell. See DNA.

Nutrient loading (see also Loading)

-changes in 42

-relationship to loss of plants 45, 46

Nutrients 73

Substances absolutely required by living organisms. In the context of this book, the term is largely confined to substances of nitrogen and phosphorus, which are generally scarce in available forms in relation to need, but substances of about 20 elements are ultimately needed for growth and maintenance. Most are in relatively abundant supply.

-control 73, 124

-cycling 29, 30

-internal diversion 147

-internal loading 30, 62, 63, 84, 91

-limiting 22-24

-loadings (See Loading)

-risk of restoration reversion 46, 60, 62

-sewage (See Sewage)

-sources, diffuse 78, 79, 80, 81 84

-sources, point 74-78, 82

-stock 76, 77

Nymphaeids (See Water Lily)

Aquatic plants rooted on the bottom but with large, rounded floating leaves. They may also have completely submerged leaves. Most typical are the water lilies.

Oligochaetes 31

Thin worms, a few mm or cm long, often pinkish from contained haemoglobin, found in sediments. They are segmented, like earthworms.

Ormesby Broad 125, 143-145

Oxidised microzone 29, 30

Surface few mm of sediment into which oxygen can penetrate rapidly enough from the overlying water to maintain aerobic conditions. Usually brown in colour reflecting the presence of oxidised iron compounds. The underlying sediment is black and deoxygenated by bacterial activity.

Palaeolimnology 56, 57, 65, 153, 154, 155

Study of the past history of lakes (GK, limnos) from an investigation of the contents of their sediments. 'Limnology' includes also the study of the current characteristics of freshwaters.

Parasites 104

Peat 27, 37, 57

Organic remains, largely of plants, preserved in bulk under waterlogged conditions.

-digging 55, 124, 152

Pelagial zone 28

That part of a lake so deep that light cannot penetrate sufficiently to support growth of plants or algae on the bottom. The term includes both the bottom and the overlying water. See 'littoral zone' for contrast.

Perch 33, 67, 93, 98, 99, 100, 118, 119, 144

Periphyton 26, 27, 31, 46, 48, 57, 103

Complex of attached algae, bacteria, Protozoa, organic detritus and marl (q.v.) which develops on plant surfaces underwater. The term is increasingly used to include similar complexes on any underwater surface (e.g rocks, sediments, beer bottles). Because 'phytos' is very definitely Greek for plant, this reflects inadequacies in the linguistic training of current generations. (See also 'eutrophication').

-grazing on 31

-shading by 26

Pesticides 47, 48, 67, 76

Substances deliberately introduced into the environment to kill organisms deleterious to crop plants.

pH 57, 88, 132, 135

A measure of acidity, defined as minus the logarithm to the base 10 of the molar concentration of hydrogen ions. The scale runs from 0 to 14, with each successive unit representing a tenfold decline in hydrogen ion concentration. Thus the lower the pH value, the higher the acidity.

-and fish feeding 34

Phosphate 16, 29, 40

-detergents 73, 77

-effluent 16, 40, 42, 44, 73-75, 76-78, 126

-run off from land 16, 22, 23, 40-42, 78, 79, 143

-solubility 22, 23, 30, 73, 79

-sugar 22

Phosphorus 16, 17, 21, 30, 39, 41, 61, 73, 74, 76, 79, 84, 126, 130, 134, 146, 141, 142, 153

-chlorophyll relationship 43

-compounds 22

-control 73-81, 126, 134, 144, 150, 153, 154

-dissolved 22, 78, 102, 121, 127

- human population 16

-particulate 22

-stripping 44, 74, 75, 78, 91, 149, 153

-total 22, 23, 57, 60, 75, 90, 117, 121, 127, 130, 133, 138, 141, 142, 143, 150, 151, 153

-transfer between land and water 23, 61

Phytoplankton 16, 20, 26, 30, 31, 32, 45, 47, 47, 51, 57, 90, 102, 121, 127, 130, 139, 144, 153

Community of largely microscopic algae suspended or floating in natural waters. Most species are denser than water and tend to sink, but are maintained in suspension by wind-generated water currents. Some species have flagella, with which they move and are able to counteract their tendency to sink. Only a few species have buoyancy mechanisms and actually float. These are primarily the bloom (qv)-forming blue green algae.

Pike 33, 35, 67, 93, 94, 105, 118, 119, 138, 140, 141, 144,

Pikeperch (syn, zander) 35, 50, 93, 118, 119

Piscivore 34, 47, 49, 67, 100, 117, 119

Animal that eats fish

-to zooplanktivore ratio 48, 49 63, 99, 133, 142

Point sources 73, 82

Supplies of nutrients or other pollutants that come from well-defined clearly located origins (e.g. a sewage treatment works) that are individually usually comparatively large compared with a myriad of small-sized locations (e.g the land surface). See 'Diffuse source'.

Polder 141

Low-lying area, reclaimed from the sea, in the Netherlands.

Polyphemus 103

Pondweed 46, 146

-sago 46

Potentially Damaging Operations 76

Actions by a tenant or landowner that may, in the opinion of the statutory conservation agency, endanger the conservation value of a Site of Special Scientific Interest.

Pristine state 23, 37

Nature of an ecosystem that is not influenced by any human activity, or at least by technologically sophisticated activity. In many parts of the world, traditional, sustainable influences on the system might be construed as part of the pristine state.

Protein 22, 36, 73

Protozoa 29, 39

Microscopic unicellular or sometimes colonial animals.

Prymnesium parvum 49

Pumped drainage 49

System of draining land by active pumping, often against gravity. Such land is thus generally lower than the water body to which the water is pumped.

Rainbow trout 118

Ranworth Broad 86

Reconstruction of the past 56, 57

Reed (See Comm on Reed)

-die back 50, 51

-planting 113, 114

Reedmace 108

Reedswamp 27, 37, 50, 51, 52, 56, 65, 74, 80, 98, 104

Vegetation dominated by emergent plants, often tall grasses, rooted in water standing substantially above the soil surface for at least part of the year.

-loss of 51, 52

-nutrient transfers 31

Refuge concept 100, 101

Provision of habitat by aquatic plants in which predation rates of fish on zooplankton, or fish on other fish, are reduced compared with those in the open water.

Rehabilitation 53

Improvement in the amenity or conservation value of a habitat falling short of the potential maximum possibilities.

Replacement 53, 55

Creation of entirely new habitats as substitutes for others damaged beyond practicable rehabilitation or restoration.

Restoration 17, 20, 53, 117

Strictly the process of returning a habitat to its pristine state (q.v.) under current environmental conditions or some former pristine state. This is usually impossible for theoretical and practical reasons. However, the term is widely used in the sense of 'Rehabilitation' (q.v.).

-failure 18

-permanency 20, 117, 118

-stability of 117

-steps in 63, 64

-strategy 63,64

Rhizomes 112, 113, 114

Underground stems, often storing nutrients and energy, from which many perennial plants propagate, following the winter or dry-season period of little growth.

Riplox 86, 87

Process of sealing sediments against release of phosphate by injecting chemicals.

River corridor vegetation 81

Natural (usually woody) or semi-natural vegetation bordering streams or rivers.

Roach 35, 93, 98, 118, 119, 120, 141, 144, 151

Rock 21, 24

-**igneous** 24

Formed from cooling of molten lavas within or at the Earth's surface.

-**metamorphic** 24

Formed from the heating, often under pressure, then cooling of sedimentary rocks.

-**sedimentary** 24

Formed from the accumulation, compression and sometimes moderate heating of debris of other rocks or organic deposits laid down originally as sediments in a marine or freshwater basin.

-**weathering** 24

Process of biological,chemical and physical decomposition of rocks.

Rockland Broad 51

Rostherne Mere 25, 134

Rotenone 96, 100

Natural product of the African derris plant, used for poisoning fish.

Rotifers 31, 32, 33

A group of small, multicellular animals which feed on small particles in natural waters, often by a ring of cilia whose individual movements give the impression of a rotating wheel. The currents so created bring a supply of particles to the mouth of the animal.

Rudd 35, 99, 100, 118, 138, 139, 144

Ruffe 141, 144

Salinity 48, 49, 57, 65, 66, 103, 104, 129, 142

Concentration of salts in a natural water. Sea water has about 35 grams per litre, freshwaters only a few percent of this.

Sallows 109

Salmon and Freshwater Fisheries Act 67, 96, 120

Scare lines 98, 99, 144

Ropes bearing coloured flutters towed through the water to drive fish into waiting nets.

Scottish Environmental Protection Agency 67

Secchi disc 26, 121, 130, 131, 133, 137, 139

White circular plate lowered into waters to measure visibility through the water column (transparency).

Sediments 26, 154

-aerobic 29

-anaerobic 29

-chemistry 29, 88, 108

-disposal 87, 88, 108

-dredging 84, 86, 147, 148, 150

-lagoons 88, 89

-nutrient cycling 27, 29

-nutrient release from 29, 91

-sealing 84-86

Sedge 34, 109

Seining 97, 122, 130, 141

Fishing technique in which a net is suspended at the water surface and extends to the bottom, where it is weighted. The net is paid out over a large arc, then drawn in to the bank to concentrate the fish which are then removed live.

Sensitive Areas (Eutrophic) 75

UK Government designation to describe areas damaged by eutrophication, or likely to be so, under the EC Urban Wastewater Treatment Directive.

Set Aside Regulations 81

Rules of a scheme to remove land from production of conventional commercial crops in Europe so as to avoid overproduction.

Sewage 39, 40, 134

-effluent 15, 50, 57, 60, 61, 74, 124, 138, 146, 149, 153

-treatment 15, 39, 42, 44, 78

Silica 56

Site of Special Scientific Interest 15, 71, 82

An area in the UK identified by the statutory conservation agencies as containing features (biological or physiographical or geological) worthy of conservation. Sites are graded in value, Grade 1 sites being equivalent to National Nature Reserves (q.v.).

Slapton Ley 25

Snails 31, 47, 57, 139

-grazing on periphyton 31

Sodium tripolyphosphate 73, 77

Spawning 97, 98, 99, 100, 132

Special Areas of Conservation 71

Sites of conservation importance designated under the EC Habitats Directive.

Special Protection Areas 71

Sites of special importance for wild birds, designated under the EC Habitats Directive.

Sphagnum 37

Stock 41

-wastes 41, 76

Stocking 119

-carp 48

-following biomanipulation 118-120

-pike 93

Submerged plants (See Aquatic plants, submerged)

-associated animals 31-33

-complexity of environment in beds of 27, 28, 30

-dominance 42, 43, 45

-precariousness of existence 27, 28

Suction dredging 87, 89, 91, 151, 152, 156

Removal of sediment by pumping out a slurry of water and sediment as opposed to bulk removal by a digger.

Succession 36, 37

Process by which ecosystems develop from early, uninhabited stages through colonisation and alteration of the habitat to quasi-permanent structures.

-plant, in lakes 36, 37

Sulphide 29, 57, 85, 154, 155

Swans 35, 48, 51, 66, 70, 112, 114, 115

Swimmer's itch 139

Switches 20

Mechanisms which determine movement from one state to another in systems capable of supporting alternative stable states (q.v.).

-boats 48, 47, 65, 124

-Canada geese 48

-common carp 48, 64

-coypu 48, 66, 124

-forward, removal of 63, 65, 68

-grazing vertebrates 65, 66

-herbicides 47, 48, 66

-mechanical 47

-pesticides 48, 67, 124

-reverse 47, 50

-salinity 48, 49, 65, 124

Targets 57, 58, 62

-information needs 59

-for nutrient control 60, 62

-setting 62

Tench 35, 70, 99, 105, 118, 119, 120, 140, 144

Top-down effects **70, 119**

Mechanisms by which organisms at the upper levels of food webs (predators) determine the nature and production of intermediate and lower (photosynthetic) levels.

Transition from clear water to turbid water 19-20, 46-48

Trawling 98, 141, 150, 151

Fishing method in which bag-like nets are dragged by powered boats through the water, or over the bottom, to capture fish which are then hauled out into the boat.

Trematodes 104

Trophic states (see Lake trophic state)

Trout 118, 119

-brown 118, 119

-rainbow 118

Turbidity 44, 104

Measure of the degree to which suspended particles reduce light penetration through natural waters.

Turions 110, 112

Free-living buds (stem plus leaf initiators) of aquatic plants, by which they disperse or overwinter.

Turkey Broad 152, 154, 155

Water Act 77

Water fleas (See Cladocera)

Cladocerans, particularly those that feed by filtering the water.

Water level manipulation 94

Water lilies 27, 34, 46, 47, 50, 56, 65, 107, 108, 115, 127, 134, 146, 152

Water milfoil 46

Water Resources Act 76, 84

Water soldier 46, 115

Water treatment 16, 41

Waterside Habitat Scheme 82

Wildlife & Countryside Act 71, 93, 96

Willow 101, 109, 114, 138, 140

Zander (see pikeperch)

Zeolite 78

Artificial clay-like substance used in domestic detergents to absorb metal ions and remove hardness from water. The ions are thus prevented from combining with the surfactant to form a scum. Other such 'builders' are sodium tripolyphosphate and nitrilotriacetic acid (q.v.).

Zooplanktivore 48, 130

Consumer of zooplankton

Zooplankton 48, 130

Animal community free swimming or suspended in the open water.

-grazing 31, 32, 135

-predation on 32, 33, 103, 104